Shadows of War

Silence lies between forgetting and remembering. This book explores the ways in which different societies have constructed silences to enable men and women to survive and make sense of the catastrophic consequences of armed conflict. Using a range of disciplinary approaches, it examines the silences that have followed violence in twentieth-century Europe, the Middle East, and Africa. These essays show that silence is a powerful language of remembrance and commemoration and a cultural practice with its own rules. This broad-ranging book discloses the universality of silence in the ways we think about war through examples ranging from the Spanish Civil War and the Israeli-Palestinian conflict to the Armenian Genocide and South Africa's Truth and Reconciliation Commission. Bringing together scholarship on varied practices in different cultures, this book breaks new ground in the vast literature on memory, and opens up new avenues of reflection and research on the lingering aftermath of war.

EFRAT BEN-ZE'EV is Senior Lecturer in Anthropology at the Department of Behavioral Sciences, Ruppin Academic Center, Israel. She has published on Palestinian-Arab and Jewish-Israeli memories of the war of 1948.

RUTH GINIO is Senior Lecturer in History at Ben Gurion University of the Negev and a research fellow at the Harry S. Truman Research Institute for the Advancement of Peace in Jerusalem. Her recent publications include *French Colonialism Unmasked: The Vichy Years in French West Africa* (2006) and *Violence and Non-Violence in Africa* (as co-editor, 2007).

JAY WINTER is Charles J. Stille Professor of History at Yale University. He is the author of *Sites of Memory, Sites of Mourning: The Great War in European Cultural History* (1995), and *War and Remembrance in the Twentieth Century* (as editor, with Emmanuel Sivan, 1999).

Shadows of War

*A Social History of Silence
in the Twentieth Century*

Edited by

Efrat Ben-Ze'ev,

Ruth Ginio

and

Jay Winter

CAMBRIDGE
UNIVERSITY PRESS

CAMBRIDGE UNIVERSITY PRESS
Cambridge, New York, Melbourne, Madrid, Cape Town, Singapore,
São Paulo, Delhi

Cambridge University Press
The Edinburgh Building, Cambridge CB2 8RU, UK

Published in the United States of America by Cambridge University Press,
New York

www.cambridge.org
Information on this title: www.cambridge.org/9780521196581

First published 2010

Printed in the United Kingdom at the University Press, Cambridge

A catalogue record for this publication is available from the British Library

ISBN 978-0-521-19658-1 Hardback

Contents

Notes on contributors

TANER AKÇAM is Professor of History, Center for Holocaust and Genocide Studies, Clark University. He is the author of *A Shameful Act: The Armenian Genocide and the Question of Turkish Responsibility* (New York, 2006). With Vahakn B. Dadrian, he has published (in Turkish) *The Armenian Issue is Resolved: Policies Towards Armenians during the War Years, Based on Ottoman Documents* (Istanbul, 2008) and *Deportation and Massacres. The Protocols of the Istanbul Military Tribunals on the Investigation against the Union and Progress Party* (Istanbul, 2009).

EFRAT BEN-ZE'EV is Senior Lecturer in Anthropology at the Department of Behavioral Sciences, Ruppin Academic Center, Israel. She has published on Palestinian-Arab and Jewish-Israeli memories of the war of 1948.

LOUISE BETHLEHEM is Senior Lecturer in the Program in Cultural Studies and in the Department of English at the Hebrew University of Jerusalem. She has published widely on South African literary and cultural history, postcolonialism, and gender studies. Her recent volumes include *Skin Tight: Apartheid Literary Culture and its Aftermath*, (Pretoria and Leiden, 2006) and *Violence and Non-Violence in Africa*, co-edited with Pal Ahluwalia and Ruth Ginio (Abingdon and New York, 2007).

RAPHAËLLE BRANCHE is Lecturer in Modern History at the University of Paris-1. She is currently working on French colonialism in Algeria and the Algerian War of Independence.

RUTH GINIO is Senior Lecturer in History at Ben Gurion University of the Negev and a research fellow at the Harry S. Truman Research Institute for the Advancement of Peace in Jerusalem. Her recent publications include *French Colonialism Unmasked: The Vichy Years in French West Africa* (Lincoln, Neb. 2006) and *Violence and Non-Violence in Africa*, co-edited with Pal Ahluwalia and Louise Bethlehem (Abingdon and New York, 2007).

SVENJA GOLTERMANN teaches history at the University of Freiburg. She is author of *Die Gesellschaft der Überlebenden: Kriegsheimkehrer und ihre Gewalter fahrungen im Zweiten Weltkrieg* (Munich, 2009) and a number of articles, including "The Imagination of Disaster: Death and Survival in Post-War West Germany," in Paul Betts, Alon Confino, and Dirk Schumann (eds.), *Between Mass Death and Individual Loss: The Place of the Dead in Twentieth-Century Germany* (Oxford, 2008).

JIM HOUSE is Senior Lecturer in French at the University of Leeds. His recent publications include (with Neil MacMaster) *Paris 1961: Algerians, State Terror, and Memory* (Oxford, 2006).

ASHER KAUFMAN is Assistant Professor of History at the University of Notre Dame. He is currently working on border dynamics between Syria, Lebanon, and Israel. His recent publications include "From the Litani to Beirut: Israel's Invasions of Lebanon, 1978–1985: Causes and Consequences," in Clive Jones and Sergio Catignani (eds.), *Israel and Lebanon 1976–2006: An Interstate and Asymmetric Conflict in Perspective* (2009).

JEFFREY K. OLICK is Professor of Sociology and History at the University of Virginia. His books include, among others, *In the House of the Hangman: The Agonies of German Defeat, 1943–1949* (Chicago, 2005), and (with Andrew J. Perrin) *Guilt and Defense: Theodor Adorno on Postwar German Society* (Cambridge, Mass., 2009).

MARY VINCENT is Professor of Modern European History at the University of Sheffield. Her recent publications include *Spain 1833–2002: People and State* (Oxford, 2007) and she is currently working on a study of Franco's "Crusade."

JAY WINTER is Charles J. Stille Professor of History at Yale University. He is the author of *Sites of Memory, Sites of Mourning: The Great War in European Cultural History* (Cambridge, 1995), and (with Emmanuel Sivan) the editor of *War and Remembrance in the Twentieth Century* (Cambridge, 1999).

EVIATAR ZERUBAVEL is Board of Governors Professor of Sociology at Rutgers University. He is the author of nine books, including *The Fine Line: Making Distinctions in Everyday Life* (Chicago, 1991), *Social Mindscapes: An Invitation to Cognitive Sociology* (Cambridge, Mass., 1997), *Time Maps: Collective Memory and the Social Shape of the Past* (Chicago, 2003), and *The Elephant in the Room: Silence and Denial in Everyday Life* (New York, 2006).

Preface and acknowledgments

We are grateful for the aid and support of the Harry S. Truman Research Institute for the Advancement of Peace of the Hebrew University of Jerusalem, and of the Konrad Adenauer Foundation, without which the development of this book would not have been possible. We thank colleagues who contributed to early meetings and discussions of this theme, and Mishkenot Sha'ananim, which offered a congenial venue for completing this project.

The structure of the book is straightforward. We have aimed at a shift of emphasis in discussions of the general themes of memory and forgetting, by privileging a third element, that surrounding silence and silencing in the way individuals and groups reconfigure the past. In the first part of the book, we offer two multi-disciplinary approaches to silence. We then divide the chapters geographically, into those discussing European, African, and Middle Eastern wars and their aftermath. We have included a chapter on the South African Truth and Reconciliation Commission, on the grounds that the Apartheid regime waged war brutally against its own people. To deny this fact is tantamount to denying the war the Nazis waged against the Jews. To be sure, the institutions of war changed over the twentieth century, but that very mutation is one of the themes of this book.

Recognizing that no one volume can do justice to a subject of manifest importance, we believe these studies, taken as a whole, offer a point of scholarly departure for further research in a field which has become central to our understanding of the ways wars' survivors make sense of the violent times in which they lived and live.

EFRAT BEN-ZE'EV,
RUTH GINIO,
JAY WINTER
Jerusalem
January 2009

Part I

Framing the problem: Multi-disciplinary approaches

1 Thinking about silence*

Jay Winter

Les souvenirs sont façonnés par l'oubli comme les contours du rivage sur la mer.
Memory is framed by forgetting in the same way as the contours of the shoreline are framed by the sea.   Marc Augé[1]

To be silent is still to speak.   Maurice Blanchot[2]

Below the surface

Marc Augé's elegant formulation of the embrace of memory and forgetting draws upon a long tradition of philosophical and literary reflection. It is time, though, to go beyond it, in the effort to transcend the now saturated field of memory studies dominated by scholarship which adopts this binary approach. For the topographical metaphor employed here is clearly incomplete. We need to see the landscape of the shoreline in all three dimensions. Doing so enables us to observe a vertical dimension to the creation and erosion of the shoreline which is dynamic, unstable, and at times, intrusive. We speak of those deposits below the surface of the water which emerge with the tides or with other environmental changes. In the framework of how we think about memory and forgetting, these hidden shapes cannot simply be ignored because they are concealed at some moments and revealed at others. They must be examined as part of the cartography of recollection and remembrance.

Silences: liturgical, political, essentialist

We call these hidden deposits silence. The composer John Cage said all that needs to be said about the performative nature of silence. It exists in

* I am grateful to Efrat Ben-Ze'ev and Ruth Ginio for contributions to and extensive discussions on this chapter.
[1] Marc Augé, *Les formes de l'oubli* (Paris: Payot & Rivages, 1998), p. 4.
[2] Maurice Blanchot, *The writing of the disaster*, trans. Anne Smock (Lincoln, Neb. and London: University of Nebraska Press, 1986), p. 11. Thanks are due to Kate McLoughlin for drawing this reference to our attention.

the world, and is defined by the world according to certain arbitrary but powerfully reinforced conventions. Those who first heard his composition *4'33"* in 1952 were stupefied by silence. What Cage did was to invite concert-goers to come together facing a pianist who sits at a piano and does not touch the keyboard for four minutes and thirty-three seconds precisely. What Cage showed them, much to their discomfort, was that silence is 'the presence of ambient and unintentional noise rather than the complete absence of sound'.[3] Our subject in this book is focused, directed and purposeful silence, not conceived of as the absence of sound, but as the absence of conventional verbal exchanges.

In the landscape we survey, silences are spaces either beyond words or conventionally delimited as left out of what we talk about. Topographically, they are there whether or not they come to the surface; and their re-emergence into our line of sight can occasion a reiteration of the interdiction on talking about them or the end of the interdiction itself.

Critically, therefore, we cannot accept the commonplace view that silence is the space of forgetting and speech the realm of remembrance. Instead, we offer the following definition of silence. Silence, we hold, is a socially constructed space in which and about which subjects and words normally used in everyday life are not spoken. The circle around this space is described by groups of people who at one point in time deem it appropriate that there is a difference between the sayable and the unsayable, or the spoken and the unspoken, and that such a distinction can and should be maintained and observed over time. Such people codify and enforce norms which reinforce the injunction against breaking into the inner space of the circle of silence.

The reasons for this cultural practice are multiple, but in the context of war and violence, the subject of this book of essays, the primary impulses underlying the social construction of silence are three. In the first place, silence is always part of the framing of public understandings of war and violence, since these touch on the sacred, and on eternal themes of loss, mourning, sacrifice and redemption. We term these uses of silence as 'liturgical silences'. They are clearly linked to fundamental moral problems, described in reflections on theodicy, or the conundrum as to why, if God is all good, evil exists in the world. Such liturgical silences are essential parts of mourning practices in many religious traditions, since not speaking enables those experiencing loss to engage with their grief in their own time and in their own ways.

---

[3] Branden W. Joseph, 'John Cage and the architecture of silence', *October*, LXXXI (Summer, 1997), pp. 80–104.

Consider, for example, the paradox that the Hebrew prayer for the dead, the Kaddish, does not mention the word 'death' or 'dying' or 'grief' or 'bereavement', all conditions or states of mind associated with the seven days of mourning passed together by families in mourning. The prayer is silent over the critical reality this practice marks. Mourning practices always touch on such matters, since they perform the fragility of life and the limitations of our own understandings of our mortal existence.

The second impulse behind the social construction of silence addresses problems of social conflict more directly. Here silence is chosen in order to suspend or truncate open conflict over the meaning and/or justification of violence, either domestic or trans-national. The hope here is that the passage of time can lower the temperature of disputes about these events, or even heal the wounds they cause. We term these practices as yielding 'political' or strategic silences.

One example, related to Vincent's essay below (see pp. 47–67), may suffice to illustrate this usage, and stand for a host of other instances, many of which are surveyed in the essays in this book. In the late 1970s, the forty years' reign of Franco's dictatorship in Spain came to an end peacefully. In short order, a socialist government came to power, and proceeded to refashion the country as a dynamic and stable member of the new European order. The price of that transition was the postponement or adjournment *sine die* – that is permanently – of any formal and public inquiry into atrocities committed during and after the civil war of 1936–9. Spain's new democracy chose peace over justice, order over the open investigation of the abundant evidence on atrocities which – like the underwater sand bars to which we referred above – was present but invisible. Not seeing what everyone saw and not saying what everyone knew became a strategy accepted by everyone at the time to ensure the success of a peaceful transition to democratic rule (see chapter 3). As we will see, such accords are matters of negotiation and thus suffer from all the faults of political compromise. With time, their hold over the parties begins to loosen, a new generation comes to power, and though silence is still ordained at the national level as wise and necessary, people start talking, looking, digging, writing and inevitably accusing. And how could it be otherwise when the scale of accusations is monumental? Here we can see that silence, like memory and forgetting, has a life history, and – when new pressures or circumstances emerge – can be transformed into its opposite in very rapid order.

Such transformative moments are examined in many essays in this book. Heidegger's silence about Nazi crimes, and his complicity in them, echoed similar lacunae in many German discursive fields after

1945. But more recently, silence about war and violence ends when victims are invited to come forward, and are given a forum ensuring that what they say will be heard. This is evidently the case in South Africa and in numerous other 'truth commissions' established for this purpose (see chapter 8).

The third impulse behind strategies of silence arises from considerations of privilege. That is, who has the right to speak about the violent past? One nearly universal answer is to privilege one group of people who pass through an experience and who thereby have the right to speak about it, as against others who were not there, and thereby cannot know and cannot judge. Only those who have been there, so this argument goes, can claim the authority of direct experience required to speak about these matters. These are what we term 'essentialist' silences.

There are many examples of such distinctions. Soldiers frequently speak about their war experiences only to other soldiers. Ben-Ze'ev's chapter refers to an annual reunion of the members of a unit in the Israeli army of 1948; these events continue to this day (see pp. 181–96). In other cases, soldiers express a kind of sexist rejection of the very capacity of women to enter and understand this masculine realm. Others take an essentialist line, in defining experience as internal and ineffable. When I addressed a conference on the First World War in the Royal Military College, Sandhurst, forty years ago, one of the participants, Charles Carrington, who was a noted author and survivor of the Great War, urged me to choose another profession. The reason: 'You will never know the war; only we who were there can know what it was like.' This was said with avuncular kindness.

Other such strictures are more acerbic. Time and again, patriots ask how can anyone criticise soldiers and the choices they make under fire if they haven't been there? And when the fighting is still unfolding, what right do civilians have to criticise what they do? Then there is the charge that moral issues are too easily framed by those who had the moral luck to avoid extreme or violent situations. And even among those who endured suffering, there were distinctions between those who knew the worst and those who luckily never reached such a point. Primo Levi said that even survivors like him did not know the worst; that knowledge was restricted only to those at the bottom of the world he inhabited in Auschwitz, those who had already become the living dead.[4]

---

[4] Primo Levi, *Survival in Auschwitz* (New York: Basic Books, 2002), p. 90.

Furthermore, others pose the question as to how we judge those who survived the war and kept secrets about their past? Condemnation is the easy way out for people who live comfortable lives. Shoshana Felman took this tack in considering the puzzle that her colleague and great literary critic Paul de Man had written anti-Semitic prose in a Belgian newspaper in 1940. This unsavory fact came to light only after de Man's death in 1982. How do we interpret his behaviour? Felman sees his scrupulous scholarship as distinct from his earlier behaviour, and goes further in suggesting his silence about his own past was a profound philosophical reflection on the terrible difficulty of all moral judgment, including judging those who as young men and women fell into the trap of the fascist temptation.[5] While not sharing this conclusion, we feel Felman's argument does offer a telling riposte to what E. P. Thompson termed the 'enormous condescension of posterity',[6] or the tendency to look down upon those stuck in predicaments we ourselves might not have resolved in any morally superior manner.

The problem with this approach to silence is its characteristic essentialism. Few any longer subscribe to the romantic definition of experience as ingested, visceral and objectively present in the lives and minds of only some individuals. According to this view, experience is theirs and theirs alone. In contradistinction, experience is much more fruitfully defined as a set of events whose character changes when there are changes – through age, migration, illness, marriage, religious conversion and so on – in the subject position of the person or group which had shared those events.[7] Students of memory in the cognitive and neurosciences no longer view their subject as fixed, as in a computer's hard drive, but more as dynamic and unstable, as in a collage. The work of Elizabeth Loftus has deepened our understanding of implanted memories, ones suggested to individuals by outsiders and sometimes by clinicians in therapeutic relationships. The danger of such interventions is evident.[8] If memory changes radically over time, then we must abandon the notion that not only memory but the right to speak about memory is the property of only a chosen few who recall the

[5] Shoshana Felman, 'Paul de Man's silence', *Critical Inquiry*, XV, 4 (Summer 1989), pp. 704–44.
[6] E. P. Thompson, *The making of the English working class* (London: Victor Gollancz, 1963), p. 18.
[7] Joan W. Scott, 'The evidence of experience', *Critical Inquiry*, XVII, 4 (1991), pp. 773–97.
[8] Daniel Schacter, *The seven sins of memory* (Cambridge, Mass.: Harvard University Press, 1999), pp. 20–3; Elizabeth Loftus, *Eyewitness testimony* (Cambridge, Mass: Harvard University Press, 1979), and Veronica Nourkova, Daniel M. Bernstein and Elizabeth Loftus, 'Biography becomes autobiography: Distorting the subjective past', *American Journal of Psychology*, CXVII, 1 (2004), pp. 65–80.

experience of what Calvin termed 'election'.[9] Relegating the rest of us to silence must be seen as a strategy of control, of cutting off debate, of *ad hominem* assertions of a kind unworthy of serious reflection.

Who has the right to speak is a question many of the essays in this volume pose. War stories are never uncontested, and over time, they change as the people who frame them grow old, move on and pass away. When the victims of violence have the sanction to speak out, as in a court of law or truth commission, then they become the authors not only of their stories, but also of their lives. Not speaking can entail accepting someone else's story about what happened to you. Or, as Bethlehem shows, it may be an assertion of dignity by those who, like rape victims, pass through indignity (see chapter 8). The central point is that the entitlement to speak about war and violence is in no sense universal. Some have the right; others do not. The difference between the two categories is a matter of social and cultural codes, which can and do change over time.

The advantages of silence

These preliminary reflections indicate the thinking behind the gathering together of the essays in this book. We intend to show in this book that the vast array of writing on memory and forgetting has reached an impasse, one imbedded in the time of its creation. We also claim that introducing the category of socially constructed silence into the literature provides a way out of some of the difficulties in the current literature, where memory and forgetting are constructed as polar opposites.

The memory/forgetting divide is a matter of perennial philosophical reflection. Paul Ricoeur's magisterial survey of this literature goes back to Plato and Aristotle and the extent to which the *eikon* and the *topos*, the trace and the place, have been understood differently in the domain of memory and in the domain of history. But even his extraordinary survey is a tract for the times, reflecting many of the intellectual currents behind the current memory boom. His book was published in 2000, and reflected decades of thought on this subject. 'I am troubled', he wrote, 'by the disturbing spectacle that gives an excess of memory here and an excess of oblivion there.'[10] This comment echoed similar remarks by the French historian/publisher Pierre Nora on our surfeit of ersatz memory, in *lieux de mémoire*, and a lack of imbedded, lived memory, in *milieu de mémoire*.[11]

---

[9] Jay Winter, *Remembering war: The Great War between history and memory in the twentieth century* (New Haven: Yale University Press, 2006), ch. 1.
[10] Paul Ricoeur, *La mémoire, l'histoire, l'oubli* (Paris: Seuil, 2000), p. xi.
[11] Winter, *Remembering war*, p. 33.

Memory, according to these and other French commentators, had become a commodity, an unavoidable sign of ethnic identity, a repository for romantic wishful thinking about the past, for which people paid substantial sums in theme parks, museums and historic sites around the world.

The memory boom is the outcome of many different processes, some commercial, some technological, some political. We do not share the critical viewpoint of these French writers, since the growth in interest in commemorative projects arises from changing political circumstances as much as market opportunities. There is a substantial literature on this subject, which we need not summarise here.[12]

In this discussion, it is evident that the Holocaust has been at the heart of the huge spiral of publications, lectures, exhibitions, museums and internet sites we have today. Initial oblivion, eventual entry into the realm of public memory: these two phases of public acknowledgment of the Holocaust have unfolded in sequence, and have inflected many other inquiries into other crimes and other abuses elsewhere in the world.[13]

It is impossible to miss the shadow of the Holocaust in the philosophical realm inhabited by Ricoeur. The third part of his study is on forgiveness, on the need to recognise the moral fallibility of all who judge the past, and therefore the necessity to aim at a kind of redemptive approach to history and memory, the effort to construct what he terms 'happy memory'. In English, the term appears absurd; in French it has more resonance, but it still has the scent of incense about it, the notion that to remember is to understand, and to understand is to forgive. There is also a psychoanalytic form of this position. To know is to heal is a premise of some forms of psychotherapy. But we must bear in mind that Freud said that his hope was to turn neurosis into normal unhappiness; no 'happy memories' here.

Healing, acknowledgement, recognition, forgiveness: these are the hallmarks of the memory boom in the 1990s, the time when Nelson Mandela moved from prison to the presidency of South Africa and when Bishop Desmond Tutu drove forward the notion of a Truth and Reconciliation process for the victims and the perpetrators of the crimes of the former regime. In this environment, remembering is the key to repentance and forgiveness, while oblivion is complicity in crimes still hidden from sight.

---

[12] Nancy Wood, *Vectors of memory: Legacies of trauma in postwar Europe* (Oxford: Berg, 1999), is a good place to begin. See also Aleida Assmann, *Erinnerungsräume: Formen und Wandlungen des kulturellen Gedächtnisses* (Munich: C. H. Beck, 1999).

[13] Andreas Huyssen, *Twilight memories: marking time in a culture of amnesia* (New York: Routledge, 1995); Lawrence Langer, *Holocaust and the literary imagination* (New Haven: Yale University Press, 1975); James E. Young, *At memory's edge: After-images of the Holocaust in contemporary art and architecture* (New Haven: Yale University Press, 2000).

Suffice it to say that there are huge problems imbedded in this approach; why repentance follows remembrance, indeed why healing follows remembrance are questions with no easy answers. Many survivors of the Holocaust, as well as many of those born long after the end of the Second World War, are uncomfortable with this fundamentally religious or spiritual approach to these matters. Primo Levi did not forgive those who told him that in Auschwitz, there was no 'why'; neither did Paul Celan forget those who destroyed his family, indeed his entire world. They wrote; they remembered, but healing was not their purpose or their fate. Victims insist on attention to other issues as well. Compensation for truncated lives and for stolen property matter too, as Bethlehem's essay suggests. The difficulties with this nearly sanctified part of the memory boom are endless, and require us to seek another way. As long as we stay in this morally charged domain, we are unlikely to emerge with anything other than an updated version of Foxe's *Book of Martyrs*.

It is our contention that by privileging the category of silence and the socially sanctioning activity of silencing, we can get beyond this moralised and moralising moment. The prime advantage of this approach is that we escape from the shadow of the Holocaust which, while unavoidable as a subject of moral significance, has tended to frame our subject in terms of the sanctification of speech and the denigration of silence about war, violence and the victims of both. Speech, we claim, is morally neutral, and so is silence. Both can be deployed in morally defensible and in morally deplorable ways.

Silence and war

If we see the question as to how to remember war and violence as one which both antedated and has continued long after the Holocaust, we can also escape from an exclusively Eurocentric approach to this matter. Since the Second World War, the institutions of war have fragmented. That is to say that unlike in the years before 1945, now our attention is fixed less on international than on trans-national or internal conflict. We focus more than ever before on organised violence within states and between non-state agents and territorial states. This is in part because the post-1945 period was one dominated by wars of national liberation, leaving in their wake fundamental social, ethnic and political cleavages, which in turn bred armed conflicts of many different kinds. The genocide in Rwanda, and the ongoing massacres – some say genocide – in Darfur are two African examples of the terrible plight of people caught in these post-colonial ethnic conflicts. Crimes committed in Bosnia during the Yugoslav civil war, in Colombia, in Lebanon, in Sri Lanka, in Kashmir, in Afghanistan and in Iraq arise from what may be termed the post-national and post-colonial setting of armed conflict.

Clearly, as war evolves, the stories we tell about it evolve in turn. Today the collage of organised violence and the suffering it entails is much more complex, even dizzying in its shifting character. The tale of war can no longer be told primarily or exclusively within the unfolding saga of nationalism and the achievement of self-determination and national dignity.

When thinking about contemporary warfare, it is essential to take a step back from our current preoccupations. The Westphalian system of conflicts between states which we tend to take for granted as the natural order of things was nothing of the kind. It was not universal and not timeless. African warfare developed its own character outside of a European system of states. And efforts by colonial powers to keep their hold on colonies struggling for independence usually took on the kind of fragmentary character we mistake as unprecedented. Nothing could be further from the case. Still, the catastrophe of the two world wars has left its imprint on what Samuel Hynes terms our 'war in the head', our shared assumptions about what war is.[14]

It follows that we may need to adjust our notions of remembrance while we adjust our attitudes towards war. The de-centring of the experience of war and violence may make it less useful to apply the categories of memory and forgetting, which frequently assume that the story is determined by a top/down approach to political power configured in a national state. This is the landscape of Orwell's *1984*, which was a dystopia set in London during the Second World War, and of Camus' *The Plague*, set in Algiers in the same time period. Shifting our attention away from the hegemonic state or police apparatus to a broader social landscape may help reconfigure our understanding of subtler processes of the framing of debate through the construction of silence. This shift could also help us chart the life cycle of silence, in such a way as to show how different memory agents use different means to puncture the balloon of silence and put words in its place.

Attention to silence and silencing also helps us turn the tense of our discussion from the passive to the active. Elsewhere we have called for greater rigor in the use of the terms 'memory' and 'forgetting', such as to point to the person or group remembering or forgetting whenever possible.[15] Unfortunately, the terms 'collective memory' and 'national memory' are parts of everyday speech, and as such lose any concrete meaning

---

[14] Samuel Hynes, *The soldiers' tale* (New York: Penguin, 2000).
[15] Jay Winter and Emmanuel Sivan (eds.), *War and remembrance in the twentieth century* (Cambridge University Press, 1999), ch. 1.

they may once have had. If we turn our discussion towards silence and silencing, there is usually someone not speaking and frequently someone making sure that those who break the rules know the consequences of doing so. Those individuals the historian Carol Gluck has termed 'memory activists' are also those who break silences and change the boundaries between what can and cannot be said. Social agency is the domain of the social construction of silence. On this point, we side with Michel de Certeau as against Michel Foucault in asserting that not all cultural practices can be collapsed into discourse.[16] Silence is one such practice with a life history of its own.

Why now?

One reason to adopt a different optic in the field of memory studies is that the social context in which we think about the subject is changing. From the time of Ernest Renan[17] at the end of the nineteenth century to Benedict Anderson's seminal study of *Imagined Communities*,[18] the nation state and the mobilising power of nationalism have provided the force and focus of several generations of scholarship on memory and remembrance.

Since the 1960s, though, a different international environment has emerged. In some respects, what we term globalisation is merely the reiteration of trends in motion before the First World War. But the huge movements of capital, goods and labour in the late twentieth century and after present us with a changing demographic landscape. To be sure, the nation state has not died; but its power has been eroded in part by a surge in emigration from what we now term the 'South' and to the 'North'. An unspecified but very large part of this population movement is illegal. That is, people have moved from 'developing' to 'developed' nations through normal visa channels if they can, but through illicit channels when they must.

This dramatic move in population history is a challenge to the integrity of the nation state. In many parts of the world, the state is less that institution with the authority to declare war than that institution with the power to determine who enters its territory. That power is now in question. The result is the presence among us of very large 'silent' populations. They are silent, in that they are not supposed to be here. If they speak up, they are likely to call attention to their illicit presence. They occupy menial jobs in developed economies, and constitute a huge

---

[16] For a fuller discussion, see Winter, *Remembering war*, ch. 1.
[17] Philippe Forest (ed.), *Qu'est-ce qu'une nation?* (Paris: Pierre Bordas et fils éditeur, 1991).
[18] Benedict Anderson, *Imagined communities* (London: Verso, 1983).

reservoir of poorly paid labour. They are silent too, in that they have no political voice in the country to which they have come. On occasion, that can mean they have no rights at all, and face hostility, harassment, arrest and deportation. Stephen Frears' 2002 film *Dirty Pretty Things* opened a window onto this subterranean world, one which is hard to look at. Our silence about the presence of these people among us is something on which we should reflect.

If the readers of this book anywhere in the developed world take an evening off, and dine in a local café, they are likely to be in the company of these newcomers, just off stage, washing dishes or cleaning up. Most of the time, we too are silent about them, preferring to avoid a direct confrontation with the problem of undocumented immigrants, who consequently lead a shadow life, filled with dangers and uncertainties.

This changing demographic reality is bound to have an effect on the way we look at the nation state, and at the historical questions we ask about our common cultural heritage. If 'memory' and 'forgetting' bracketed our understanding of nationhood and nationalism at the high water mark of what Charles Maier termed the 'age of territoriality',[19] then it may be possible to see that now, in a trans-national age, it makes sense not to dispense with memory and forgetting, but to develop a wider vocabulary to explore the sphere of signifying practices in the contemporary world. We suggest that exploring the subject of silence and its social construction is one such analytical development.

Silence as a cultural practice

Now that we have established the value, indeed the necessity, of the study of silence, we need to understand that the processes of silencing and respecting silences are socially conditioned in a host of ways. Let us consider a number of them.

Speech: free and unfree

The courts help enforce silence in many different societies. In this domain, some rules apply, and some of these rules are coercive. Even in liberal societies, there are limits to free speech. No one has the right to shout 'Fire' frivolously in a crowded space; in some countries, a speaker who denies that the Holocaust happened can be prosecuted and imprisoned. There are other, well-known instances in which the law itself

---

[19] Charles Maier, 'Consigning the twentieth century to history: Alternative narratives for the modern era', *American Historical Review*, CV, 3 (2000), pp. 807–31.

inscribes and enforces boundaries as to what can be said with impunity. Until May 2008, blasphemy was a crime in Britain. A charge of offending Muslim beliefs brought opprobrium (and calls for his death) on the head of Salman Rushdie after he published in 1998 his novel *Satanic Verses*, a work of satirical fiction which was not at all funny to devout Muslims. His book was burned in Yorkshire, but outside of Britain, some religious authorities went further. The Ayatollah Khomeini issued a 'fatwa' or judgment rooted in Islamic law, calling for Rushdie's death. He went into hiding for a decade.

The normative enforcement of silence is a much more subtle and multifaceted domain. British libel laws were notoriously more advantageous to the prosecution than were American libel laws. This difference permitted the British publisher Robert Maxwell to cover up his crimes for decades before his death. The risks of prosecution for libel were simply too great for the whistle-blowers or the newspapers who knew that he was a charlatan and a thief. The law is an important domain in the social construction of silence, one which like all others, changes over time and place.

The confessional is a site of speech, the content of which is privileged, even in a court of law. The same is true for exchanges with a doctor, a lawyer or a spouse. All inhabit a space in which what is said is – and must remain – no one else's business. At times, we accept the validity, even the necessity of violating these rules, but only in extremis. Victims of rape or sexual abuse can anticipate a veil of silence draped over their suffering in everyday conversation, though in a court of law, they may have to speak about torture or injury which outside the courthouse is 'unspeakable'. Even in this case, though, victims may remain silent, since the speech act may be performative; that is, the pain described is inflicted once again through testimony. As Bethlehem's essay shows, all such statements mix revelation with silences, and who are we to say that the damaged person who refuses to speak even then is mistaken or culpable?

Poetic licence

Are writers among the unseen legislators of rules about silence? Do they help us break it? In some respects, the answer is yes to both questions. But the realm of silence with which writers deal is imbedded in complex social practices of specifying and obeying codes of delicacy or tact. Consider this mundane instance of socially censored speech: even though there is no legal obstacle to discussing in public a painful divorce with one of the parties to it, many people would hesitate long before doing so. In contemporary Britain, polite conversation may avoid many subjects, aside from the weather, on the grounds that the primary purpose of social exchanges is the avoidance of embarrassing anyone. Why embarrassment is a state to be avoided at all costs is a question we need not entertain here, though it raises clearly the differences which exist between societies' rules of decency and proper comportment.

Humour frequently describes and violates such rules of tact. We have already noted the Rushdie case, but there is a much longer tradition of vicious denunciation of injustices through black comedy. Humour, even the savage kind, provides a cover of indirection for statements which, if said in bland prose, could result in accusations of slander, libel or treason. Jonathan Swift's 'A Modest Proposal' is a recipe book for tasty dishes with unusual ingredients – the bodies of Irish children in an over-populated country. Voltaire's *Candide* hid moral indignation in the folds of his modest tale. More recently, a completely different sensibility made anti-Semitism into the stuff of brilliant fiction. Céline's prose is filled with anti-Semitism of an unmistakable kind. 'The delirium of words' is how Céline described these diatribes, which did not prevent his masterpiece *Voyage au bout de la nuit* from appearing in the 'classic' series the Pleiades, in 1952.

What can be said in a joke is not at all what should be said in 'polite' conversation. Consider the following joke about Alzheimer's disease. We should not fear this illness, the joke begins, because when you have it, every day you meet new and interesting people. Is this mockery of the mentally disabled, or of the suffering of their loved ones? Yes, on both counts. Is it a way of talking about a condition most people prefer to leave in the shadows? Yes again. And perhaps too, mockery is a gentle form of the recognition of fallibility, like ethnic jokes one makes about one's own people, to puncture piousness or self-importance. Tact or taste or good breeding or sensitivity or manners describe the comportment of those who do not say such things. And it is precisely this silence which gives satirists and comedians their challenge.

Sometimes, it is said, they go too far. But where is too far? There are no hard and fast rules. The Monty Python team ended their 1979 film *The Life of Brian*, a spoof on the New Testament, with a scene in which a chorus of men bound to crosses sing together: 'Always look on the bright side of life.' This ditty drove traditionalists in Britain up the proverbial wall, at least initially. Thereafter Anglican clergymen urged their congregants to sing along. Travesty, or cross-dressing, is another Python specialty. Here the prejudices against homosexuality and the blurring of conventional sexual roles and postures are exposed by deliberately vulgar exaggeration, in which comedy speaks the unspoken social prejudices and self-deceptions of what we term mainstream or 'polite' society. In this case, though, it is unclear whether mockery undermines or fortifies the boundaries against talking about certain subjects. Laughter can reduce tensions, but it rarely eliminates them.

Indeed, in some contexts, buffoonery can carry a message others fear to voice. There is a long tradition of granting licence to liminal characters, like court jesters and fools, who can speak truth to power. Consider this exchange between Shakespeare's King Lear and his Fool:

FOOL: Dost thou know the difference, my boy, between a bitter fool and a
    sweet fool?
LEAR: No, lad; teach me.
FOOL: That lord that counselled thee
  To give away thy land,
  Come place him here by me-
  Do thou for him stand.
  The sweet and bitter fool
  Will presently appear;
  The one in motley here,
  The other found out there.
LEAR: Dost thou call me fool, boy?
FOOL: All thy other titles thou hast given away; that thou wast
  born with.

'This is not altogether fool, my lord,' the loyal Kent tells the baffled King. The Fool prods further:

FOOL: Prithee, nuncle, keep a schoolmaster that can teach thy fool to lie. I would
    fain learn to lie.
LEAR: And you lie, sirrah, we'll have you whipp'd.
FOOL: I marvel what kin thou and thy daughters are. They'll have me whipp'd for
    speaking true; thou'lt have me whipp'd for lying; and sometimes I am whipp'd
    for holding my peace. I had rather be any kind o' thing than a fool! And yet I
    would not be thee, nuncle. Thou hast pared thy wit o' both sides and left
    nothing i' th' middle.

A risky thing for a courtier to say? Yes, but not for a fool, who knows what everyone else knows, but has a socially sanctioned transgressive role. He tells Lear what he comes to learn – that once he lets go of the reins of power, his royal trappings amount to nothing. He is but an old man, dependent upon his children to keep him alive. And yet no one in court would ever dare to say such a thing. Comedy speaks truth to power, and lives to tell the tale another day.

I have dwelt on this text because it shows the extent to which social deviants may be permitted to defy the rules of 'polite' society, and call the 'great ones' to book for their crimes and misdemeanours. Clowns can mimic; comics, mock; and the mentally ill can point out what others prefer to leave unsaid. It was no accident that the Soviet Secret Police used the drug haldol to silence dissidents; it was the chemical 'straightjacket' used to control psychotic people, and therefore very effective in silencing dissent.[20] The patients discussed in Goltermann's chapter (see chapter 5) were in this category of deviant speech: they could express fears others left unsaid.

Silence can be shocking, and intentionally so. Harold Pinter's plays redefined theatre as a space dominated by silences occasionally interrupted by words. The menace imbedded in the relations between the characters in his plays was heightened, at times excruciatingly so, by long periods of wordlessness. Again, humour cloaked some painful issues. In *The Homecoming*, a son comes to his father's house to introduce his new bride, who says nothing. The father takes his time, and then responds that he had asked his son never to bring his whores home. Outrageous, to be sure, but also a very probing jab at the London Jewish world which Pinter offended by his marriage to a non-Jewish woman, Vivien Merchant. Theatre has exposed hypocrisy, especially sexual hypocrisy, since Shaw and Ibsen, but what Pinter added to the mix was the potent brew of silence, one which has endured. His Nobel Prize for Literature is in part a recognition of this achievement.

All the arts have the potential for speaking without words. In a performance of Verdi's opera *The Lombards and the First Crusade* in the Florence Opera in 2005, the scene in which the Crusaders take the city of Jerusalem took the form of total darkness and background sounds of battle, punctuated by silent cameos of three or four members of the cast fixed in poses of prisoners under torture in Abu Ghraib prison in Iraq. The sight of a man on a box, with a pointed cap on his head and electrodes attached to his arms needed no commentary. The image is now iconic; it tells its own story.

The same is true with respect to the photograph taken of Che Guevara's dead body in 1967, though here the image took on a life of its own. Instead of silently saying, 'We got him. He is dead. One less revolutionary to worry about.', the photograph of a handsome man laid out like Christ after the crucifixion, unintentionally but powerfully sacralised his death and turned his death mask into a revolutionary icon. Images speak in ways which are hard to control.

Amnesty

Amnesty comes from the Greek *amnēstia* meaning oblivion. It is a legal remedy providing a way in which societies wrestling with intractable

---

[20] Paul Calloway, *Soviet and Western psychiatry* (London: Moor Press, 1992).

political and social conflicts can draw an arbitrary line separating a *then* when legal and other grievances were pursued and a *now* when, in the interest of the collective, no further reckoning is permitted. Amnesty is not synonymous with forgetting. It tries to bypass the paralysis which can attend to the settling of scores *ad infinitum*. After an amnesty, the words 'I accuse' may still be uttered, but they have no legal force.

Drawing a legal line in the sand in this way requires a consensus that more justice is done by ceasing open conflict over the past than would be done by continuing to pursue one's enemies. Over time, that consensus may break down, leading to a renegotiation of the terms of amnesty. This happened in Argentina in 2005, when the country's Supreme Court struck down as unconstitutional the amnesty laws covering crimes committed by the government in the pursuit of its 'Dirty War' in the late 1970s and 1980s. Legislative nullification is underway today (2009) to do the same in Chile.

The recent uncovering of mass graves in Spain shows the way in which amnesties may begin to unravel. Fernandez notes that 'the public disclosure of caches of bones, products of the tragic legacies of war and violent conflict, elicits heartbreaking stories that had previously been suppressed or only whispered'. Older people may have preferred to live with a past 'thrown into oblivion', but their children and grandchildren may think otherwise.[21]

As Vincent shows in this book, the stabilising effect of amnesty itself is unstable over time. Indeed in November 2007, the Spanish parliament passed a 'Law of National Memory' opening up the whole subject of injustice and atrocities committed during the civil war seventy years before. Sentences handed down by Franco's courts were declared 'illegitimate', and local and national authorities were instructed to help individuals to locate and exhume the bodies of Franco's victims still buried in mass graves. In addition, all statues and other symbols of the Franco regime were to be removed from public places. The Spanish prime minister drove this measure through, in part on principle, and in part because his own grandfather had been executed during the civil war. His silences – and indeed Spain's silences – were now transformed into both words and deeds.[22] Amnesty is not eternal.

Amnesty of a different kind was practised in South Africa's Truth and Reconciliation Commission. Here we deal with the purging of individual

---

[21] Francisco Fernandez, 'The return of Civil War ghosts. The ethnography of exhumations in contemporary Spain', *Anthropology Today*, XXII, 3 (2006), pp. 7–12.
[22] 'Spain confronts past under Franco', *Spiegel online International*, 1 November 2007. See: www.spiegel.de/international/europe/0,1518,514796,00.html.

guilt through the public and complete admission of guilt by those who come forward. The Christian character of this form of truth-telling instead of judicial punishment made it attractive to some, but not to others. Those who suffered injury still have to find healing; others have to find a home or other forms of material comfort. The performance of guilt may or may not yield the reconciliation of the victim and the perpetrator. What happens instead is that the victim gets to the microphone, seizes his or her own story and therefore becomes a subject and not just an object in history. This is of great importance, but what the victim says may itself contain silences. Here Bethlehem's chapter offers much to think about when contemplating the legacies of amnesty.

Transitional silences

Some silences arise from a new state of belief or affiliation. Women's maiden names vanish in some cultures when they marry and choose to use their husband's family name. In the Sora tribe in India, the period embracing their conversion to Baptist Christianity, and their leaving behind shamanistic practices, is marked by what Vitebsky describes as 'moments of inarticulacy'. What has been silenced are their conversations with their ancestors, mediated by shamans and anathema to Christian practice. They have not forgotten how to talk with their ancestors; they now choose not to speak in this way, since their new religion precludes it. And yet they remain troubled, since they have lost much by renouncing their older sacred language. In this respect, their linguistic and religious transition leaves them speechless.[23] It is unclear what sanctions Baptist ministers have if there is any backsliding among their congregants. In seventeenth-century Yucatan, the sanctions were horrifying, but then, conversion was hardly a choice. Franciscans tortured and killed thousands of Mayans who reverted to the old ways of speaking the language of their gods.[24] Many Jews who converted to Christianity were in danger of being burnt at the stake should they return to the old ways. Indeed, at times these ways of speaking survived in muted form, as a Friday night festive meal without any associated ritual practices. The shadow of a language repressed is evidence once again that silence is not synonymous with forgetting.

---

[23] Piers Vitebsky, 'Loving and forgetting: Moments of inarticulacy in tribal India', *Journal of the Royal Anthropological Institute*, XIV, 2 (2008), pp. 243–61.

[24] Inga Clendinnen, *Ambivalent conquests: Maya and Spaniard in Yucatan, 1517–1570* (Cambridge University Press, 1987).

Commemorative silences

Commemoration is the collective representation of a shared view of a past worth recalling. As such, it is performative; it selects elements of a narrative and necessarily suppresses other sides of the story. It is difficult for any nation to commemorate inglorious events or acts committed in its name. Military disasters and war crimes fall into this category.When a society decides to commemorate a happier chapter in its history – a victorious war, for instance – the difficulties of deciding what to say and what not to say are immediately apparent. The key problems arise when wars become democratic. Before the early nineteenth century, nobles or mercenaries waged wars out of a sense of personal honour or for more pecuniary reasons. Only the great or the powerful were immortalised in stone or on canvas. But by the twentieth century, war had become everyone's business. The extension of casualty lists to the thousands, then to millions, made commemoration much more difficult. The question arose as to how to glorify those who die in war without glorifying war itself?

One way to do so is to ensure that the names of everyone – and not only the generals – are listed and honoured. And yet even this format does not solve all the problems of remembering war in the modern age. In French, a war memorial is a memorial to the dead – *monument aux morts*; in English, it is the more equivocal 'war memorial'. Which part of war does it commemorate? The justice of its outbreak? The justice of its outcome? The honourable treatment given to enemy prisoners or the wounded? No one knows the answer to these questions, and all commemorators start with the same puzzle: what do we leave out?

Consider but two examples of the problem. The war memorial in New College, Oxford, commemorates all those members of the college who died in the Great War. The question arose, what about German former students who died for the Kaiser? Do they get on the list of the fallen? In this college, the answer is yes; in others the answer is no. A second problem is of more recent vintage. In 2006, the British Ministry of Defence said that all those shot for cowardice in the 1914–18 war would be pardoned. This decision opened the door to the addition of these 343 names to war memorials commemorating those who died in that war. To date (2009) it is not at all clear what individual towns and villages will do when asked by a family to put recently pardoned great, great Uncle Harry's name on the town war memorial. These local authorities may choose silence on the issue; but this is hardly surprising, since every decision to commemorate is a decision to simplify and clarify a message by leaving out substantial parts of the story surrounding it.

Silent topoi: erasure and recovery

Over time, most commemorative sites fade into the landscape and return to silence. This is because the people who use them and animate them get old, sick, die, move away or turn their attention to other activities. Other buildings, usually of vernacular construction, need special work to mark them off as places where something special happened. Dolores Hayden has examined a host of buildings now landmarked, but not otherwise noteworthy. What sets them apart is the decision of groups of people to point out something important: here is where a union held its meetings; there is the site of the first childcare centre in our town.[25]

Sometimes, the vernacular carries a silent message whether or not anyone puts a plaque on a wall or doorway. The town of Kars in Turkish Anatolia is the setting of Orhan Pamuk's novel *Snow*. Nowadays a peripheral Turkish town, where the government is trying to maintain political stability in light of tensions both with Islamists and with Kurds, its dilapidated old buildings stand as reminders of another past. These buildings, Armenian and Russian mansions and churches, loom in the background of the story. They are dark presences, which embody absence and silence. Looking at these buildings, the author suggests, who can deny that something terrible happened to the people who lived in them?[26]

Pre-1948 Arab villages play this role in today's Israel. Some villages were completely destroyed during the conflict. Others housed newly arrived Jewish immigrants after the war. This process of expulsion and repopulation by new inhabitants was not the subject of much comment in the decades following 1948. Yet as the Palestinians slowly found the means to voice their demands for recognition and return, the remains of their villages took on new meanings. They turned into sites of collective pilgrimage, of reminiscence and of stories. Ruins attract words, even when the stones are silent.[27]

Destruction of physical artifacts can erase the traces of a people and their cultural practices. How much do we know today of North American Indian settlement? We have pottery and fabulous funerary monuments left by the Etruscans, but not a word they wrote or spoke. Language is both more and less than an artifact. In Europe, Yiddish is now a nostalgic language, since the Nazis succeeded in destroying the physical and cultural world of Eastern European Jewry. Equally lost are hundreds of villages where that language was spoken, erased or covered by the rubble of violence and war.[28]

[25] Dolores Hayden, *The power of place* (Berkeley: University of California Press, 1992).
[26] Orhan Pamuk, *Snow*, trans. Maureen Freely (New York: Knopf, 2004).
[27] Efrat Ben-Ze'ev, 'The politics of taste and smell: Palestinian rites of return', in Marianne Lien and Brigitte Nerlich (eds.), *The politics of food* (Oxford: Berg, 2004).
[28] Simon Schama, *Landscape and memory* (New York: Knopf, 1995).

But even the notion that some forms of vandalism are irreversible needs qualification. What matters more than the physical environment is the way people attach cultural and political meanings to it. The giant stone Buddhas of Afghanistan were destroyed by the Taliban, who attached one set of meanings to these sculptures. In the very act of destruction, they both drew attention to the site, and stimulated others to try to restore the site and replace the images. Sometimes, these acts of restoration are out of place. Though the full physical presence of Jewish life before 1933 cannot be restored in today's Berlin, some inhabitants want to retrieve the sounds of that vanished world. There is a revival of Klezmer music in Berlin these days, even though Klezmer music was not heard in Berlin before the Nazis came to power. Nostalgia can be entirely misleading, producing images of a lost culture which never existed in the first place.[29]

But at times, we reaffirm the existence of a world we thought was gone. A group of shepherds found the Dead Sea Scrolls in an abandoned cave in the Judean desert in the 1940s. Merchants and then scholars acquired them, and through these texts, the Essene sect began to speak again, after two millennia of silence. The building of a memorial to the vanished Jews of Vienna in the centre of the city in 2000 turned up the site of a medieval cemetery, which now too is a site of memory. Discoveries happen, as do wanton acts of vandalism erasing treasures the world will never see.

Political contestation

This brief excursion into the complex field of cultural practices surrounding silence and speech acts is in no sense exhaustive. There are many other cultural practices we need to attend to; many are evident within family life. Family secrets are known to us all, and so are the euphemistic ways our relatives speak about them. Basso has shown how silence denotes courtesy, reticence, a sense of social discomfort and caution among Apache tribesmen. Thus we need not look only at art or poetry to find nuance and delicacy conveyed by silence. In addition vernacular silences describe those times when words are ineffective in defusing conflict or anger.[30] In many different cultural settings, perfectly ordinary occasions require silences as signs of respect and diffidence.

Nonetheless, the overwhelming majority of cases examined in the recent literature concern silences in the arena of politics and public affairs. A common thread that runs through the pages of this book is indeed the

[29] Svetlana Boym, *The future of nostalgia* (New York: Basic Books, 2002).
[30] Keith Basso, '"To give up on words:" Silence in Western Apache culture', *Southwestern Journal of Anthropology*, XXVI, 3 (1970), pp. 215–30.

politics of silence. These chapters depict wars or violent events the moral character of which was contested both at the time of the conflict and in its aftermath. In the case of Nazi Germany, which is discussed in two of the chapters (chapters 4 and 5), while there is a consensus regarding the immoral character of the German regime and the crimes it committed, there was and still is disagreement regarding the ways in which Germans should deal with this immoral past. In this section, we will examine how the transformation of moral and political judgments over time can lead to the breaking of silences or to the changing of their boundaries. The unsayable and the unsaid rarely stay fixed.

Another subject examined below is the selection or occlusion of those aspects of past violence which are problematic. Groups of people construct scripts which omit, correct and occasionally lie about the past. Repeated frequently enough, these scripts become formulaic or iconic, which is to say, they tell truths rather than the truth. Consensual silence is one way in which people construct the mythical stories they need to live with.

Silences break down when time passes and needs change. As in personal loss, groups of people need time in order to face collective loss or disaster. We have already noted that in many cultures, the initial stage of mourning demands silence. Thereafter men and women may be so busy rehabilitating themselves after a war or a violent conflict that they do not have the time, energy or will to speak about what happened. At such moments, they may be tempted to absorb and disseminate heroic stories without much factual basis.

The post-1945 period in Western Europe is a good example. Pieter Lagrou has documented the construction of the myth of national resistance in Belgium, the Netherlands and France. This heroic tapestry hid a much darker story, one whose emergence Henry Rousso has sketched in the case of France.[31] By the 1970s, it was possible to face some of the unpalatable history of the Second World War. Political and economic stability created the conditions for examining some of the hidden facets of the recent past.

What happens to societies happens to veterans of conflicts too. Young ex-soldiers grow old and tend to go over the ground of their youth. Grandchildren ask questions in ways grandparents may feel able at this stage of their lives to answer more fully and sometimes more honestly than

---

[31] Pieter Lagrou, *The legacy of Nazi occupation: Patriotic memory and national recovery in Western Europe, 1945–1965* (Cambridge University Press, 2000); Henry Rousso, *The Vichy syndrome: History and memory in France since 1944*, trans. Arthur Goldhammer (Cambridge, Mass.: Harvard University Press, 1994), p. 10.

they had done in the past. This is evident in the case of the young Israeli soldiers of 1948 interviewed fifty-five years later by Ben-Ze'ev. In their old age, they tended to speak of their war experiences differently from the ways they had done in the past. Their youthful certainty about their morality and the justness of their cause had faded (chapter 10).

Generational change may work in other ways too. Benjamin Stora describes how the *harkis* (Muslim Algerians who fought on the French side during the Algerian War) kept silent both about 'their' war and about the shabby treatment they received after they came to France in the mid-1960s. Their children felt no such compunction, and by demanding their rights, they helped draw aside the veil of silence on the war in Algeria as a whole. Such generational elements are among the many facets of the construction and deconstruction of silences about the Algerian war and about the violent suppression of Algerian demonstrations in Paris in October 1961, discussed by Raphaëlle Branche and Jim House in chapter 6.[32]

The passage of time alone is not always enough to change the boundaries of silence. Sometimes other catalysts are needed. Academic research, for instance, can occasionally bring certain silenced events into public attention. Henry Reynolds showed that Aborigines in Australia had fought against the seizure of their land. This eviscerated the argument of the Australian government that what they took was *terra nullus*, an empty landscape, and therefore gave Aborigines grounds to sue the Crown for failing to act responsibly as holders of the land in trust. Under some of that land lay uranium and other mineral deposits; it did not take more than a second or two for everyone to see the implications of Reynolds' research. While disputed by other scholars, Henry Reynolds helped expose the myths and lies about the past underlying Australian racism.[33]

The passage of time has finally uncovered many family secrets kept hidden in Stalinist Russia. Couples long married only recently told each other the truth about their family histories, about which both had lied to each other for decades. Why did they do so?: to cover the shame and the danger of admitting that fathers and mothers had been purged or murdered by the regime.[34] Here oral history and the 'memory activists' who conduct it can be the trigger which precipitates the ending of the reign of silence.

---

[32] Benjamin Stora, *La gangrène et l'oubli: La mémoire de la guerre d'Algérie* (Paris: La Découverte, 1991), pp. 261–5.

[33] Henry Reynolds, *The other side of the frontier: Aboriginal resistance to the European invasion of Australia* (Boulder, Colo.: Westview Press, 1998).

[34] Orlando Figes, *Whisperers: Private life in Stalin's Russia* (New York: Metropolitan Books, 2007).

Sometimes outsiders can do the research which changes the way insiders talk about the past. Insiders risk being labelled as outcasts for 'dwelling' too much on the 'negative' history of their country; outsiders have more freedom and less social pressure to confirm self-serving narratives about the past. Doing research on Vichy France in the 1960s and 1970s was a risky matter; there were (and are) too many sensitivities to respect and too many secrets to hide. Young scholars and archivists risked their careers if they started actively snooping around. An American historian faced none of these problems. Robert Paxton wrote his *Vichy France* (1972) on the basis of German archives while important parts of French archives were still closed. Paxton's thesis, which has stood the test of time, was that Vichy policy, including its harsh measures against Jews, was first and foremost a French matter and not a German diktat.[35] Collaboration was thus not primarily an attempt to defend the country against an occupier, but a consciously worked-out vision of a 'better' future, one purged of communists, trade unionists and Jews.

New academic 'fashions' can also induce discussion of silenced issues. Oral history emerged as a sub-discipline when feminists and subaltern scholars insisted on bringing women's voices and the voices of subject people into the study of the past. Sticking to conventional archives would ensure that they would never be heard. The official silence in Indonesia regarding the violence that Indonesian 'freedom fighters' inflicted on their fellow villagers during the 1945–9 war of independence against the Netherlands was not easily maintained in the face of sustained research and publications by younger historians and anthropologists using life histories and oral sources. The Indonesian war produced long-lasting silences on the Dutch side as well. The ugliness of the end of colonial rule has never been easy to face. These evasions, silences and outright lies could not be sustained in light of new research on war told from the soldiers' point of view, rather than from the politicians' or generals' perspective.[36]

Even though academic research can draw public attention to silenced past events, of much greater effect are 'memory agents' using trade publications, magazines, television, film and the internet to broadcast their historical narratives. Filmmakers, journalists, television series producers and fiction writers can reach a very wider public, and can make a

---

[35] John F. Sweets, 'Hold that pendulum! Redefining Fascism, collaborationism and resistance in France', *French Historical Studies*, XV, 4 (1988), p. 745.

[36] Stef Scagliola, 'The silences and myths of a "dirty war": Coming to terms with the Dutch-Indonesian decolonization war (1945–1949)', *European Review of History*, XIV, 2 (2007), pp. 249–51.

difference in broader currents of opinion about what can and cannot be said about the past. Marcel Ophüls' 1971 documentary *Le Chagrin et la pitié* (*The Sorrow and the Pity*) dealt with French life under Nazi occupation, focusing on the town of Clermont-Ferrand, and emphasised the active collaboration of many French men and women with the Germans. The film was criticised by some historians as largely distorted and as replacing the myth of a nation of resisters with another one – that of a nation of collaborators. Nevertheless, through skilful interviewing techniques, Ophüls effectively broke the silence regarding French collaboration under Nazi occupation and helped open a debate in France over this subject, a debate which is still alive today (2009). The Italian filmmaker Gillo Pontecorvo's 1966 *Bateglia di Algeri* (*Battle of Algiers*) produced considerable political controversy in France, and although banned from film theatres in France for five years, it helped to draw public attention to the Algerian war and to stimulate further discussion of dark subjects such as torture (see chapter 6). The Senegalese director, Ousmane Sembene's 1987 film, *Camp Thiaroye*, contributed to the initial breaking of the silence in Senegal and in France around the French brutal repression of an African soldiers' revolt in December 1944, a subject discussed by Ginio below (see chapter 7).

The most obvious political change that can alter the boundaries of silence is a departure of a leader, and/or a change of regime. Nikita Khrushchev's speech to the twentieth communist party congress in 1956, three years after Stalin's death, in which he criticised actions taken by the deceased leader is a prominent example. Even though knowledge of his speech was confined initially to the forum of party members, Khrushchev had accomplished something no one had dared to do while Stalin was still alive. His euphemism for mass murder – the cult of personality – fooled no one. Six years later, in 1962, the publication of Solzhenitsyn's *One Day in the Life of Ivan Denisovitch* broadcast the message in a story devastating in that it is simply the story of a good day; readers had little difficulty imagining what a bad day – or thirty years of bad days – was like.

The death or departure of a dictator does not always end the silence surrounding crimes committed under his rule. Indonesian historians and journalists may treat Suharto's role in the Indonesian revolution in a more critical light now that he has gone, but there is still much that cannot be said, at least in public, about many facets of his rule.[37] The same is true for the succession of rulers who have come to power in Ankara. The role of a

---

[37] Scagliola, 'The silences and myths of a "dirty war"', pp. 250–1.

long-defunct regime – that of the Ottoman empire – in the Armenian genocide of 1915 still today cannot be discussed in public, as Akçam shows (see chapter 9).

The May 1968 student revolt helped break a number of silences. Here was a generation's protest against a certain type of society and therefore, implicitly, of a certain vision of its history. French students challenged a society that had taken refuge behind the 'myth of the resistance' promoted, indeed embodied, by the then president Charles de Gaulle.[38] When he resigned, the obstacles to uncovering the silence of the Vichy years shrank considerably.

Social movements can throw a searchlight on the past and uncover corners hitherto darkened by consent or conspiracy. In Germany and Austria in 1968, the student revolt had many targets, including the war in Vietnam. But at its core, these protesters pointed an accusing finger at their parents' generation, not just with respect to their materialism, but with respect to what they had done or had not done during the Third Reich.[39] In Vienna, a group of young medical students and doctors exposed the experiments on Jewish children conducted in the Nazi period by Dr Heinrich Gross in the Spiegelgrund Children's Hospital in Vienna. He never went to jail, but his exposure was characteristic of the accusatory nature of inter-generational conflict in 1968 and after.[40]

Immigrant groups protesting their treatment in North America and Europe heightened interest in the slave trade and the wealth distinguished institutions gained from traffic in human beings. Consequently, a veil of silence was lifted in distinguished universities. Brown University formally acknowledged that its founders participated in the slave trade and that this institution had profited from it. Earlier histories of the university had not even mentioned the slave trade, but by 2004, times had changed.[41]

One essay in this book shows the way morally ambiguous chapters in the history of Israel become tied up in silences. Ariel Sharon was deemed by an Israeli judicial commission to be indirectly responsible for war crimes committed at Sabra and Shatilah refugee camps in 1982, during the Israeli invasion of Lebanon. Kaufman demonstrates that the focus on his culpability drew attention away from many other morally dubious episodes in that campaign, while ultimately not preventing his reemergence twenty years later as a man of peace and prime minister of his

---

[38] Rousso, *The Vichy syndrome*, pp. 98–9.
[39] Michael A. Schmidtke, 'Cultural revolution or culture shock? Student radicalism and 1968 in Germany', *South Central Review*, XVI, 4 (2000), pp. 77–89.
[40] I am grateful to Helmut Konrad, of the University of Graz, who drew this story to my attention during a visit to the site of the crime in 2008.
[41] *Slavery and justice* (Providence, RI: Brown University, 2004).

country (see chapter 11). On the contrary; everyone knew about Sharon and Sabra and Shatila, but no one talked about it.

Once more, it is important to emphasise that speech acts can be performative. They can be sufficiently overblown as to obscure or obliterate recollection of particular events. Silence too is performative; understanding its meaning depends on the aim of the the individual and the groups framing and performing it.[42]

There are those who believe that commemoration can entail a turning away from political action, a kind of anaesthesia which deadens sensibilities and the will to act in the world.[43] What I have called the 'memory boom' of the later twentieth century followed the events of 1968, which both shook and left standing the foundations of political power in the developed world.[44] Is remembering therefore a kind of silencing of political will? Yes and no; what the French call 'le devoir de mémoire', the duty to remember, is both more prevalent today and more likely to include within politically or socially necessary acts of collective remembrance hidden silences which marginalise or eliminate uncomfortable readings of the subject being commemorated. The general rule is that the closer to the centres of power in the state are such acts of commemoration, the more likely is it that ulterior political motives will lead to a highjacking of the event and its deployment as a means of legitimating the current order. Small-scale commemoration is much less likely to be coopted in this way. Remembering can lead to action just as easily as it can lead to inaction; it all depends on who does the work of remembrance.[45]

Conclusion

Our interpretation of the way silences are constructed and maintained may be summarised in two parts. First, morally ambiguous chapters of a country's history cannot be faced easily, and which country does not have them? This is recognised by small groups, by larger populations, and by societies as a whole; talking about the past presents the danger of a

---

[42] Jay Winter, 'The performance of the past: Memory, history, identity', in Karin Tilmans, Frank van Vree and Jay Winter (eds.), *Performing the past* (University of Chicago Press, 2010), ch. 1.

[43] Charles S. Maier, 'A surfeit of memory? Reflections on history, melancholy and denial', *History and memory*, V, 2 (1993), pp. 136–51; see also Charles S. Maier, 'Hot memory ... cold memory: On the political half-life of fascist and communist memory', paper delivered to conference on 'The Memory of the century', Institut für die Wissenschaften vom Menschen, Vienna, 9–11 March 2001.

[44] Winter, *Remembering war*, ch. 1.   [45] Ibid., ch. 6.

breakdown of the legitimacy or the authority of a regime. In one respect, silence then is the insurance policy people take to protect the given order, even at the cost of the truth. This is the motor force behind what we term political silence.

Secondly, over time such veils of silence fray, tear, disintegrate or are torn apart. Memory activists are critical players in this process, and they work against the backdrop of the movement of time and the inevitable passage of generations. New technologies for the archiving and retrieval of testimony help dispel some silences, though not all.

A rough rule of thumb is that the process of democratisation entails an ending of socially accepted silences about what happened in a pre-democratic period. The gradual democratisation process in Senegal beginning in 1974 and accelerating with the resignation of Léopold Sédar Senghor in 1980 allowed playwrights and filmmakers to criticise neo-colonial relations with France and reevaluate the French presence in this African country before and after independence (see chapter 7). The Spanish transition from Franco's dictatorship to a constitutional monarchy shows, though, that some silences may linger long after the new institutions of a democratic state have been established (see chapter 3). Democracies have their silences too, and they are perhaps more insidious because they appear to be enforced without visible coercion.

All those who posit rules of thumb must immediately admit to exceptions. In some cases, silence follows completely unambiguous narratives of a regime's crimes. In 2005, the new Georgian Ministry of Education, eager to display its democratic credentials and await its entry into the European Union, constructed a syllabus of twentieth-century history for their schools and universities without mentioning one of their most distinguished native sons – Josef Stalin.[46] Silence here is another word for lying about the past, a practice which shows no sign of going out of fashion. While taking account of such practices, we do not wish to reduce all forms of silence to this level. Silence, like shadows, best describes the grey areas of the past.

There are always people in a position to violate codes of silence, in a way denied to or rejected by the rest of us. Madmen, actors, comedians, holy men, poets, troubadours frequently occupy liminal positions within society, and sometimes manage to say the unsayable, and live to tell the tale again. They renew, so to speak, our poetic licence, and help us, perhaps force us, to hear the silences built into the language we use to describe the past. Even under the most horrifying conditions, some individuals who

---

[46] Bellagio conference on History and Memory in Georgia, July 2005.

perform language still have the courage and the conviction to speak out, and by doing so, point to what everyone else knows but is not saying.

Two stories from the worst of Stalin's years illustrate this point. The first is in a story Solzhenitsyn tells of a great meeting in a Soviet city to celebrate the heroic output of a factory. At the end of the speech the party hack gave, the audience to a man rose and thunderously applauded. They stood standing and applauding, and soon realised that someone had to be the first to stop, but no one wanted to be that individual. Hands grew sore, and at one point, a man stopped clapping and sat down. The next day he vanished into the Gulag. In that mad world, his hands had condemned him by ceasing to signal his applause; he had lapsed into lethal silence.[47]

The second illustration is also Russian from the Stalin period. There is today in St Petersburg a statue of Anna Akhmatova, standing mute in front of the prison where in 1938 her son or knowledge of her son lay hidden. Her poem 'Requiem' recalls the 300 hours of her frozen vigil at that very place. Her words are there, rooted to the spot, as she had been, silently, hoping against hope, seventy years ago. She asked in her poem that if there would be a monument to her, it would be placed there, and so it is. Poets live with silence; they help us feel it and see where it starts and where it ends.[48]

Our intention in this book is to place the social construction of silence alongside remembering and forgetting the events of war and violence in different parts of the world. We show that silence has liturgical and essentialist functions, as much as political ones, and that while the political domain is essential in this field, we should also note that the subject of war and violence always touches the sphere of the sacred, and in that sphere there are always silences. We note that many veterans of wars insist that only those who 'know' through direct experience can speak about war, but that this claim is filled with contradictions and flaws. We show that there are agents of silencing, intent on keeping the lid on certain topics or words, just as there are memory agents equally dedicated to blowing the lid off. We draw attention to liminal figures, like writers, comedians, actors, who live in a special space accorded to risky speech, one which can offend and provoke by saying things which everyone knows but no one says in public. All of these people live their lives surrounded by a cloud of socially produced silence, a cloud which can be opaque or vanish in a flash.

[47] Aleksandr I. Solzhenitsyn, *The Gulag Archipelago* (New York: Harper & Row, 1973), pp. 69ff.
[48] Robin Kemball, 'Anna Akhmatova's "Requiem, 1935–1940"', *Russian Review*, XXXIII (1974), pp. 303–12.

Silence is not one but many things, and all occupy and frame the landscape of remembrance. The French writer Maurice Blanchot summed up our subject with uncharacteristic Gallic directness. 'To be silent is still to speak', he wrote in 1952.[49] And to speak of silence as a social phenomenon, as we have done in this book, is to speak of the myriad ways in which we all observe silences, and thereby agree to deal with moral ambiguities, to live with and through contradictions, by both remembering *and* forgetting the past.

---

[49] Blanchot, 'The Writing of the disaster', p. 11.

2   The social sound of silence: Toward a sociology of denial

Eviatar Zerubavel

A foremost manifestation of the social construction of silence is the phenomenon commonly known as a *conspiracy of silence*, whereby people collectively ignore something of which each one of them is personally aware.[1] Whether it takes place in an alcoholic family, a corrupt organization, or a country ruled by an incompetent leader, such "silent witnessing"[2] involves situations where each "conspirator" is aware of something yet nevertheless unwilling to publicly acknowledge it. Essentially underscoring the difference between knowing and acknowledging, conspiracies of silence thus highlight the fundamental yet undertheorized tension between personal awareness and public discourse.

Whether they are generated by pain, shame, embarrassment, or fear,[3] conspiracies of silence revolve around *undiscussables*, let alone *unmentionables*, that are "generally known but cannot be spoken."[4] In other words, they revolve around so-called *open secrets* that, unlike ordinary ones, are actually known by everyone thereby constituting "uncomfortable truths hidden in plain sight."[5]

Being both aware and (at least publicly) unaware of something at the same time implies a certain amount of *denial*, yet studying conspiracies of silence requires approaching this notoriously elusive concept from a sociological rather than a more traditional psychological perspective. Whereas psychologists are essentially interested in the *intra*personal dynamics of blocking information from entering individuals' awareness, a *sociology* of denial would highlight the *inter*personal dynamics of keeping it from entering their public discourse.

---

[1] See Eviatar Zerubavel, *The Elephant in the Room: Silence and Denial in Everyday Life* (New York: Oxford University Press, 2006).
[2] Stanley Cohen, *States of Denial: Knowing about Atrocities and Suffering* (Cambridge: Polity, 2001), p. 75.
[3] Zerubavel, *The Elephant in the Room*, pp. 5–8.
[4] Michael Taussig, *Defacement: Public Secrecy and the Labor of the Negative* (Stanford University Press, 1999), pp. 50–1.
[5] Paul Krugman, "Gotta Have Faith," *New York Times*, December 17, 2002, p. A35.

The simplest way to refrain from publicly acknowledging something of which one is personally aware is to remain silent about it. And indeed, the foremost public form of denial is silence. Silence is more than simply absence of sound. As Paul Simon points out in his famous song, it actually has a rather clear sound. In fact, as our conventional images of "thick," "heavy," "deafening," or "resounding" silence seem to imply, it often speaks louder than words.

In his short story "Silence," Leonid Andreyev explicitly contrasts stillness, or "the mere absence of noise," with silence, which actually implies "that those who kept silent could ... have spoken if they had pleased."[6] Being silent, in other words, involves more than just absence of action, since the things we are silent about are in fact actively *avoided*.

Rather than simply failing to notice something, denial too involves an effort to actively avoid noticing it. Moreover, it involves avoiding things that actually beg for our attention, thereby reminding us that conspiracies of silence revolve not around unnoticeable matters we simply overlook but actually around highly conspicuous ones we actively avoid.[7] That explains our choice of the proverbial "elephant in the room," a creature of imposing stature and therefore highly noticeable presence, to represent metaphorically the object of such conspiracies. Like the emperor's naked body in "The Emperor's New Clothes,"[8] it is highly visible to anyone willing to keep his eyes open. Thus, if we ignore its presence, it can only be as a result of active avoidance, as otherwise it would be impossible *not* to notice it. To ignore an "elephant," in short, is to ignore the obvious.

Ignoring an "elephant" is not a result of simply failing to notice it but of some actual *pressure to disregard* it. Such pressure is for the most part a product of unmistakably social traditions, conventions, and norms of attending which we internalize as part of our socialization.[9]

To appreciate the normative, and thus social, underpinnings of the mental act of ignoring something, consider, for example, the norms of

---

[6] Leonid N. Andreyev, "Silence," in *The Little Angel and Other Stories* (Freeport, NY: Books for Libraries Press, 1971 [1910]), p. 130. See also pp. 131–2, 140, 142, 144.

[7] See also Włodzimierz Sobkowiak, "Silence and Markedness Theory," in Adam Jaworski (ed.), *Silence: Interdisciplinary Perspectives* (Berlin and New York: Mouton de Gruyter, 1997), pp. 39–61.

[8] Don Juan Manuel, "What Happened to the King and the Tricksters Who Made Cloth," in John E. Keller and L. Clark Keating (trans.), *The Book of Count Lucanor and Patronio* (Lexington: University Press of Kentucky, 1977 [1335]), pp. 130–3, famously retold by Hans Christian Andersen in "The Emperor's New Clothes," in *The Complete Fairy Tales and Stories* (Garden City, NY: Doubleday, 1974 [1836]), pp. 77–81.

[9] On the social organization of human attention, see Eviatar Zerubavel, *Social Mindscapes: An Invitation to Cognitive Sociology* (Cambridge, Mass: Harvard University Press, 1997), pp. 35–52.

attention that so often determine what we regard as irrelevant. Separating the "relevant" from the "irrelevant," after all, is for the most part a *socio-mental* act performed by members of particular social communities who are socialized to focus on, and thereby notice, certain things while systematically disregarding others.

Consider, for example, the way juries are socially expected and even formally instructed to focus their attention in court. Under the exclusionary rule, for instance, illegally obtained evidence, compelling as it may be, is considered inadmissible, and if it is ever brought up in court the judge can actually order the jury to disregard it. Along similar lines, consider also the tacit social norms that govern the way people focus their attention in gynecological examinations. Medical practitioners, for example, are socialized to regard "the pelvic area ... like any other part of the body" to the point where its "sexual connotations are left behind," and, as one would expect, they therefore want it clearly understood that "they are not concerned with an aesthetic inspection of a patient's body" and that "their gazes take in only medically pertinent facts." For the same reason, however, patients too are expected "to have an attentive glance upward, at the ceiling or at other persons in the room, eyes open, not dreamy or 'away.' [They are] supposed to avoid looking into the doctor's eyes during the actual examination because direct eye contact between the two at this time is [considered] provocative."[10]

What we are socially expected to ignore is often articulated in the form of various *taboos against looking, listening, as well as speaking.* Those who defy or even simply ignore such prohibitions are considered social deviants. As such, they are often targets of social sanctions.

A most effective way to ensure that we would in fact stay away from tabooed objects and not discuss, let alone even mention them is keeping them *nameless.*[11] A somewhat milder form of verbal avoidance involves the use of *euphemisms* ("the ladies' room," "the F word"), which basically allow us to invoke them indirectly while technically refraining from mentioning them. By using an innocuous brand name such as Tampax, for example, advertisers can thus effectively invoke a subject like menstruation while still keeping it technically unmentionable (so convincingly, indeed, that only a naive little boy might actually start craving this

---

[10] Joan P. Emerson, "Behavior in Private Places: Sustaining Definitions of Reality in Gynecological Examinations," in Hans-Peter Dreitzel (ed.), *Recent Sociology No.2: Patterns of Communicative Behavior* (London: Macmillan, 1970), pp. 78, 83. See also p. 86.

[11] See, for example, Mark Jordan, *The Silence of Sodom: Homosexuality in Modern Catholicism* (University of Chicago Press, 2000), p. 16.

seemingly magical product after seeing on a television commercial that one can do practically anything – swim, bowl, ski, play tennis – with it).

Yet much of what we are expected to ignore is socially articulated in the even milder form of *tact*, which, although sociologists have yet to note the connection between them, is but a "soft" version of taboo. As evident from etiquette rules prohibiting us from either asking or commenting about others' marital problems, miscarriages, or suicide attempts, that involves staying away from "delicate" information we have not been invited to access. Being tactless is considered a form of social deviance, and friends and neighbors may even turn a blind eye to possible signs of domestic violence (bruises, loud altercations) just to avoid being labeled "nosy."

Not only are we expected to refrain from asking embarrassing questions, we are also supposed to pretend not to have heard embarrassing "answers" even when we actually have. By not acknowledging what we in fact do see or hear, we thus tactfully *pretend not to notice* it. Pretending not to notice things we "know but ... are supposed not to know"[12] is at the heart of what it means to be tactful, as so perfectly captured in the tongue-in-cheek definition of a gentleman as someone who, having mistakenly entered the ladies' showers, tells the naked woman he sees there: "Excuse me, sir." That also explains why the first person in "The Emperor's New Clothes" who announces that the emperor has no clothes is in fact a child who has yet to learn what one is supposed to pretend not to notice even when one does notice it.

Yet the social pressure to ignore the elephant in the room is only partly produced by norms. The scope of our attention and the bounds of acceptable discourse are socially delineated by normative as well as political constraints, and what we look at, listen to, and talk about is therefore actually affected by *both normative and political pressures.*[13] Indeed, appreciating the prohibitive political circumstances that typically promote silence is necessary for understanding why it is actually the emperor's (and not, say, one of his attendants') lack of clothing that the metaphor of the elephant in the room so evocatively captures.

As we proceed to examine the phenomenon of denial from a sociological rather than a more traditional psychological perspective we soon realize that it often involves more than just one person and that we are actually dealing with *co-denial*, an unmistakably social phenomenon that involves *mutual* avoidance. Indeed, only when the elephant in the room is

---

[12] Lily Pincus and Christopher Dare, *Secrets in the Family* (New York: Pantheon Books, 1978), p. 145.

[13] Zerubavel, *The Elephant in the Room*, pp. 33–45.

jointly avoided can we actually talk about a "conspiracy" of silence. No wonder we often represent such conspiracies in the form of a *team* of three monkeys who see no evil, hear no evil, and speak no evil. The fact that they are always presented together clearly points to social systems rather than individuals as the most appropriate context for studying silence.

As the foremost manifestation of co-denial, silence is a *collective* endeavor. While "it takes only one person to produce speech ... it requires the *cooperation of all* to produce silence."[14] The silence surrounding marital violence, for example, thus involves not only the perpetrator who wants to keep it secret, but also the victim who feels too embarrassed to tell anyone about it as well as other family members, neighbors, and friends who are quite aware of it yet nevertheless unwilling to acknowledge it publicly. Indeed, it is the *collaborative* efforts of those who avoid mentioning the elephant and those who refrain from asking about it that make it a conspiracy. In other words, it takes at least two persons to "dance the familiar conspiracy tango – one not to tell, the other not to ask."[15]

At first glance, it is only the monkey who speaks no evil who seems to be responsible for generating the silence, yet a more nuanced understanding of the dynamics of co-denial calls for examining the intricate relations among all three members of this simian trio. Consider, for instance, the essentially symbiotic relationship between not speaking and not listening. After all, in order for Bill Clinton to be able to keep his affair with Monica Lewinsky secret, it was critical that people around him would also not be too curious about it. Though evidently somewhat suspicious about the nature of their relationship, his personal secretary Betty Currie thus nevertheless tried to "avoid learning the details." Even Treasury Secretary Robert Rubin, who was in charge of the White House Secret Service, made a conscious effort not to find out what its agents actually knew about it: "I wouldn't sit in the same room if they wanted to tell me."[16]

Furthermore, as one is reminded by the discreet manner in which Thomas Jefferson conducted his relationship with his slave Sally Hemings, thereby making it easier for his family to pretend not to know about it and thus avoiding public humiliation, being tactful toward others requires some preventive display of tact on *their* part as well.[17] After all, if they expect me to pretend to ignore them, they need to be careful not to

---

[14] Robert E. Pittenger et al., *The First Five Minutes: A Sample of Microscopic Interview Analysis* (Ithaca, NY: Paul Martineau, 1960), p. 88. Emphasis added.

[15] I. F. Stone, "It Pays To Be Ignorant," *New York Review of Books*, August 9, 1973, p. 8.

[16] David E. Sanger, "Lewinsky Was Familiar Face to Agents near Clinton's Door," *New York Times*, September 13, 1998, National Section, p. 35.

[17] See also Erving Goffman, *The Presentation of Self in Everyday Life* (Garden City, NY: Doubleday Anchor, 1959), pp. 234–7.

force themselves on my attention. It is easier to hear no evil when others speak no evil, and to see no evil when they "show no evil," as the highly collaborative manner in which our society's discomfort with nudity is jointly expressed by (at least seemingly) incurious non-voyeurs and discreet non-exhibitionists seems to suggest. By being tactful we thus also help others avoid embarrassing us.

The equal protection provided to those who speak and those who hear no evil is the result of the rather symmetrical relations between the opposing social forces generating conspiracies of silence. Such symmetry is exemplified by the reluctance of *both* children and parents to discuss sexual matters with each other, the former feeling uncomfortable asking and the latter feeling equally uncomfortable telling. Along similar lines, consider also the chillingly symmetrical dynamics of silence between the fearsome perpetrators and fearful witnesses of atrocities, as evidenced, for example, by the Nazis' efforts to hide the horrors of their concentration camps from nearby residents who in turn tried to turn a blind eye and disregard them.[18]

By collaboratively seeing and showing, or hearing and speaking, no evil we thus construct a *double wall of silence*,[19] so perfectly exemplified by the proverbial closet surrounding homosexuality, which is an unmistakably collaborative construction built by gays and straights *together* and, as is quite evident in the infamous US military "Don't ask, don't tell" policy, designed to prevent those inside it from speaking as well as those outside it from hearing.[20] Consider also, along these lines, the structurally as well as functionally similar wall of silence jointly constructed by doctors and terminal patients around the patient's imminent death, when "both doctor and patient know of the latter's fatal illness, and both know the other knows, but they do not talk to each other about it,"[21] or the heavy silence hanging over many Holocaust survivors' homes, which is essentially a product of the tragic "interweaving of two kinds of conflicted energy: on the part of the survivor, [the] suppression of telling; on the part of the descendant, [the] fear of finding out."[22]

[18] See, for example, Gordon J. Horwitz, *In the Shadow of Death: Living Outside the Gates of Mauthausen* (New York: Free Press, 1990), p. 175. See also pp. 36–7, 92–6.

[19] Dan Bar-On, *Legacy of Silence: Encounters with Children of the Third Reich* (Cambridge, Mass: Harvard University Press, 1989), p. 328.

[20] See also Jordan, *The Silence of Sodom*, pp. 90, 107.

[21] Barney G. Glaser and Anselm L. Strauss, *Awareness of Dying* (University of Chicago Press, 1965), p. 125.

[22] Ruth Wajnryb, *The Silence: How Tragedy Shapes Talk* (Crows Nest, Australia: Allen and Unwin, 2001), p. 32.

One of the major factors affecting the likelihood of participating in a conspiracy of silence is the amount of social distance among the participants. The "closer" we feel, the more we trust (and the more likely therefore we are to talk more openly with) one another. Formal relations, on the other hand, stifle openness and thus promote silence.

Equally significant are the power relations among the participants. We generally trust our equals more than our superiors, and social systems with particularly hierarchical structures (and thus more pronounced power differences) therefore make open discourse much less likely.

Needless to say, there is also a significant difference between private and public settings. After all, while co-workers may quite readily discuss their higher-ups' corrupt or incompetent behavior "behind the safety of closed doors and in veiled whispers ... only the foolish or naive dare to speak of it in public."[23] That also explains why the norms of political correctness are more likely to be breached in restroom graffiti than in public lectures.

Yet the structural factor that most dramatically affects the likelihood of participating in conspiracies of silence is the number of conspirators involved. In marked contrast to ordinary secrets, "open" ones are actually more tightly guarded as *more*, rather than fewer, people know them. Indeed, the larger the number of participants in the conspiracy, the more prohibitive the silence.

As so chillingly portrayed in the film *The Incident*, two young hoodlums can actually terrorize an entire subway car not despite, but precisely as a result of, the presence of so many passengers silently watching them together.[24] By implicitly exemplifying the undiscussability of atrocities and abuse, such *silent bystanders* essentially enable their denial. Women who remain silent when their husbands molest their daughters thus help perpetuate the abuse (as do many "supervising" bishops in cases of pedophile priests) by the very fact that they refrain from explicitly acknowledging that it is happening. So, for that matter, do friends and co-workers who look the other way and pretend not to notice obvious signs of one's alcohol addiction.

Watching others ignore the elephant in the room increases the likelihood that one will also ignore it, and the social pressure to join the conspiracy is compounded as the number of those silent bystanders

---

[23] Elizabeth W. Morrison and Frances J. Milliken, "Organizational Silence: A Barrier to Change and Development in a Pluralistic World," *Academy of Management Review* XXV (2000), p. 706.

[24] See also Bibb Latané and John M. Darley, *The Unresponsive Bystander: Why Doesn't He Help?* (New York: Appleton-Century-Crofts, 1970).

increases. Broaching an unmentionable subject is much more difficult when there are thirty rather than just three other persons around, none of whom seems particularly eager to discuss it.

Watching several people ignore the elephant together is also quite different from watching each of them ignore it by himself, as it involves *watching each of them watch the others ignore it* as well. In fact, these are situations in which each participant is essentially surrounded by an entire social system (rather than just a bunch of isolated individuals) in denial. Moving from two-person to wider conspiracies of silence thus also involves a significant shift from strictly interpersonal pressure to actual *group pressure*, where breaking the silence seems to violate not just some individuals' personal sense of comfort but a collectively imposed taboo, thereby also evoking a somewhat heightened sense of fear.

Yet what often determines the intensity of a silence is not only the number of persons conspiring to maintain it but also how long they manage to do so. Like other forms of denial, silence is self-reinforcing, and the longer we remain silent, the more necessary it becomes "to cover [our] silence with further silence."[25] In other words, *silence becomes more prohibitive the longer it lasts*. As Samuel Johnson said, "silence propagates itself [and] the longer talk has been suspended the more difficult it is to find anything to say."[26] By the same token, "the longer [things] remain undiscussed, the harder it becomes to talk about them."[27]

Furthermore, as I watch others ignore a comment made at a meeting and, as a result, disregard it as well, the social pressure on them to further disregard it is in turn intensified by my own disregard. A vicious cycle is thus generated where each conspirator's denial in turn bolsters the others', their collective silence thereby increasingly reverberating as more people join the conspiracy. Indeed, that is how an entire society comes collectively to deny its leader's incompetence, glaring atrocities, or impending environmental disasters.

Yet what ultimately makes conspiracies of silence even more insidious is the underlying *meta-silence*, the fact that the silence itself is never actually discussed among the conspirators. Unlike situations where we explicitly agree not to talk about something ("let's not get into that"), the very fact that they are avoiding it thus also remains unacknowledged.

---

[25] Frederick B. Bird, *The Muted Conscience: Moral Silence and the Practice of Ethics in Business* (Westport, Conn.: Quorum Books, 1996), p. 51.

[26] Rudolf Flesch, *The New Book of Unusual Quotations* (New York: Harper and Row, 1966), pp. 349–50.

[27] Kathleen D. Ryan and Daniel K. Oestreich, *Driving Fear Out of the Office: How To Overcome the Invisible Barriers to Quality, Productivity, and Innovation* (San Francisco: Jossey-Bass, 1991), p. 30.

Indeed, the reason it is so difficult to talk about the elephant in the room is that "not only does no one want to listen, but no one wants to talk about not listening."[28] We thus avoid it without acknowledging that we are actually doing so – a perfect example of *meta-denial*. The very act of avoiding the elephant, in other words, is itself an "elephant".

Yet though the likelihood of participating in conspiracies of silence increases as they become wider or longer, the opportunities for ending them increase as well. And even if none of the conspirators actually try to break the silence, there is always a chance, however small, that they might.

Breaking a conspiracy of silence involves *acknowledging the presence of the elephant in the room* by making it part of the public discourse. While many people throughout the Soviet Union had been personally aware of the atrocities committed under Stalin, for example, only with Khrushchev's speech about "the cult of the personality" to the twentieth party congress in 1956, and even more so, with the publication of Aleksandr Solzhenitsyn's harrowing account of the Gulag system in *One Day in the Life of Ivan Denisovich* (1962) was the deafening silence surrounding them *publicly* broken. By the same token, although many Americans may have noticed George W. Bush's poor judgment, callousness, and lack of accountability following the 2003 US invasion of Iraq, not until the 2005 flooding of the city of New Orleans did those blatant features of his presidency fully enter the public discourse.

To appreciate the role of publicity in combating denial, consider, for example, the attempts made by gay activists during the AIDS epidemic of the 1980s to force prominent gay public figures out of their closets in a deliberate effort to expose the hitherto unsuspected prevalence of homo-sexuality in American society. Note, however, the subtle yet significant difference between the acts of "outing" particular individuals and expos-ing the prevalence of homosexuality in general. This is similar to the distinction between laws that require local authorities to publicize the identities of sex offenders and attempts to raise our general awareness of child pornography. This contrast underscores the fundamental yet under-theorized distinction between silence breaking and whistle-blowing.

After all, what silence breakers such as Émile Zola (whose open letter "*J'accuse*" broke the public silence surrounding the rather blatant yet unacknowledged anti-semitic undertones of the Dreyfus affair) or Rolf Hochhuth (whose 1963 play *The Deputy* opened public discussion over the question of the Vatican's complicity in the Holocaust) essentially do is

[28] C. Fred Alford, *Whistleblowers: Broken Lives and Organizational Power* (Ithaca, NY: Cornell University Press, 2001), pp. 20–1.

quite different from what whistle-blowers such as Daniel Ellsberg, Erin Brockovich, or the *60 Minutes* team do. Rather than ordinary secrets the very existence of which most of us are unaware, they try to unveil "open" ones of which we are all personally aware yet unwilling to publicly acknowledge. In publicizing "back*ground*" (yet nevertheless overt) rather than back*stage* (and therefore covert) information, they thus help uncover "elephants" rather than closeted "skeletons."

It is not only individuals, however, who break conspiracies of silence. Indeed, there are many social movements whose entire raison d'être is to raise public awareness of ubiquitous yet nevertheless collectively ignored "elephants." The public demonstrations held by the Mothers of the Plaza de Mayo to protest Argentina's infamous "Dirty War" against its political dissidents in the late 1970s and 1980s perfectly exemplify such group silence-breaking. So do "Take Back the Night" rallies aimed at raising public awareness of a traditionally ignored issue like rape, and efforts made by "alternative" newspapers and human rights organizations to call attention to the plight of traditionally ignored groups like sweatshop workers and refugees.

In order for their presence to be publicly acknowledged "elephants" need to be pulled out of the socio-perceptual "background" and turned into "figures" of explicit attention. Breaking conspiracies of silence, in other words, involves *foregrounding* the elephant in the room. That entails enhancing its social visibility by turning the proverbial spotlight on it as well as by metaphorically opening people's eyes so that they cannot help but "see" it. It also involves making it figuratively audible by being *outspoken*, as exemplified by documentary filmmaker Michael Moore's 2003 Oscar acceptance speech, where he bluntly declared at a ceremony marked by its organizers' effort to politely ignore the fact that it was being held only a few days after the US invasion of Iraq:

We like non-fiction [yet] we live in fictitious times. We live in a time where we have fictitious election results that elect a fictitious president. We live in a time where we have a man who's sending us to war for fictitious reasons. Whether it's the fiction of duct tape or fiction of orange alerts, we are against this war, Mr. Bush. Shame on you, Mr. Bush, shame on you.[29]

Silence-breaking presupposes *straightforwardness*. Essentially reversing pronouncedly evasive denial-enhancing tactics, such as using euphemisms and "beating around the bush," one normally breaks conspiracies

---

[29] "Moore Fires Oscar Anti-War Salvo," March 24, 2003, http://news.bbc.co.uk/1/hi/entertainment/film/2879857.stm.

of silence by "calling a spade a spade." This often involves *naming* the "elephant" thereby making it more explicitly discussable, as famously exemplified by Betty Friedan's critique of the resounding silence surrounding the reality of being a housewife, the first chapter of which is actually titled "The Problem That Has No Name" and opens with the words, "The problem lay buried, unspoken, for many years in the minds of American women."[30] Consider also, along these lines, the 2004 *Nightline* segment where Ted Koppel simply read the names of all the 700 or so American soldiers who had died in the Iraq War up to that point thereby explicitly foregrounding the war's widely known yet at the time still publicly invisible and inadmissible human cost.[31]

"Elephants" are also foregrounded artistically, as exemplified by protest songs and anti-war exhibits such as the "Arlington West" mock cemeteries in Santa Barbara and Santa Monica,[32] as well as through humor. Consider, for instance, a 2003 *Daily Show with Jon Stewart* skit where a 28-page section officially blanked out from a congressional report in a lame effort to "unmention" Saudi Arabia's highly conspicuous role in the 9/11 attacks is satirically hailed by Stephen Colbert as an artistic tour de force:

> But look at the report. I mean really look at it. Notice the use of bold black lines ... This piece asks us: 'What is a government report? Does it need to contain information?' It forces the reader into an agonizing reappraisal of our societal dependency upon facts, names, dates, places ... I say 'Bravo, Bush Administration, for this remarkable report!'[33]

No wonder so much of our humor revolves around taboo subjects such as sex, bodily functions, and social groups ordinarily protected by the norms of political correctness. Indeed, it may sometimes become the only legitimate form of discourse in which "elephants" can be safely foregrounded. After all, even in Nazi Germany one could at least tacitly point to the glaring discrepancy between one's leaders' actual looks and the "Aryan" ideal of manhood they so vigorously championed through jokes suggesting, tongue in cheek, that the ideal German ought to be "as blond as Hitler, as tall as Goebbels, [and] as slim as Göring."[34]

Like silence itself, breaking it is a collective endeavor. Like the child in "The Emperor's New Clothes," the first person who mentions the elephant in the room only begins the collective process of publicly

---

[30] Betty Friedan, *The Feminine Mystique* (New York: W. W. Norton, 1963), p. 15.
[31] "Nightline," April 30, 2004.
[32] www.arlingtonwestfilm.com. See also www.breakingthesilence.org.il/index_en.asp.
[33] "The Daily Show with Jon Stewart," July 28, 2003.
[34] Fritz K. M. Hillenbrandt, *Underground Humour in Nazi Germany 1933–1945* (London: Routledge, 1995), p. 11. See also the cartoon on p. 37.

acknowledging its presence. After all, for a conspiracy of silence to actually end there ultimately must be no more conspirators left who want to keep it alive.

Essentially counteracting the group pressure to maintain the silence, silence breakers too use the weight of numbers. As evidenced by family intervention tactics of overcoming drug addicts' denial of their addiction, while "it is fairly easy to discount or dismiss the claims of one person ... it becomes harder when these claims are made by a chorus. A group carries the necessary weight to break through to reality."[35]

As we have seen, the situation of a numerical minority facing pressure from the majority to join a conspiracy of silence becomes more pronounced as the number of conspirators increases. Yet for the very same reason, as more people join the first person who tries to break the silence, the increasing social pressure on the remaining conspirators to acknowledge the elephant's presence may ultimately override the social pressure to keep denying it.

In order for that to happen, however, they need to be ready actually to hear the announcement that the emperor has no clothes. Yet as the Trojans' reaction to Cassandra's prophetic warnings about the wooden horse seems to suggest, our initial response to those who try to open our eyes is quite often to actually ignore them. Essentially expanding the conspiracy of silence also to encompass anyone who tries to break it, we thus resist the pressure to acknowledge the presence of the foregrounded elephant by trying to push it back to the background.

As if to test the limits of cynicism, conspirators of silence may in fact even ask everybody nevertheless to keep ignoring the unveiled elephant, as exemplified by George W. Bush's attempt to use the "This is no time to play the blame game" tactic to deflect public criticism following Hurricane Katrina. They may also try to divert attention away from the silence breakers, question their credibility (and thereby also the reality of the elephant), or even actually silence them.

Silence breakers are also ridiculed, vilified, and ostracized.[36] Aside from their immediate punitive function, such retaliatory tactics are also designed to intimidate anyone else who might contemplate breaking the silence. Yet actual or potential silence breakers are not the only designated targets of such intimidation; so, in fact, is anybody who pays attention to

---

[35] Vernon E. Johnson, *Intervention: How To Help Someone Who Doesn't Want Help* (Minneapolis, Minn.: Johnson Institute Books, 1986), p. 66.
[36] On why we often consider silence breakers social deviants, see Zerubavel, *The Elephant in the Room*, pp. 73–8.

them. After all, only when our mouths *as well as our eyes and ears* are kept tightly shut will the elephant in the room remain unnoticed.

Ironically, it is precisely our collective efforts to keep them closed that make it so big. As soon as we open our eyes, ears and mouths and jointly acknowledge its presence, it actually begins to shrink. And only then, when we no longer collude to ignore it, would the proverbial elephant finally get out of the room.

Part II

Europe

3   Breaking the silence? Memory and oblivion
     since the Spanish Civil War*

Mary Vincent

> The late rebellion need not be remembered since it is impossible it
> should be forgotten.[1]

On 28 October 2007, Spain's congress of deputies voted in favour of a
'law to recognise and broaden the rights of and support for those who
suffered persecution or violence during the Civil War and dictatorship'.[2]
Universally known as the law of historical memory, the legislation
was approved by the Senate on 10 December 2007 and published on 2
December as Ley 52/2007,[3] the culmination of a much longer process of
'recovering' a public memory of civil war. King Juan Carlos had, for
example, declared 2006 – the seventieth anniversary of the outbreak of
the Civil War – to be Spain's 'year of historical memory'. Significantly,
2006 was also the seventy-fifth anniversary of the coming to power of the
Second Spanish Republic and, as the king's declaration made clear, the
historical experience of democracy was the foundation for any recovery of
historical memory.

In the decree, 'over 25 years of democracy' was treated as the stable
foundation that now allowed Spaniards to address the question of historical memory.[4] Such an assumption is validated by the scholarly literature: it has become commonplace to assert that this concern with
a traumatic past attests to the robustness of consolidated democracy.
Far from being fragile or transitional, Spanish democracy now has

---

* I would like to thank Mike Braddick, Paul Heywood and Gary Rivett for their help with this
  chapter.
[1] Quoted in Jonathan Scott, *England's Troubles: Seventeenth-Century English Political
  Instability in European Context* (Cambridge University Press, 2000), 162.
[2] *Ley por la que se reconocen y amplían derechos y se establecen medidas a favor de quienes
  padecieron persecución o violencia durante la Guerra Civil y la dictadura.*
[3] http://noticias.juridicas.com/base_datos/Admin/l52-2007.html consulted 22 January 2008.
[4] www.boe.es/g/es/bases_datos/doc.php?coleccion=iberlex&id=2006/12309 consulted 22
  January 2008.

the legitimacy that allows its citizens to pursue difficult issues.[5] Recuperating historical memory is testimony to the maturity of the democratic system and a guarantee of its future; it is, in the king's words, 'the surest way of ensuring our future of coexistence'. *Convivencia,* one of the key tropes of the transition,[6] thus becomes integral to the potentially divisive process of incorporating past conflict into present coexistence. This is significant, as the memory that was being recovered in the public memory campaigns of 2006 was explicitly that of the Second Republic. The year of historical memory was dedicated to remembering and honouring 'those who struggled to establish a democratic regime in Spain, those who suffered the consequences of civil conflict and those who fought against the dictatorship to defend the liberties and basic rights that we enjoy today'.

The 'recovery' of historical memory was thus not only rehabilitating the reputation of the Second Republic – previously seen simply as the antechamber of the Civil War – but also positing a historical continuity between that regime and the stable democracy of post-1978 Spain. Such comparisons had deliberately been avoided during the transition to democracy that followed General Franco's death in November 1975. Indeed, the years of transition had been marked by a public tendency to subsume the Republic into the period of civil war and paint both as a tragedy. The collective experience of civil conflict was depicted as a time when terrible mistakes were made. It was generally agreed that crimes were committed by both sides, a device which divided responsibility between them and so effectively absolved both of blame.[7]

The Civil War had been seen as a time of troubles, to be lamented rather than addressed. Indeed, the sense that the conflicts of the 1930s had become something that could not be talked about – or, at least, not talked about in particular ways – underlay the common notion of a *pacto del olvido* or 'pact of forgetting' that had formed an essential part of the transition. Also called the *pacto de silencio,* this was not a legislative project – still less a law – but a tacit and generally unspoken agreement not to rake up the past. Such a 'pact' was, it is argued, fundamental in ensuring the peaceful and *legal* construction of a democratic regime in Spain, allowing Spaniards to look forwards rather than back and

---

[5] For example, Georgina Blakeley, 'Digging Up Spain's Past: Consequences of Truth and Reconciliation', *Democratization* 12 (2005), 44–59.

[6] Laura Edles, *Symbol and Ritual in the New Spain: The Transition to Democracy after Franco* (Cambridge University Press, 1998), 43–62.

[7] This is a major theme in the work of Paloma Aguilar Fernández; see in particular, *Memoria y olvido de la Guerra Civil española* (Madrid: Alianza, 1996).

changing former adversaries into interlocutors in a common dialogue.[8] There was only one, highly significant, piece of legislation underpinning this 'pact', the 1977 Amnesty Law.[9] This granted a general and reciprocal amnesty that made the democratic monarchy the first twentieth-century Spanish regime not to call to account those associated with the preceding regime. The law was thus not simply a break with the past as it provided the legislative means that allowed the country 'to pretend that it had forgotten the past'.[10]

The only way that people have of pretending that they have forgotten is to keep quiet. What the historian is faced with is thus not text, but the absence of text, not speech but silence. These moments of silence should be recognised for what they are, and cultural history has done much to ensure that historians 'read' these silences in a way that cannot be done for simple gaps in the historical record. Lacunae are unknowable; silences supposedly are not. Indeed, interpreting silence now features so regularly in historical works that it is easy to forget just how problematic this is. For how do we ascribe meaning to silence when all that can be heard is the absence of speech? We use the term as both metaphor and description, invoking it in both a literary and a historic sense. Yet, even as description, silence has multiple facets. This does not pose the historian with a simple taxonomic task. Rather the uncertainty – the *unknowableness* – of its meaning gives silence an intrinsic ambivalence.

In the case of the *pacto del olvido*, silence is the signifier both of pretending to forget and of actually forgetting. This profound ambiguity is reinforced by both the name and the nature of the *pacto del olvido*, not least the fact that it did not actually exist. Despite its almost ubiquitous reification, there was never a binding, enforceable, or even written agreement not to rake over the past, a feature that helps to explain why, when most care was being taken to construct a consensual politics, the Civil War was routinely made a subject of discussion both in academic studies and through the products of popular culture, notably feature films.[11] Unlike the Act of

---

[8] For accounts of the period, see José María Maravall, *The Transition to Democracy in Spain* (London: Croom Helm, 1982), Paul Preston, *The Triumph of Democracy in Spain* (London: Methuen, 1986), 53ff. and Mary Vincent, *Spain 1833–2002: People and State* (Oxford University Press, 2007), 199–224.

[9] http://noticias.juridicas.com/base_datos/Penal/l46-1977.html.

[10] Paloma Aguilar Fernández, 'Justice, Politics, and Memory in the Spanish Transition', in Alexandra Barahona de Brito, Carmen González-Enríquez, and Paloma Aguilar (eds.), *The Politics of Memory: Transitional Justice in Democratizing Societies* (Oxford University Press, 2001), 98–9.

[11] Santos Juliá, 'Presentación' and Paloma Aguilar Fernández, 'La evocación de la guerra y del franquismo en la política, la cultura y la sociedad españolas', in Santos Juliá (ed.),

Indemnity and Oblivion that succeeded the English Civil War – and with which the *pacto del olvido* is often semantically confused – there was no attempt in Spain to enforce the 'burial of what is passed' or to legislate 'against raking up painful memories of civil war'.[12] No one could be brought before the courts to answer for political crimes committed before 15 December 1976 but there was never any attempt to restrict speech, historical investigation or fictional representation.

Yet, the *pacto del olvido* is often rendered into English as the Pact of Oblivion. The frequent use of this translation is, I think, curious, although it is supported by any dictionary one cares to look at and has often been used by professional translators. Marc Augé's *Les formes de l'oubli*, for example, has been translated into English under the title *Oblivion*.[13] It is not that we can dismiss 'oblivion' as a stilted dictionary definition, even though in everyday speech, *olvido* means 'forgetting' or 'forgetfulness' far more often than it does 'oblivion'. The 'pact of forgetting' is both a more natural translation and one that comes closer to the way the phrase is used in Spanish. Yet, the hyperbolic notion of oblivion persists, even though this confuses not only the name but also the nature of the agreement that is being undertaken. For, while oblivion is absolute, forgetting is not. And when, as in the case of Spain, there is no specific legislation or formal agreement and the 'pact' itself remains tacit and unspoken, the 'oblivion' is actually structured by silence rather than by forgetting.

This is highlighted if we compare the Spanish example with formal, legislative attempts to induce forgetting, such as that which occurred in England during the 1660s. Even these, however, should be understood as a range of spoken interventions, understandings and 'illocutionary acts' that form the political and cultural context of the legislative text.[14] The Act of Free and General Pardon, Indemnity and Oblivion

Memoria de la Guerra y del Franquismo (Madrid: Taurus, 2006), 15–26 and 279–318, esp. 288–98; Jo Labanyi, 'History and Hauntology; or, What Does One Do with the Ghosts of the Past? Reflections on Spanish Film and Fiction of the Post-Franco Period', in Joan Ramón Resina (ed.), *Disremembering the Dictatorship: The Politics of Memory in the Spanish Transition to Democracy* (Amsterdam and Atlanta: Rodopi, 2000), 65–82.

[12] Charles II, quoted Scott, *England's Troubles*, 410; see also Paulina Kewes, 'Introduction: The Uses of History in Early Modern England', *Huntington Library Quarterly* 68, 1/2 (2005), 18.

[13] Marc Augé, *Oblivion*, trans. Marjolijn de Jager (Minneapolis: University of Minnesota Press, 2004). See also the translator's note, Nicole Loraux, *The Divided City: On Memory and Forgetting in Ancient Athens*, trans. Corinne Pache with Jeff Fort (New York: Zone, 2002), 265.

[14] See further David Norbrook, 'Introduction: Acts of Oblivion and Republican Speech-Acts', in Norbrook, *Writing the English Republic: Poetry, Rhetoric and Politics, 1627–60* (Cambridge University Press, 2000), 1–22.

that supposedly brought a final end to the English Civil War was part of a wider rhetoric of remembrance that both contributed to and was structured by the political flux of the time. Examples from the tumultuous past were frequently invoked, particularly awful examples. The cry '1641 is come again' rang out at the threat of political unrest while public holidays introduced by the restored Stuart monarchy all commemorated England's deliverance from various past threats.[15] The question was thus not that of forgetting – still less of oblivion – but of what could be remembered (or at least spoken about) and how this could be invoked. And this rather banal observation again raises the relationship between silence and forgetting. In Augé's words, '[m]emories are crafted by oblivion as the outlines of the shore are created by the sea' and precisely the same contouring determines the relationship between speech and silence.

Why then the rhetorical desire to consign past events to oblivion – 'raz'd out of the Book of Time'[16] – when what was actually being striven for was the act of not remembering? The answer lies, of course, in the relationship between memory and forgetting. The need to forget or lay aside the past has constituted part of the process of recovering from civil war since classical times. Ancient Athens, the polity that gave us the concept of civil war as 'a deep wound in the body of the city', also patterned the process by which such a wound could be healed.[17] Reuniting the polis, and eschewing the language of victory for that of unanimity, would allow citizens to forget the divisions that lay at the heart of the city. Hence the Athenian citizens' decision in 403 BC 'not to recall misfortunes of the past' and so not only bring about an end to civil war but also theorise, and thus fix in political discourse the importance of emphasising unity over accommodating division.[18]

The rediscovery of classical learning in the Renaissance cemented the association in political thought between unity and harmony. The peaceful polity was ordered and harmonious, both virtues that depended on the observance of hierarchy. In seventeenth-century England, the classical ideal of political unity was consciously observed. A veneration for classical learning enabled men to evoke Athenian precedent and to imagine a time, even during the Civil War, when those currently fighting each other would agree to 'look forward and not back and never think of what is past'.[19] History provided an example of how the aftermath of civil war could be

---

[15] Kewes, 'The Uses of History', 18–19; Scott, *England's Troubles*, 164.
[16] Quoted Scott, *England's Troubles*, 26.   [17] Loraux, *The Divided City*, 15–44 at 24.
[18] Ibid., 15, 29.
[19] Charles I on passing the Act of Oblivion, quoted Kewes, 'The Uses of History', 18.

imagined even as hostilities continued. The agreement to forget, to consign the past to oblivion, was the precedent for how to construct peace. And as these seventeenth-century protagonists were, like the Athenian citizens, an elite group of political actors, the emphasis on the unity of the polis had more than historical precedent to recommend it.

In contrast, in an age of mass politics, the civil wars of the twentieth century have been large-scale mobilisations looking towards outright victory. Indeed, the Spanish Civil War is, at least in the initial stages of resistance to the rebel military coup and the defence of Madrid, a textbook example of a 'people's war'.[20] Yet, this popular defence of progressive, Republican social change was immediately depicted by the rebels as the uncontrolled actions of a rabble. An awareness of the political importance of unity, order and harmony persisted, playing a particular role in Francoist Spain. In 1879, the Vatican had reaffirmed the teachings of St Thomas Aquinas as the basis of Christian scholarship and social teaching.[21] Aquinas' Aristotelian premises led to a firm principle that the purpose of government was to assure internal peace, an injunction that was easily related to 'the peace of Franco'.[22] Yet, while this notion of peace was expanded over the long years of Franco's reign to encompass some kind of social consensus, in the 1940s, peace was simply a euphemism for victory. The question that needs to be explored is, then, why the principle of oblivion was eschewed in the immediate aftermath of the Spanish Civil War even though the silence that characterised the post-war was itself a constitutive part of forgetting (or pretending to forget).[23]

The Franco regime rested upon military victory. The material sinews of power marshalled by the New State enabled it to impose its will upon a subject population, enforcing control of the national territory and registering the movement and activity of its citizens to an extent previously unknown in Spain. A fearsome repression made manifest the brutal fact of state power: Republican Spain would be subdued by violence and even the last refuges – the mountainous sierras where Republican guerrillas waged war on the New State – would be brought under control. This was

---

[20] Charles Townshend (ed.), *The Oxford Illustrated History of Modern War* (Oxford University Press, 1997), 163.

[21] Leo XIII, *Aeterni Patris*.

[22] Mary Vincent, 'La paz de Franco: el concepto de jerarquía en la España de la posguerra', in Carolyn Boyd (ed.), *Religión y política en la España contemporánea* (Madrid: Centro de Estudios Políticos y Constitucionales, 2007), 83–105.

[23] For a literary depiction of the period see Luis Martín-Santos, *Tiempo de Silencio* (Barcelona: Seiz Barral, 1961) and, for an account by a historian, Michael Richards, *Time of Silence: Civil War and the Culture of Repression in Franco's Spain, 1936–1945* (Cambridge University Press, 1998).

achieved relatively quickly and, with the regime secure in power, violent repression eased. The Francoist dictatorship undoubtedly has a place among the twentieth century's murderous regimes, but it is conspicuous by a lack of plans for grandiose transformative change. The Spanish regime thus remains apart from the 'high modernist' schemes of Hitler, Stalin or Mao, and not simply in terms of the great differential in numbers killed.[24] Its essential pragmatism – the military use of repression to subdue territory, the accommodation with the Catholic Church, the tolerance of protected private space for the family – led to fascism being tamed well before the defeat of the Axis in the Second World War became inevitable.[25] Once the pace of killing slackened, Spain settled into a state of mute acquiescence.

Rhetorically, the regime continued to fight the Civil War. The division of Spain and, in particular, the threat posed by 'anti-Spain' remained a trope of official discourse even down to the 1970s. By then, the anachronistic rhetoric of the Civil War had little resonance outside Francoist circles, but it persisted. The date of the military coup against the Second Republic, 18 July, was a national holiday until being formally abolished in 1977. Similarly, a military 'Victory Parade' was held annually until 197ᶠ even though the day of the victory, 1 April, had ceased to be a national holiday in the 1960s. These celebrations had undergone their own process of evolution during the long years of the Franco regime. The Victory Parade had been moved to mid May even while 1 April was still an official holiday and there was no additional commemoration of 18 July by the Francoist Cortes after 1958.[26] Nevertheless, it was the case that, despite some decay in the 1960s, the dictatorship's festive calendar perpetuated the public memory of the Civil War. Parades, commemorations and public holidays acted as mnemonics in a restructuring of public life that was intended to enforce remembering rather than allow forgetting.

By the mid twentieth century, the politicisation of public life had become inevitable. It was expected that the Francoist regime would change street names, festivals, public statuary and official commemorations. The Second Republic had done the same, as had the Primo de Rivera dictatorship of

---

[24] On 'high modernist' schemes to transform society, see James Scott, *Seeing Like a State: How Certain Schemes to Improve the Human Condition Have Failed* (New Haven: Yale University Press, 1998). For a discussion of the Spanish case, see Vincent, *Spain*, 160–9.

[25] On the place of fascism in the regime see Ismael Saz Campos, *España contra España: los nacionalismos franquistas* (Madrid: Marcial Pons, 2003) and *Fascismo y Franquismo* (Valencia: Universitat de València, 2004).

[26] A military parade continued to be held on 'Armed Forces Day', Paloma Aguilar and Carsten Humleback, 'Collective Memory and National Identity in the Spanish Democracy', *History and Memory* 14, 1/2 (2002), 124–6.

the 1920s. But the endless victory celebrations of the Franco regime specifically recalled a traumatic past, which was used didactically (and repressively) as a 'remembered abyss' from which the Nationalist victory had providentially saved Spain.[27] This abyss encompassed both the past and the future: the moment of redemption lay in the past but Spain's salvation, her glorious present, was contrasted with the imagined fate that would have awaited the country if Franco had lost the Civil War. Yet, by conjuring up this notion of what might have been, the regime admitted the possibility of other alternative futures. The commemoration of civil war, no matter how controlled or how politicised, thus inevitably transmitted a memory of the defeated Republic. The 'peace of silence' may have been achieved by controlling speech through censorship and fear but the Republic remained embedded within the Francoist regime, alluded to even through every attempt to forget it.

The Franco regime owed its existence to the Republic; any attempt to silence its memory thus paradoxically recalled it. Conversely, while the New State was marked by a refusal to forget the conflicts of the 1930s, preserving the panoply of victory down to the 1970s, there was an equally paradoxical attempt to erase the memory of the Second Republic. It was not just that the regime ensured a heavy police presence on days when some Spaniards sought to maintain a Republican presence by celebrating May Day, or the anniversary of the proclamation of the Second Republic on 14 April.[28] Rather, the mechanisms of repression were used to silence the spoken memory of the Republic except when invoked as a force for evil or the putative ruin of Spain. This legend persisted even though everyone knew of the spontaneous repression that marked the outbreak of civil war and the official repression that succeeded it. During the 'hot summer' of 1936 when, as Francoist apologists endlessly recounted, revolutionary violence had claimed the lives of thousands in the Republican zone, known left-wingers were being picked off by Falangist death squads in the Nationalist zone.[29] Their victims were left shrouded in silence, their communal graves unidentified and unmarked. One of the first accounts we have is by Gerald Brenan, who in 1949 visited the unmarked *pozos* in Víznar, outside Granada, where Federico García Lorca's body lay along-side hundreds of others. Brenan pieced together the story of the poet's

[27] The quotation is Scott's, *England's Troubles*, 162. For a study of the often ambivalent meanings of political festivals, see David Cressy, *Bonfires and Bells: National Memory and the Protestant Calendar in Elizabethan and Stuart England* (Berkeley and Los Angeles: University of California Press, 1989).

[28] Richards, *Time of Silence*, 157–8.

[29] See, for example, Ignacio Martín Jiménez, *La Guerra civil en Valladolid, 1936–9: amane-ceres ensangrentados* (Valladolid: Ambito, 2000).

death from muttered hints, asides and evasions. 'Among ourselves' he was told, 'we don't talk of these things, but we haven't forgotten them.'[30] Lorca's literary stature assured his immortality. His grave was unmarked and his death unrecorded but the fact of it was both known and mourned around the world. His execution had been reported, condemned and commemorated, notably in Antonio Machado's poem 'El crimen fué en Granada: a Federico García Lorca'.[31] Machado also died a victim of the Civil War, in exile in the French border town of Collioure in February 1939.[32] Though an unambiguously Republican figure – his poem to Lorca was perhaps the best-known Spanish-language piece to emerge from the war – Machado's work remained available in Spain, with collected editions of his poetry published through the 1940s. In contrast, Lorca's work remained banned by the Franco regime until 1953, although it never went out of print abroad. By the time of democracy, Lorca had become Spain's most translated author, but during the Civil War Machado was the more authoritative figure, and his death made a significant impact. The stories of other poets – notably Miguel Hernández who died in a Francoist gaol in 1942 – added to the wider narratives of dislocation and displacement. However, a Republican cultural tradition was maintained in exile, by publishing houses, an intelligentsia now largely based in Mexico, and perhaps above all, by the stature of writers such as Machado and Lorca.[33] Their towering position in twentieth-century Spanish literature made the Republican literary tradition impossible to obliterate, just as Milton's place in the English canon had preserved the memory of protestant radicalism.

Few, however, shared in this immortality. Those buried alongside Lorca had no such mantle of fame; officially at least they remained unnamed and unknown. When a process of recuperating 'historical memory' began in earnest at the turn of the twenty-first century, identifying and reburying those silent dead was a powerful impetus. They were to be named, their stories told, and their deaths recorded.[34] This was, in part,

---

[30] Gerald Brenan, *The Face of Spain* (London: Turnstile, 1950), 122–48; quote at 139.

[31] Aurora de Albórnoz (ed.), *Poesias de Guerra de Antonio Machado* (San Juan de Puerto Rico: Asopmante, 1961); Valentine Cunningham (ed.), *The Penguin Book of Spanish Civil War Verse* (Harmondsworth: Penguin, 1980), 205–8.

[32] Ian Gibson, *Cuatro poetas en Guerra* (Barcelona: Planeta, 2007) and *Federico García Lorca: A Life* (London: Faber, 1989).

[33] Serge Salaün, 'Las voces del exilio: La poesía española, 1938–46', in Josefina Cuesta and Benito Bermejo (eds.), *Emigración y exilio: Españoles en Francia, 1936–1946* (Madrid: Eudema, 1996), 355–65; Alicia Alted, *La voz de los vencidos: El exilio republicano de 1939* (Madrid: Aguilar, 2005), 201–56.

[34] See Emilio Silva Barrera, *Las fosas de Franco: los españoles que el dictador dejó en las cunetas* (Madrid: Temas de Hoy, 2003) and Emilio Silva, Asunción Esteban, Javier Castán and Pancho Salvador (eds.), *La memoria de los olvidados: Un debate sobre el silencio de la represión franquista* (Valladolid: Ambito, 2004).

a process of restitution. Since their violent and unlawful deaths, and through nearly four decades of dictatorship, these Republican victims of Francoism had lain unrecognised and uncommemorated, 'perished as though they had never been'. Now they were to be named, an honour that had been accorded to the Nationalist dead since the first moments of victory. In contrast to those who lay in the unmarked communal graves that dotted the pueblos of Castile, the victims of Republican violence were endlessly commemorated. Every revolutionary atrocity was investigated: the names of the victims, the manner of their deaths and the names of their killers were recorded for both police purposes and for posterity in the *Causa General*. This 'informative' lawsuit, begun in April 1940, was kept in the Tribunal Supremo until 1980, when it was opened and transferred to the Archivo Histórico Nacional.[35] The process of naming did not end there: the names of Nationalist war dead were inscribed on the walls of all parish churches (including cathedrals) in celebration of both their deeds and the heroism of their deaths.

The forms of commemoration chosen by the Franco regime to honour its dead explicitly denied the nature of the conflict that had torn the country asunder in the 1930s. This was not a civil war but a crusade, fought to save and liberate the 'true' Spain from a foreign, atheistic and un-Spanish yoke. The titanic nature of that struggle required an equally titanic memorial. On 1 April 1940 the construction of a national monument was announced, an underground basilica church, hewn out of the living rock at Cuelgamuros outside Madrid, within sight of El Escorial. As the decree put it, 'the stones to be erected must have the grandeur of the monuments of old, which defy time and forgetfulness'.[36] Built in part by Republican prisoners forced to begin the construction of a nave longer than that of St Peter's and a cross 150 metres high, the church dominated the site known as the Valley of the Fallen, which became an enormous burial ground.[37] Few, however, are acknowledged by name: only the

---

[35] Isidro Sánchez, Maneul Ortíz and David Ruíz (eds.), *España Franquista: Causa General y actitudes sociales ante la dictadura* (Ciudad Real: Universidad de Castilla la Mancha, 1993); José Luis Ledesma, 'La "Causa General": Fuente sobre la "represión", la guerra civil (y el Franquismo)', *Spagna Contemporanea* 28 (2005), 203–30. A selection of documents was published as *Causa General: La dominación roja en España, avance de la información instruida por el Ministerio público* (Madrid: Ministerio de Justicia, [1944]) and is available online at www.causageneral.com/.

[36] Quoted Paul Preston, *Franco: A Biography* (London, HarperCollins, 1993), 351.

[37] See Nicolás Sánchez-Albórnoz, 'Cuelgamuros: presos políticos para un mausoleo', in C. Molinero, M. Sala and J. Sobrequés (eds.), *Una inmensa prisión: los campos de concentración y las prisiones durante la guerra civil y el Franquismo* (Barcelona, 2003), 3–17 and Daniel Sueros, *El Valle de los Caídos: Los secretos de la cripta franquista* (Barcelona: Argos Verdara, 1983).

graves of Franco and the Fascist leader José Antonio Primo de Rivera, which flank the high altar, are identified, although tens of thousands of others 'fallen for God and Spain' fill the ossuary niches built into the walls behind the side altars.

The exact number of dead who lie at Cuelgamuros is unknown: the figure of 50,000 is often quoted but estimates range from 40 to 70,000. Human remains were collected and moved to the basilica from 1958, the year before it was officially inaugurated with a requiem mass on 1 April 1959, the twentieth anniversary of Franco's victory.[38] Reburial had been a commemorative motif during the very early post-war years, when those killed in the revolutionary violence of 1936–7 were identified, traced and their bodies recovered for reburial by their families. Those killed in and around Madrid – which included the Paracuellos massacres of November 1936 – were even made the subject of a special investigation by the Causa General.[39] The deaths were painstakingly reconstructed, with physical evidence such as scraps of clothing placed in the archives alongside skeletal diagrams documenting injury and cause of death. Identity was confirmed whenever possible, with some corpses being exhumed in the presence of relatives.[40] All unidentified bodies were given Christian burial in the 'Martyrs Graveyard of Paracuellos de Jarama'; some relatives also chose this option, though others requested that the deceased be reburied closer to home, often in Madrid's Almudena cemetery.[41]

This was one of the cemeteries where, in 1958, collective wartime graves were opened and their contents taken to fill the gargantuan *columbarios* in the Valley of the Fallen. The remains were moved indiscriminately. Few were identified and mistakes were common even in the counting of bodies. The register for 23 March 1959, for instance, recounted the arrival of 'the following caskets with the remains of our dead from the War of Liberation: Navarre 16 caskets; Vitoria, 37; Palencia, 26; Alicante, 16; Avila, 18'. In addition, the register noted the arrival of several bodies from Aldeaseca, a pueblo in Avila: an 'unknown woman' and five men, also 'unknown'. In fact, though, there were six male bodies (a skull had been left behind in the original grave) and the names of all were known locally. Far from being

[38] *La Vanguardia*, 2 April 1959.
[39] 'Pieza especial de exhumaciones de mártires de la Cruzada' Archivo Histórico Nacional, Fondos Contemporáneos, Causa General (henceforth AHN CG) legajo 1536. The Paracuellos massacres were a staple of Francoist historiography and continue to generate polemic rather than historical scholarship. See, however, Ian Gibson, *Parcuellos, como fue: La verdad objetiva de la matanza de presos en Madrid en 1936* (Madrid: Temas de Hoy, 2005).
[40] E.g. the exhumation carried out at El Pardo, 24 January 1944, AHN CG legajo 1536, ramo 3, carpeta 5.
[41] E.g. AHN CG legajo 1536, ramo 3, carpeta 3.

those 'fallen for God and for Spain' in the 'War of Liberation', these were Republican victims, shot by Nationalist gunmen, usually Falangists, in the extra-legal repression that marked the outbreak of civil war in Castile. In 1959, they were re-interred in the regime's grandiose memorial, remaining there, unnamed and unknown, until their families began to campaign against the horrible irony of having those killed by Franco's repression buried in his mausoleum.[42]

This transfer of Republican as well as Nationalist dead did, however, mark a change from the policies of the early post-war years, providing some sort of basis for the regime's rhetorical claims that the Valley was a monument to *all* the Civil War dead. These claims were always hollow: the inclusion of Republican remains never signified reconciliation, as the architectural rhetoric of the basilica made clear. The Republican dead were left undifferentiated and unmarked. Indeed, the physical structures of the walls of niches that made up the *columbarios*, meant that the dead were quite literally built into the walls of the basilica. Their presence was alluded to but never truly recognised. Rather, they were subsumed into another group of dead, those 'fallen for God and Spain'. This inscription was carved into the side chapel of the Holy Sepulchre just as it was into the plaques listing the Nationalist dead that were put up on the outside walls of parish churches. Similarly, the funeral liturgy that opened the Valley of the Fallen was held in honour of 'our' dead, an occasion 'when our prayers rise to heaven beseeching Divine protection for our fallen'.[43]

The Republicans laid to 'rest' in the Valley of the Fallen thus represent another silence, one of many silences interwoven even into the proclamation of victory. They were incorporated into the fabric of the church, but no reference was made either to them or to how they died. As the vast mausoleum at Cuelgamuros dramatically demonstrated, the aftermath of the Spanish Civil War was characterised by a refusal to forget. The silences of victory were sharply differentiated from any attempt at reconciliation as they *subsumed* the defeated, declaring the unity of victory at the same time as they denied any genuine attempt to construct such a unity. A parallel liturgical example had come during the war itself when various Catholic agencies, including many clergy, had campaigned against the practice of commemorating the dead with the 'emptiness' of a minute's silence.[44] Silence should not be something in itself; it was rather a space that allowed for contemplation, the examination of conscience, or, in this case, prayer.

---

[42] '¡Rojos interrados con Franco!', *El Mundo*, 19 September 2004.
[43] Franco's address, *La Vanguardia*, 2 April 1959.
[44] *Signo* (Organo de la Juventud de Acción Católica), 20 November 1936.

The oblivion sought by the victorious Francoist regime was thus erasure rather than reconciliation. 'Empty' silence was to be filled with Catholic spirituality or regime doctrine; Republican victims of Nationalist violence were incorporated into the glorious body of the martyred fallen. This obliteration of the Republican past is perhaps the only aspect of 'oblivion' that the Franco regime had in common with the earlier English attempt at reconciliation after civil war. The disinterred body of Oliver Cromwell was posthumously 'executed' in 1660 along with those of two other regicides. The following year, when the Act of Oblivion was passed, the bodies of other distinguished Republicans were exhumed from Westminster Abbey and permanently expelled from their places of honour there.[45] The past that could be accommodated by the Restoration monarchy was one that acknowledged and moved on from the divisions of the past but not one that preserved the memory of a radical tradition. As Franco had said at the inauguration of the building that was to be his own tomb, 'The anti-Spain was defeated and beaten, but it is not dead.'

Several historians of seventeenth-century England maintain that the erasure promised by the sub-texts of the Act of Oblivion did indeed come to pass. The 'national forgetting' finally achieved by the Restoration settlement distorted the historical record by downplaying the importance of both radical republicanism and, in particular, religious conflict. English literature has, for example, 'never entirely undone' the Republican poets' expulsion from Westminster Abbey.[46] Such erasure, in the sense of determining the narrative of history, was quite clearly an aspiration of the Franco regime. The first published studies of the Civil War were martyrologies, which, under titles such as *Este es el Cortejo … heroes y martires de la cruzada española* or *La gran víctima*, presented a civil war as a transcendental drama enacted throughout and outside historical time. The redemptive sufferings of the martyrs made the war into an episode in the eternal struggle between good and evil; those who inflicted such suffering were simply anonymous agents of evil. The secular equivalent of these pious volumes had titles such as *La guerra de reconquista española … y el criminal comunismo* and, like Joaquín Arrarás's monumental *Historia de la Cruzada Española*, published in fascicles in 1943, they served a similar purpose.[47] Clerics and laymen,

---

[45] Norbrook, *Writing the English Republic*, 3, 432. Blair Worden, *Roundhead Reputations: the English Civil Wars and the Passions of Posterity* (London: Penguin, 2001), 215–42.

[46] Scott, *England's Troubles*, 46, 393; Norbrook, *Writing the English Republic*, 432.

[47] Aniceto Castro Alabarrán, *Este es el Cortejo … heroes y martires de la cruzada española* (Salamanca: no publisher, 1938); Enrique Esperabé de Arteaga, *La guerra de reconquista española que ha salvado a Europa y el criminal comunismo* (Madrid: no publisher, 1940); Joaquín Arrarás and Carlos Sáenz de Tejada, *Historia de la Cruzada Española* (Madrid: Ediciones Españoles, 1940–42). See further David K. Herzberger, *Narrating the Past:*

historians and artists, professionals and amateurs, together developed a
National Catholic historical discourse that rediscovered 'an immutable
and immanent national tradition' and used this to silence all reference to
alternative discourse or interpretations of the past.[48]

The writing of history thus reflected the purging and purification that
characterised the violent and repressive years of the early Franco regime.
Republicanism and the liberal tradition were to be expunged from the new
Spain. Yet, in David Norbrook's words, 'the more violent the erasure ...
the more it can be seen that there was something to hide'.[49] There was
much that could not be said about the Civil War; far more, in fact, than
could not be *known* about the war. As the writers of the histories of the
'Crusade' showed time and again, the silences of the Franco regime were
deliberate, interwoven into a dictatorship that neither forgot the past nor
truly acknowledged it. For what was explicitly being denied was that the
country had fought a civil war, that the divisions within the body politic
had become so great that Spaniards had taken up arms against each other
and fought to the death to determine the future shape of Spain. The
externalisation of the enemy as 'anti-Spain' denied the internal origins
of civil war and so maintained the idea of harmonious politics in the post-
war. The memory of division was thus denied.[50]

The Franco regime's ceaseless depiction of the Civil War as a cataclysmic struggle between 'Spain' and 'anti-Spain' rejected historical time in
favour of mythic time. The 'true' Spain – an immanent, mythic body –
collapsed any sense of temporal advance and so rejected linear concepts of
time, rooted in Enlightenment notions of progress. 'Spain was, is, and will
be immortal' read one victory poster that juxtaposed the helmeted head of
a 1930s soldier against Columbus's galleons. The erasure of the
Republican past – which was to be achieved by the physical eradication
of republicanism – thus paradoxically denied the reality of civil war as did
the regime's insistence on the tropes of unity, harmony and order in the
post-war reconstruction. The triumph over the anti-Spain had simply
allowed the 'true' Spain to emerge; oblivion was embedded in this particular configuration of time. This may be true, as Augé argues, of *any*
configuration of time, but the Francoist narratives of civil war and victory –
the event that gave these narratives meaning – also suggested a temporal
stasis. 'The fascist has no memory. He learns nothing. That also means

History and Historiography in Postwar Spain (Durham, NC and London: Duke University
Press, 1995), 15–38; Carolyn Boyd, *Historia Patria: Politics, History and National Identity
in Spain 1875–1975* (Princeton University Press, 1997), 232–72.
[48] Boyd, *Historia Patria*, 235.   [49] Norbrook, *Writing the English Republic*, 3.
[50] Loraux, *The Divided City*, 25–6.

that he forgets nothing and that he lives in the perpetual present of his obsessions.'[51]

There is thus a sense in which only with Franco's death on 20 November 1975 did the aftermath of the Civil War actually begin. A long-lasting period of conflict in Spanish history had – at least potentially – finally come to an end. This sense of terminus – of a temporal division between what had gone before and what was now to come – found expression in repeated references to a new beginning. The new age that had dawned in Spain meant both democratic politics and national reconciliation.[52] The politics of forgetting were thus intertwined with the processes of restitution. And while the restitution that characterised the transition was in part about confining a troubled and divisive past to oblivion – the 'pact of silence' – it was also about establishing the political arrangements that would allow Spaniards to move on from that past. The process of restitution after a time of conflict thus served a dual purpose. At one level, it raised issues of public memory, and changed what could and could not be said about the Civil War. Francoist embargos were lifted: things that could not be said were now uttered; books that had been banned now circulated. The new interpretation of the Civil War avoided the Francoist insistence on triumph and victory and moved instead to an uncertain emphasis on tragedy.

The 1930s became a period of 'collective madness', a time of unreasonable and extreme behaviour when neither side fully understood its actions.[53] This is not a convincing, or even plausible, historical understanding of the Civil War, but it was both useful and politically convenient. Interpreting the war as a tragedy allowed the construction of 'a memory without an adversary'. The Franco regime may have been the antithesis of the new democracy, but many of those who had once supported and staffed that regime – including Prime Minister Adolfo Suárez – were now constructing the transition. No new democratic memory could thus take Francoists as an enemy or even as an opposite.[54] The notion of the Civil War as a collective tragedy was another instance of 'the changing rhetoric of political commentary conducted through the medium of history'.[55] Against Franco's relentless insistence on victors and vanquished, Spain and anti-Spain, the device of tragedy divided responsibility for the conflict and thereby exonerated both sides.

---

[51] Augé, *Oblivion*, esp. 25–6, 50–2; quote at 52.
[52] Edles, *Symbol and Ritual in the New Spain*, 41–3.
[53] Aguilar Fernández, *Memoria y olvido*, 284–6.
[54] Salvador Caredús i Ros, 'Politics and the Invention of Memory. For a Sociology of the Transition to Democracy in Spain', in Resina (ed.), *Disremembering the Dictatorship*, 25–6.
[55] Kewes, 'The Uses of History', 14; she is referring to the Act of Oblivion as an early example of this.

As is always the case during periods of reconstruction, the political imperatives of the transition lay in the present rather than the past. And, while the Spanish transition is always dated to the dictator's death, if not before, it is of course the case that, in these early uncertain times, both democracy and transition only actually existed as aspirations. The process of political transformation remained fragile, as is schematically indicated by the distinction made by political scientists between democratic transition and its consolidation.[56] It is, perhaps, such fragility that determined the scrupulous adherence to legality that distinguished several historical instances of reconstruction, from England in the 1660s to Spain in the 1970s, rather than the public memory of a traumatic and conflictive past. As is well known, the Spanish transition to democracy was accomplished legally and that meant that, in at least the early stages, it had to be brought about within a Francoist legality. While change was symbolised by occasional dramatic events – most famously when the Francoist Cortes voted itself out of existence on 18 November 1976 – the insistence on legal change emphasised continuity, and a surprising respect for the immediate past.[57]

It is often suggested that the legal, consensual, *pacted* nature of the transition to democracy was ultimately governed by the fear of failure, by the memory of the Civil War and, specifically, the knowledge of what might happen should consensus fail. '[E]ven when civic thought considers the time of conflict a thing of the past ... conflict is endlessly reborn as a threat.'[58] Yet a threat does not necessarily signify a real possibility. A reminder of the horrors of civil war is not the same as the imminent danger of civil war. The conditions under which countries dissolve into armed conflict were not present in Spain in the 1970s, even though both political violence and military intervention were genuine dangers. There was, of course, no guarantee that democracy would be achieved peacefully or consensually in Spain, but neither was civil war the only – or even a likely – alternative. Indeed, the strength of both popular and elite consensus around the need for democratic change always made the establishment of representative politics the most likely outcome.[59] Conjuring up

[56] E.g. Leonardo Morlino, *Democracy between Consolidation and Crisis* (Oxford University Press, 1998). On the uncertainty of the transition, see Elías Díaz, 'Ideologies in the Making of the Spanish Transition', *West European Politics* 21, 4 (1998), 26–39.

[57] Similarly, according to Scott, the 'fabric' of the English Restoration was 'government by law', *England's Troubles*, 409.

[58] Loraux, *The Divided City*, 57.

[59] Víctor Pérez-Díaz, *The Return of Civil Society: the Emergence of Democratic Spain* (Cambridge, Mass. and London: Harvard University Press, 1993); Manuel Castells, *The City and the Grassroots* (London: Edward Arnold, 1983); Vincent, *Spain*, 199–224.

spectres from the past served a useful political purpose in maintaining the transition as a controlled, consensual and elite process.

The long shadow of the past was thus deployed during the transition as part of a political discourse intended to prevent violence and any potentially uncontrollable popular dynamic. This is rather different from the claims made for traumatic memory; the kind of public memory that, we are told, governed the English Restoration 'far more securely than did Charles II'. This meant that 'the first and final imperative of restoration was forgetting'; only oblivion would end this 'tyranny of memory'. At the same time, however, only when 'the troubles' began to disappear in practice, could they 'begin to disappear from the public mind'.[60] Such an interpretation would, though, surely suggest that the process of reconstruction was actually governed by political rather than historical or temporal imperatives. The decision to put the past aside – whether framed tacitly, as in the *pacto del olvido* or legislatively, as was the case with the Act of Oblivion – was an essentially pragmatic arrangement that allowed the political architecture of a new system to be constructed behind the façade of the old.

The historiography of silence, forgetting and oblivion thus itself occludes, in these cases, the political history of the times. Though widely cited simply as the Act of Oblivion, England's Act of Indemnity and Oblivion not only proclaimed that none would speak about the Civil War but also made practical provision for those who had served in it. Similarly, in Spain, issues of indemnity were addressed during the early years of democracy, albeit in a piecemeal fashion. The 1977 Amnesty Law was clearly a vital piece of legislation in this regard. Defined groups were specifically rehabilitated: army officers purged by the dictatorship were reinstated, enabling them to claim their pensions; disabled Republican veterans became eligible for pensions; compensation was given to those gaoled for more than three years. By 1991, twenty-six per cent of social security payments were related to the Civil War.[61] Yet, despite this substantial, if largely untrumpeted, restitution, the 2007 'law of historical memory' was directly intended to *broaden* the rights of those who suffered. The law extends the categories of those eligible for compensation to include, for instance, orphans, injured civilians and those who had served lesser sentences.

The law also explicitly covers both the Civil War and the dictatorship and so simultaneously conflates two historical periods into one.

---

[60] Scott, *England's Troubles*, 26, 43–6.

[61] José Alvarez Junco, paper given to a symposium held at Rewley House, Oxford, 29 June 2007.

Paradoxically, this may serve to clarify just what is being remembered, for while questions of historical memory have been most commonly framed in terms of the 'unquiet past' of the Civil War, they have actually usually addressed the repression of the early Franco regime. This is, indeed, where the grassroots process of creating a public memory began, with the forensic excavations of communal graves undertaken on private initiatives and with voluntary labour. Such initiatives led to the foundation of the Asociación para la Recuperación de la Memoria Histórica (Association for the Recovery of Historical Memory: ARMH) established in December 2000 by Emilio Silva and Santiago Macías, grandchildren of people who disappeared during the Civil War.[62]

The ARMH is often seen as breaking the silence that surrounded the Civil War. Its public discourse is that of discovery as well as recovery, a revelatory tone that informs much of the public debate around 'historical memory' in Spain. The emergence of the ARMH is thus seen, in the popular imagination at least, as marking the point at which the *pacto del olvido* was abandoned. Yet, the silence of the transition had only been at best partial and incomplete, particularly in terms of *historical* memory. For while work remains to be done on the numbers and identities of those who died at the hands of the incipient Franco regime, there was historical knowledge of the repression, just as there were personal memories. Some of the most celebrated stories of the repression – such as that of the young girls, known as the 'thirteen roses', who were executed in Madrid in 1939 – figured in the popular imagination as forgotten tales ignored by history, even though the facts of the case were familiar to historians.[63] The recurrent discursive trope is that of 'breaking' silence and 'confronting' the past. As Emilio Silva put it, in a quote to a British newspaper covering the 'law of historical memory', 'the story of the victims of Franco's dictatorship was buried in a ditch. They forgot the rights of these people.'[64]

This insistence on disclosure, on revealing a past kept from public knowledge, is not explained by the standard theories put forward in analyses of the end of the *pacto de silencio*. These commonly include generational change – only with the passage of time could the

---

[62] See Silva Barrera, *Las fosas de Franco*; Blakeley, 'Digging Up Spain's Past'; Madeleine Davis, 'Is Spain Recovering its Memory? Breaking the *Pacto del Olvido*', *Human Rights Quarterly* 27 (2005), 858–80. See also the ARMH website, www.memoriahistorica.org/.

[63] Juliá, 'Presentación', in Juliá (ed.), *Memoria de la Guerra y del Franquismo*, 20–21; Carlos Fonseca, *Trece rosas rojas: la historia más conmovedora de la guerra civil* (Madrid: Temas de Hoy, 2004). See also Tabea Alexa Linhard, 'The Death Story of the "Trece Rosas"', *Journal of Spanish Cultural Studies* 3, 2 (2002), 187–202.

[64] *The Observer*, 4 November 2007. See also Silva et al. (eds.), *La memoria de los olvidados*.

grandchildren of the Civil War address a past their parents could not – and the consolidation of democracy in Spain, now sufficiently robust to allow the exploration of an uncomfortable, traumatic past.[65] But the debates around historical memory are only about breaking silence in a hyperbolic sense. The revelatory tone has crept in as knowledge of the past has moved outside the rarified world of political and academic elites to become the subject of popular debate. The processes of 'historical' memory in Spain are not about historical memory at all, but about collective memory, a renegotiation of the public narratives of the dictatorship and the Civil War (and therefore also of the transition). This is not a 'recovery' of a lost past but a reordering of historical narratives accomplished in a changing present.[66]

Narratives are, of course, structured as much by what they leave out as by what they include, as much by oblivion as by remembering. The work of the ARMH is driven by the need to make restitution for wrongs committed in the past, to honour the dead, and to acknowledge the awful way in which they died. This is not unusual. The moral desire for restitution drives much public history, from Australia's 'history wars' to the recent commemoration of the abolition of the slave trade in Britain. Such debates are profoundly influenced by a new vocabulary of human rights, which is related, at least at some level, to the universalisation of the experience of war and genocide in the mid twentieth century. The vocabulary of genocide is now quite commonly applied to the Francoist repression, though it is by no means universally accepted. It is, though, an indicator of the internationalisation of the Spanish experience, as was the ARMH's submission to the United Nations Working Group on Enforced or Involuntary Disappearances, which, in 2002, included Spain among those countries still to resolve issues of 'the disappeared'.

It would clearly be wrong to see this drive for restitution simply as a foreign import and nor is it convincing to see it as a later phenomenon, shaped by international developments, notably the Pinochet case.[67] Rather, the claims for restitution of wrongs – which have unsurprisingly led to counterclaims from other interested parties, such as the veterans of Franco's Blue Division, which fought with the Wehrmacht on the Eastern Front and the campaign to preserve their own memory sites – are

---

[65] For the first explanation see Aguilar, 'La evocacíon de la guerra', 304ff; for the second see Blakeley, 'Digging Up Spain's Past'.

[66] See further, Joan Ramón Resina, 'Short of Memory: the Reclamation of the Past since the Spanish Transition to Democracy', in Resina (ed.), *Disremembering the Dictatorship*, 83–125.

[67] Davis, 'Is Spain Recovering its Memory?'; Rebecca Evans, 'Pinochet in London – Pinochet in Chile: International and Domestic Politics in Human Rights Policy', *Human Rights Quarterly* 28, 1 (2006).

profoundly related to the question of erasure. Although the official erasure of the past supposedly now lies in the past, associated with and confined to the Franco regime, the attempt to extirpate republicanism presaged the claims for the restitution of wrongs made under democracy. Such claims bring their own erasure: the false claims of Francoist Spain are to be obliterated by democratic Spain, in the same way that the last public statues of the dictator are being removed. A past, or least a version of the past, is to be rubbed out as 'true' representative Spain finally defines itself against dictatorial Francoist Spain and rediscovers its democratic antecedents in the rehabilitation of the Second Republic. Plausibly, Francoism is thereby reduced to a parenthesis in the modern history of Spain.

'A spectre is haunting Spain, the spectre of difference.'[68] Any genuine oblivion must entail an actual, rather than simply an attempted, erasure from history. To return to an earlier historical example, this is the claim made by Scott and Norbrook about England's radical religious past, obliterated by the Restoration settlement. Yet any genuine oblivion, any real erasure of the past would presumably be irrecoverable, resistant to the reminders offered by, for example, John Milton's unquestioned place in English literature. In the case of Spain, the passage of time is much shorter, which must make claims about erasure more circumspect, but the discourse of recovery and revelation is still used by those looking to recover the past that has purportedly been erased. It is, though, clear that this is not a recovery but a rewriting, a new narration of the past to reflect the agency of those in the present. And it is in these new narratives – which select and forget as well as remember, which 'discover' certain facts and stories from the past and consign others to oblivion – that the relationship between memory and silence is reworked. For in the aftermath of civil war, attempts at erasure, which are various and repeated and, inevitably, contradictory, leave a legacy of partisanship.

In both the English and the Spanish cases, despite the very different circumstances and, indeed, passage of time, partisan positions persisted despite the successful establishment of political accommodation. The salient question is that of a usable past. Political reconciliation was a pragmatic reality, but the positions of the Civil War persisted, their struggles now waged in cultural and historical debate. In Spain, such partisanship is exacerbated by a persistent tendency to frame the history of the Civil War as a moral struggle between two antithetical sociopolitical blocs, a narrative trope that structures as much academic historical writing as it does popular books.

---

[68] Resina, 'Introduction', in Resina (ed.), *Disremembering the Dictatorship*, 11.

This legacy of partisanship – structured as it is by the political divisions of left and right, victors and vanquished – reflects the fundamental problem with attempts to consign aspects of the past to oblivion. It is not just that partisan narratives are structured by what they do not say as much as by what they do but rather that these narratives, by their very nature, deny a communality of experience. In the Spanish case, the competing narratives of the Civil War, whether presented as academic history, popular sensation, or legislation, continue to present the moral claims of each side. It is, at some level, a quest for moral victors, a search for who has the right to write the history of Spain's troubled past. What is explicitly *denied* is the fact that Spain's conflict was a civil conflict, that each side struggled with a country rendered by political, social and cultural cleavage; that each side had popular support and legitimate grievances; that even so, responsibility for the conflict was not equal. As in all such cases of deep and grievous internal struggle, whoever won would have to reconstruct and re-forge the body of the nation. And, as historic examples from every historical period from classical times suggest, civil war is perceived as a deep wound. It is to be forgotten not only as a means of re-forging political life but also as a way to deny the cleavage that lies at the heart of politics. Attempts at oblivion thus retain a fundamental ambivalence. The continuing controversy over the Civil War is, in fact, still a way of denying what the Civil War was and of occluding the divisions which produced it and which, even today, echo through Spain's debates over historical memory.[69]

[69] Loraux, *Divided City*.

4   In the ashes of disgrace: Guilt versus shame revisited[1]

Jeffrey K. Olick

In 1946, the Columbia University anthropologist Ruth Benedict published a book version of a report she had written during the War for the Foreign Morale Analysis Division of the US Office of War Information. Since then, *The Chrysanthemum and the Sword* has been considered a classic, most noted for its contrast of a Japanese "shame culture" to a Western "guilt culture." "A society that includes absolute standards of morality and relies on men's developing a conscience," Benedict writes, "is a guilt culture by definition ..." "True shame cultures," in contrast, "rely on external sanctions for good behavior, not, as true guilt cultures do, on an internalized conviction of sin. Shame is a reaction to other people's criticism."[2] Perhaps the most important difference for Benedict is in how individuals in "guilt cultures" and in "shame cultures" process misdeeds: In a "guilt culture," "A man who has sinned can get relief by unburdening himself. This device of confession is used in our secular therapy and by many religious groups which have otherwise little in common. We know it brings relief." On the other hand, "Where shame is the major sanction, a man does not experience relief when he makes his fault public even to a confessor. So long as his behavior does not 'get out into the world' he need not be troubled and confession appears to him merely a way of courting trouble. Shame cultures therefore do not provide for confessions, even to gods" (p. 222). Shame thus causes one to hide or deny; guilt causes one to admit.

Certainly, the distinction between guilt cultures and shame cultures is tricky, as is any such broad schema. *The Chrysanthemum and the Sword* has generally been regarded as a relic of another age, and has been criticized for its too strong notion of national character (each nation is either one or

---

[1] "In the ashes of disgrace" is similar to the title of a memoir of post-war Germany by the sociologist Hans Speier, *From the Ashes of Disgrace: A Journal from Germany, 1945–1955* (Amherst: University of Massachusetts Press, 1981).

[2] Ruth Benedict, *The Chrysanthemum and the Sword: Patterns of Japanese Culture* (New York: Houghton Mifflin, 1989 [1946]), pp. 222–3.

the other kind of culture) and especially for its perceived implication that guilt cultures are both historically more advanced than shame cultures and morally superior to them.[3] As with most such "classics," however, the account is at least somewhat more subtle than scholarly memory indicates. Benedict points out that even in guilt cultures, one may experience shame as well, for instance "when [a person in a guilt culture] ... accuses himself of gaucheries which are in no way sins ..." She claims, moreover, that "Shame is an increasingly heavy burden in the United States and guilt is less extremely felt than in earlier generations." On the one hand, she agrees that this could rightly be interpreted as "a relaxation of morals." Her concern over the rise of shame and the decline of guilt comes from the fact that "we do not expect shame to do the heavy work of morality. We do not harness the acute personal chagrin which accompanies shame to our fundamental system of morality." On the other hand, she also admits that another interpretation is possible: After all, she notes, "Modern novelists ... who in the early years of this century celebrated the new Western individualism, became dissatisfied with the Occidental formulas and tried to celebrate sincerity ... as the only true doctrine." At very least, then, the "progression" from shame to guilt is not necessarily inevitable, and there often seems to be a mix of the two.

For all the concern with Benedict's putative national character argument and its perceived reductionism, some contemporary scholars have found this fundamental distinction useful. One can, for instance avoid the temptation to see one or the other cultural form as hegemonic in a particular kind of society or the implication that shame and guilt are stages in a developmental process. As Aleida Assmann puts it, "Shame culture and guilt culture stand ... for two forms of cultural treatment of a disruptive evil ... Instead of a historical development in which a higher guilt

---

[3] For example, "In a culture where shame is a major sanction," Benedict writes, "people are chagrined about acts which *we* [emphasis added] expect people to feel guilty about." Benedict thus dispassionately describes Japanese culture as a sort of institutionalized hypocrisy: "'Respecting yourself' often implies exactly the opposite behavior from that which it means in the United States... It had no implication, as it would in the United States, that even if thoughts are dangerous a man's self-respect requires that he think according to his own lights and his own conscience." Another such example is Benedict's argument that "*Makoto* does not mean what sincerity does in English usage... for calling a man 'sincere' in Japan has no reference to whether he is acting 'genuinely' according to love or hate, determination or amazement which is uppermost in his soul." Additionally, "In Japan 'respecting yourself' is always to show yourself the careful player. It does not mean, as it does in English usage, consciously conforming to a worthy standard of conduct – not truckling to another, not lying, not giving false testimony... When a man says 'You must respect yourself,' it means, 'You must be shrewd in estimating all the factors in the situation and do nothing that will arouse criticism or lessen your chances of success...'" (p. 220).

culture succeeds a lower shame culture, it is more reasonable to assume a dialectic in which two behavioral systems continually reactivate each other." In a study of Weimar-era German intellectuals, Helmut Lethen has argued that the First World War discredited the guilt principle for many European thinkers: "The fact that the civilized nations could engage in such horror, that individuals were able to suspend conscience for the sake of military operations, neither informed introspection nor generated confessions." As a result, "We would be much nearer the mark in saying that the collective gaze following World War One was averted from the complex of issues identified by a guilt culture."[4] According to Lethen, shame – which he follows Benedict in seeing as "fixing the genesis of internal authority in social violence" – was a more helpful framework for "the construction of a self more able to bear the immense pressures that rapid modernization placed on the bourgeois individual." It enabled the war's losers "to subvert the fiction of the self-made individual that is part of the concept of a guilt culture ..."[5]

The culture of Weimar, according to Lethen, thus depended on a manly "conduct of cool." In this light, it is not surprising that the two major philosophical alternatives of the Weimar period were, first, a dom-inant conservative embrace of Nietzschean nihilism coupled with a radical critique of modernity (supporting a shame culture) and, second, a less-successful liberal neo-Kantian existentialism coupled with a defense of humanism (supporting a guilt culture). In Germany, the former was part of the broader cultural universe of which National Socialism was a part, while the latter went underground or into exile. Indeed, many accounts of post-Second-World-War German intellectual culture either skip over the possibility of a persisting radical conservatism (part of a shame culture) or characterize it as a phenomenon so marginalized as to be nearly totally irrelevant. One manifestation of this is the place that has been ascribed to the philosopher Karl Jaspers, particularly to his 1946 book, *Die Schuldfrage* (*The Question of German Guilt*).[6] According to the German-Israeli histor-ian Dan Diner, for instance, "Jaspers's discussion of the theme [German guilt] in 1945–46 reads like a founding text for the new (West) German

---

[4] Helmut Lethen, *Cool Conduct: The Culture of Distance in Weimar Germany*, trans. Don Reneau (Berkeley: University of California Press, 2002), p. 11.

[5] Lethen, *Cool Conduct*, p. 15. See also Aleida Assmann and Ute Frevert, *Geschichtsvergessenheit/ Geschichtsversessenheit: Vom Umgang mit deutschen Vergangenheiten nach 1945* (Stuttgart: Deutsche Verlags-Anstalt, 1999), pp. 88–96.

[6] Karl Jaspers, *The Question of German Guilt*, trans. E. B. Ashton (New York: Fordham University Press, 2000). Originally published as *Die Schuldfrage: Von der Politischen Haftung Deutschlands* (Munich: Piper, 1965 [1946]).

collective identity ... Jaspers's ... confessional text," Diner claims, "acquired quasi-normative significance for the old Federal Republic."[7] In the historians' dispute of 1985, the sociologist and philosopher Jürgen Habermas attacked neo-conservatives, claiming that their attempt to limit the role of Holocaust memory in the Federal Republic violated basic commitments of West German political culture, namely – if not exactly guilt, then acknowledgment of and accepting responsibility for Germany's Nazi past. Habermas' main referent for this tradition was Karl Jaspers.[8] For Habermas, Jaspers' approach was the *sine qua non* of a healthy German political culture, and any implication that it was not obvious and untouchable was unacceptable.[9]

Even those who ascribe more power or even legitimacy to purportedly discredited conservative traditions ascribe Jaspers' guilty view to official culture and the conservative shame tradition to the private sphere: In his study of the radical conservative writer Ernst Jünger, for instance, Elliot Neaman argues that "Official unequivocal antifascism [guilt culture] repressed the legacy of pre-Nazi German culture [shame culture], seen as contaminated and compromised by the Nazi assimilation of the romantic-classicist German pantheon."[10] As Jan-Werner Mueller puts it in his study of post-war intellectuals in the Federal Republic,

Two cultures opposed each other in early postwar Germany. On the one side, there was an official public culture of guilt and democratic humanism, sanctioned by the Allies through the licensed journals, and centered on emigrants and liberals such as Jaspers. On the other side stood an obstinate culture of silence, in which honour was preserved through taboos. The culture of guilt and communication, not surprisingly, dominated in public, but the counterculture of silence became more characteristic for the private and semi-private life of the young republic.[11]

On the one hand, Lethen states that "In the context of the Nuremberg trials, the statement of the Protestant Church,[12] and denazification, a guilt

---

[7] Dan Diner, *Beyond the Conceivable: Studies on Germany, Nazism, and the Holocaust* (Berkeley: University of California Press, 2000), p. 219.

[8] See especially Jürgen Habermas, *Philosophical-Political Profiles* (Cambridge, Mass.: MIT Press, 1990).

[9] Jürgen Habermas, *The New Conservatism: Cultural Criticism and the Historians' Debate* (Cambridge, Mass.: MIT Press, 1989). Also the chapter on Jaspers in Jürgen Habermas, *Philosophical-Political Profiles*.

[10] Elliot Y. Neaman, *A Dubious Past: Ernst Jünger and the Politics of Literature after Nazism* (Berkeley: University of California Press, 1999), p. 10.

[11] Jan-Werner Mueller, *Another Country: German Intellectuals, Unification and National Identity* (New Haven: Yale University Press, 2000), p. 31.

[12] In 1945, the German Protestant Church issued the so-called "Stuttgart Declaration of Guilt," acknowledging a limited responsibility of the Protestant leadership for not having resisted more strongly (the intent, purview, and ultimate meaning of the Stuttgart Declaration was highly disputed).

culture is a matter of official prescription ..." On the other hand, he insightfully demonstrates that "The distinction between shame and guilt cultures is instructive as a myth, the reality of a wish projection that was persuasive to a generation of critical intellectuals."[13]

In the pages that follow, I reconstruct the debate between Jaspers as a proponent of inner transformation through acknowledgement of guilt and representatives of Lethen's "cool conduct"– Martin Heidegger, Ernst Jünger, and Carl Schmitt– as proponents of silence and forgetting as a way of avoiding shame. The more general question I address through this case, however, is in what ways the shame versus guilt matrix is a useful one for understanding how members of burdened collectivities can confront the challenges to their identities, both personal and collective, that such legacies raise. Clearly, Germany after the Second World War is the paradigmatic case, though the relevance for contemporary discussions of the responsibility ordinary citizens and subsequent generations bear for the legacies of authoritarianism should be clear as well. The advantage to seeing shame versus guilt as a dialectic is that it helps us avoid the cultural reductionism implied by seeing Japan as a "shame culture" and thus as culturally behind the West. Nevertheless, by examining just such a dialectical process within a particular national context, we may end up wary of dismissing the implication that guilt is more progressive than shame. Indeed, not all repudiations of Jaspers came from the right.

I.   Guilt and transfiguration

On October 25, 1945, the *Neue Zeitung*[14] carried a letter from the Nobel-Prize-winning Norwegian writer Sigrid Undset. Undset had passed the war in American exile, during which time she was active in discussions of German character and theories of re-education. Undset was deeply skeptical about the possibility of a German turnaround. For her, the horror was simply too much to be overcome with institutional restructuring or re-examination of basic values: "The greatest hindrance to German re-education," Undset argued, "is not German thinking, but rather the actual deeds which have been committed as a result of this thinking." Interestingly, Undset's inflection of "collective guilt" was more longitudinal than latitudinal (in other words, guilt shared over time rather than guilt of all present at one time): She acknowledged that in a nation of 70 million people there will be a mix of good and bad, intelligent and

---

[13] Lethen, *Cool Conduct*, pp. 13–14.
[14] The *Neue Zeitung* was a newspaper published in Germany by the US army for the German population.

stupid. The real problem is with "millions of German children," who are burdened with "fathers who took part in the atrocities against civilians, women and children ..." Moreover, beyond the legacies of actual perpetration of atrocities, "Countless German children have parents who experienced a fleeting prosperity as a result of the plunder of Europe ... pocketing some of the booty which had been taken from the dead!" And German mothers are as guilty as the fathers, having taken over "homes and properties of people in occupied territories, even keeping family portraits which they occasionally offered to sell back to their owners at a high price!"

At the request of an American editor, Karl Jaspers undertook a response to Undset, which contained the seeds of his more elaborate arguments in *Die Schuldfrage*. In the immediate aftermath of the war, Jaspers was perhaps uniquely placed to speak on behalf of positive German traditions. A former protégé of the sociologist Max Weber, Jaspers represented the liberal side of German nationalism; a neo-Kantian existentialist philosopher, Jaspers stood for humanistic ideals (yet also appreciated darker readings of Nietzsche like that of his friend Martin Heidegger); stripped of his university position in 1937 and married to a Jew, Jaspers was entirely free of National Socialist taint.

For Jaspers, there were two fundamental problems with Undset's argument. First, her condemnation appeared total and her assessment of Germany's future hopeless. Jaspers, however, believed fervently in the possibility for repentance and conversion: "The freedom, the possibility of a turn-around, remains for everyone, even the guilty." Second, Undset's condemnation appeared to Jaspers to be illegitimately collectivistic: "To condemn summarily a people as a whole or every member of this people seems to me to violate the claim of being human. No verdict on an individual person," Jaspers argued, "even less so on all members of a people is true, that claims 'that is the way they are.'" Insofar as Undset blamed a unitary German world of ideas, Jaspers said, she was employing the same logic as the Nazis, a logic which is "a means of mutual hatred of peoples and groups. It was applied in the most evil way by the National Socialists and was drummed into people's heads by their propaganda." Jaspers agreed with Undset's outrage, but argued that the issue was "in what sense every German must feel complicit." This was the central question Jaspers attempts to work out in *Die Schuldfrage*, which had its origins as a series of lectures in Heidelberg in 1945–46.

"The Question of German Guilt"

Despite its reputation as the definitive statement of post-war German guilt culture, Jaspers' *Die Schuldfrage* had none of the totalistic condemnations of Undset and other non-Germans who during the war had argued the deficits of (and remedies for) German national character. Ever the philosopher, Jaspers believed that "to arrive at truth we must differentiate." By now, knowledge of Jaspers' quadripartite distinction of criminal, political, moral, and metaphysical guilt is widely known. Criminal guilt refers to those acts for which one may be held liable in a court of law; political guilt refers to the responsibility one bears for the political system in which one lives by virtue of being a citizen (political "responsibility," Jaspers argued, is borne even by those who opposed the regime); moral guilt refers to whatever personal failings one demonstrated in attitude, demeanor, or action (for instance, enthusiasm for the regime's successes or turning a blind eye to one's suffering neighbor); metaphysical guilt is closest to the Christian notion of original sin, guilt stemming from the knowledge that such things are possible in the world. The four types of guilt, one notes, can be divided in two different ways: Criminal and political guilt are public, while moral and metaphysical guilt are private; by the same token, criminal and moral guilt are absolutely individual, whereas political and metaphysical guilt can be shared.

Types of Guilt	*Private*	*Public*
Individual	Moral	Criminal
Collective	Metaphysical	Political

But the importance of Jaspers' argument is not entirely captured by the typology, which is what has received the most attention. Jaspers' rhetorical strategy was to establish from the outset a community of discourse with his compatriots: "We must learn to talk with each other," he pleaded, "and we mutually must understand and accept one another in our extraordinary differences." The obstacle here was "the great diversity in what we believed all these years, what we took to be true, what to us was the meaning of life... What we must painfully renounce is [thus] not alike for all ... We are divided along different lines of disappointment." Jaspers thus argued from the standpoint of one suffering the same fate as his compatriots and made no effort to excuse himself from the burdens of which he spoke. Nevertheless, it remained for him to work out – both philosophically and personally– what this bond of common nationality could mean, given all the differences in disappointment.

Jaspers was at this point simultaneously more resigned to the situation *of "vae victus"* (woe to the vanquished) than many of his compatriots as well as more positively inclined towards the Western authorities, whose political culture he believed to be motivated by principles of right, law, and fairness. By the same token, Jaspers rejected – as many of his compatriots did – that anything good could come of accusations or demands for introspection from outside. "It is only human," Jaspers said, "that the accused, whether justly or unjustly, tries to defend himself." Such accusations – as we saw with the response to Sigrid Undset – Jaspers considered both crude and born of illegitimate motives: "That condemnation by the victorious powers became a means of politics and impure in its motives – this fact itself is a guilt pervading history ... Evil is evil even when inflicted as retribution." Jaspers' tone was nevertheless significantly different from that of many others who spent great time outlining the failures of Germany's enemies (though he did nevertheless mention the "guilt of others"). "The political question ..." for Jaspers, however, was "whether it is politically sensible, purposeful, safe and just to turn a whole nation into a pariah nation, to degrade it beneath all others, to dishonor further, once it had dishonored itself." From this perspective, what the Allies thought was ultimately irrelevant for Germans: "Those charges from without are no longer our concern. We must clarify the question of German guilt. This is our own business."

The reality Germans had to face, Jaspers thus argued, was that they had in fact become a "pariah people" (Undset's reaction was proof). The concept of pariahdom was for Jaspers and many others a very powerful one, not incidentally because the classical example of a "pariah people," as articulated by Max Weber, was the Jews.[15] We already saw Jaspers' charge that Undset's collectivistic condemnation drew on the same logics against Germans that the Nazis had used against Jews (and Jaspers repeated the argument in *Die Schuldfrage*). Later in the book, Jaspers continued to make the association: "A world opinion which condemns a people collectively is of a kind with the fact that for thousands of years men have thought and said, 'The Jews are guilty of the Crucifixion.' Who are the 'the Jews'? A certain group of religious and political zealots whose relative power among the Jews of that time, with the Roman occupation authorities, led to the execution of Jesus."

The crucial question, however, was what the Germans would make of their pariah status. Would it be thoroughly negative or would it yield new insight? "Here we Germans face an alternative. Either acceptance of the guilt not meant by the rest of the world but constantly repeated by our conscience comes to be a fundamental trait of our German self-consciousness – in which case our soul goes the way of transformation – or we subside into the average

---

[15] For a seminal discussion of Jaspers' use of the pariah concept in *Die Schuldfrage*, on which my account draws a great deal, see Anson Rabinbach, *In the Shadow of Catastrophe: German Intellectuals Between Apocalypse and Enlightenment* (Berkeley and Los Angeles: University of California Press, 2000), pp. 129–65.

triviality of indifferent, mere living ..." For Jaspers, the moral and political imperative was clear: "There is no other way to realize truth for the German than purification out of the depth of consciousness of guilt."

Nevertheless, this was Jaspers' vision for the future of Germany, and it is why *Die Schuldfrage* is considered a founding text for a new political culture:

Full frankness and honesty harbors not only our dignity – possible even in impotence – but our own chance. The question for every German is whether to go this way at the risk of all disappointments, at the risk of additional losses and of convenient abuse by the powerful. The answer is that this is the only way that we can save our souls from a pariah existence.

Elsewhere, however, Jaspers put a more positive inflection on the pariahdom experience, arguing that it might even produce special insights. First of all, he argued, it would have been a mistake to isolate Germany from all other nations: "What broke out in Germany was under way in the entire Western world as a crisis of faith, of the spirit. This does not diminish our guilt – for it was here in Germany that the outbreak occurred, not somewhere else – but it does free us from isolation." The point, however, was that the fact that the catastrophe occurred in Germany "makes us instructive for the others." This is the positive inflection of pariahdom – the possibility of one's own experience of transformation serving as a beacon to others who have the same long-term needs but are not pressed as much by contemporary circumstances to take up the challenge: "By our feeling of collective guilt we feel the entire task of renewing human existence from its origin – the task that is given to all men on earth but which appears more urgently, more perceptibly, as decisively as all existence, when its own guilt brings a people face to face with nothingness."

The challenge Jaspers set himself was thus truly a monumental one. His was a plea to his non-criminal compatriots to overcome their defenses and to realize where they too had incurred guilt. The four-part scheme was not merely a differentiation of guilt, but indeed an addition of guilts one may not have been willing to consider for fear that doing so would class one with the execrable. The differentiation of types of guilt thus worked in two directions: on the one hand, it made clear that only a rather narrow class of acts was criminally chargeable; Jaspers' schema thus drew a line against a concept of guilt that, like Undset's, condemned indiscriminately.[16] On the other hand, Jaspers' argument was that just because one rightly felt oneself free from the dangers of a criminal prosecution, one was not so easily finished with the matter. Jaspers' aim, put simply, was to make his

---

[16] Rabinbach, *In the Shadow of Catastrophe*.

compatriots – even those who had opposed the regime – *feel* guilty. By the same token, he wanted them to *feel* the appropriate *kind* of guilt and for the right reasons, and to do the right thing with these feelings. "True," he said, "among our people many were outraged and many deeply moved by a horror containing a presentiment of coming calamity." But this was not enough to free them from political responsibility: even if one had done almost everything one could to stop it, one still bore the burden of repairing it. This was the condition of collective identity: the only possibility would be to renounce one's Germanness, which was not possible anyway. Jaspers asked his indifferent compatriots to see the costs of their own weakness: "even more went right on with their activities, undisturbed in their social life and amusements, as if nothing had happened." For Jaspers, "This is moral guilt," and cannot be excused.

Jaspers was indeed pleading with ordinary Germans who were not criminally guilty to acknowledge the manifold ways one was tied up even with a reality one did not necessarily – or at least in all its implications – want. "To have been a good soldier," he stated bluntly as an example, "does not absolve one from all other guilt." Being German required reparation in the political world, self-examination in the moral realm, and confession in the metaphysical realm (the same applied to other peoples as well, though the circumstances of their political responsibility and moral guilt were different, and perhaps less burdensome). But a closer reading that attends to the personal origins of *Die Schuldfrage* calls attention to other passages, which might otherwise go unnoticed. Certain kinds of evasions, and certain kinds of evaders, were more irksome to Jaspers than others.

II.   The recalcitrance of shame

Jaspers was, of course, disgusted with the Nazi leaders and their equivocations. But what could one expect? More problematic for Jaspers were certain kinds of intellectuals, particularly those who "went along in 1933, sought leading positions and publicly upheld the ideology of the new power, only to become resentful later when they personally were shunted aside." Jaspers argued that the problem was that "These ... now feel that they suffered under the Nazis and are therefore called for what follows. They regard themselves as anti-Nazis." But this was pure hypocrisy for Jaspers: "In all these years, according to their self-proclaimed ideology, these intellectual Nazis were frankly speaking truth in spiritual matters, guarding the tradition of the German spirit, preventing destructions, doing good in individual cases." Jaspers, however, rejected this exculpatory version of events: "Many of these may be guilty of persisting in a mentality which, while not identical with Party tenets and even disguised as metamorphosis and opposition, still clings in fact to the mental attitude of National Socialism and fails to clear itself." Jaspers' not-so-secret target here? His former friend, Martin Heidegger.

Martin Heidegger was – and is – considered by many to be the most important philosopher of the twentieth century, credited with providing philosophical grounding for the postmodern turn *towards* language and *against* philosophical anthropology (the idea, which is the core of humanism, that man has an unalterable essence that stands outside of time). Heidegger's thought has been revered unlike virtually any other in European intellectual circles. Despite an essentially "non-political" existence in the 1920s (a common trope at the time), Heidegger came to see a transformative alternative in National Socialism. In April 1933, following Hitler's January 30, 1933 assumption of power, Heidegger was elected to the rectorship of Freiburg University; at the end of May, he delivered his now notorious address in which he praised the National Socialist agenda and declared it time for an epochal battle (later, Heidegger maintained that this battle was meant to be a philosophical one for Being, *not* literally a real, mechanized war); the speech included the rhetoric of "blood and soil" and preached a rather rousing nationalism.

Heidegger joined the Nazi Party on May 1, 1933. Scholars have shaded his activities as rector either as moderate political engagement for the National Socialists or as moderate attempts to lessen their more extreme intrusions into university life.[17] Either way, his philosophical language of the period was easily harmonizable with the National Socialist rhetoric of national renewal and cultic fervor. Nevertheless, caught up in faculty disputes and disagreements with supervising party officials, Heidegger resigned a mere ten months into his rectorship, though without a critical statement. During the remaining majority of the Third Reich, Heidegger largely avoided political activities, later complaining that his philosophical renown was exploited for political purposes without his involvement. Nevertheless, he never officially resigned from the party. Even more problematic for his reputation, however, is that he never repudiated his early National Socialism nor acknowledged any guilt for his role in legitimating the regime.

Friends since the early 1920s, who saw in each other a shared purpose which they spoke of as a community of battle, Jaspers and Heidegger

---

[17] The major line of dispute over Heidegger's reputation, especially since the 1970s, is between those who attributed Heidegger's National Socialism to political naivete of no consequence for his philosophical legacy and those who argue that Heidegger's National Socialism was wholly consistent with his philosophy, thus compromising its legacy.

continued to correspond in the early years of National Socialism, though their exchanges became more and more distanced; they ceased altogether after 1937. The next moment in their relationship, then, was when the botanist Friedrich Oehlkers wrote to Jaspers on behalf of the Freiburg University denazification committee, requesting Jaspers' evaluation of Heidegger's fitness to resume his professorial duties. In his letter, Jaspers described Heidegger this way:

Heidegger is a significant potency, not through the content of a philosophical world-view, but in the manipulation of speculative tools. He has a philosophical aptitude whose perceptions are interesting; although, in my opinion, he is extraordinarily uncritical and stands at a remove from true science. He often proceeds as if he combined the seriousness of nihilism with the mystagogy of a magician.[18]

Nevertheless, Jaspers argued that "it is absolutely necessary that those who helped place National Socialism in the saddle be called to account. Heidegger belongs among the few professors to have so acted." The question was how much was to be excused by brilliance. Jaspers concluded that "Exceptional intellectual achievement can serve as a justifiable basis for facilitating the continuation of such work; not, however, for the resumption of office and teaching duties." For Jaspers, education was simply too delicate a matter. "Heidegger's manner of thinking, which to me seems in its essence unfree, dictatorial, and incapable of communication, would today in its pedagogical effects be disastrous." Jaspers' solution, accepted by the committee, was that Heidegger be given emeritus status (including a pension) so that he could continue to work as a philosopher, but that he be prohibited from teaching.

Perhaps the most broadly relevant passage from Jaspers' evaluation letter, however, was his statement of what would have been required of Heidegger after his mistake of 1933. In his petition to the committee requesting reinstatement, Heidegger had denied all responsibility for the course of National Socialism. He explained his original motivation as stemming from his belief that "an autonomous alliance of intellectuals could deepen and transform a number of essential elements of the 'National Socialist Movement' and thereby contribute in its own way to overcoming Europe's disarray and the crisis of the Western spirit." The mistake he acknowledged was that he believed he could influence the transformation of National Socialism into something closer to what he envisioned. Heidegger thus seemed to believe not only that he was not

[18] Karl Jaspers, "Letter to the Freiburg University Denazification Committee (December 22, 1945)," in Richard Wolin, *The Heidegger Controversy: A Critical Reader* (Cambridge, Mass.: MIT Press, 1993), pp. 144–51; 148–9.

wrong, but that it was the other way around: it was the *National Socialists* who failed to understand *him*! For Jaspers, however, "A change of conviction as a result of directional shifts in the National Socialist camp can be judged according to the motivations which are in part revealed at the specific point in time. 1934, 1938, 1941 signify fundamentally different stages." In Jaspers' opinion, "for purposes of reaching a judgment, a change of conviction is almost meaningless if it resulted only after 1941, and it is of trifling value if it did not occur radically after June 30, 1934."

All this helps us understand, then, what (and whom) Jaspers had in mind when he wrote in *Die Schuldfrage* that "If a mature person in 1933 had the certainty of inner conviction – due not merely to political error but to a sense of existence heightened by National Socialism – he will be purified only by a transmutation which may have to be more thorough than any other." This he and others expected from Heidegger and never received. Heidegger's former student Herbert Marcuse even wrote to Heidegger asking for it in no uncertain terms: "You (and we) can only combat the identification of your person and your work with Nazism (and thereby the dissolution of your philosophy) if you make a public avowal of your changed views."[19] Heidegger's response did not give an inch: "... your letter shows me" he wrote back to Marcuse, "how difficult it is to converse with persons who have not been living in Germany since 1933 and who judge the beginning of National Socialism from its end."[20]

This would all amount to nothing more than intellectual-historical gossip, the pathetic tale of a broken man (if indeed that is what Heidegger was) if Heidegger's self-defense had not in fact been a highly theorized political position in the immediate post-war public discourse about the question of German guilt. Heidegger's defense certainly had its pathetic aspects, particularly when he responded to Marcuse's concerns that Heidegger had been associated with "a regime that murdered millions of Jews, that made terror into an everyday phenomenon, and that turned everything that pertains to the ideas of spirit, freedom, and truth into its bloody opposition" by equating this to the post-war treatment of Germans in the East. Even more relevant was Heidegger's argument that "An avowal after 1945 was for me impossible: the Nazi supporters announced their change of allegiance in the most loathsome way; I, however, had nothing in common with them."[21]

---

[19] Quoted in Wolin, *The Heidegger Controversy*, p. 161.   [20] Ibid., p. 162.
[21] Ibid., p. 162.

Heidegger, humanism, and responsibility

It would thus be easy to dismiss Heidegger's refusal to disavow his National Socialist associations as psychological weakness were it not that Heidegger's predisposition was both common to a particular cultural milieu and had Heidegger not offered a highly theorized version of his refusal, the famous "Letter on Humanism."[22] The "Letter on Humanism" was occasioned by Heidegger's early post-war correspondence with a young French follower, Jean Beaufret. The letter's philosophical frame, however, was Heidegger's attempt to distinguish his own position from mainstream existentialism, particularly as expressed in Sartre's lecture, "Existentialism is a Humanism." For Heidegger, it decidedly was not. Existence – or in Heidegger's language "Being" – was for Heidegger opposed to essence, which is an abstraction – or, again in Heidegger's language, a "forgetfulness of Being." For Heidegger, the core that all the diverse humanisms in the history of philosophy shared was that they privileged the *"humanitas* of *Homo humanus,* [which] is determined with regard to an already established interpretation of nature, history, world, and the ground of the world." For Heidegger, this was the fundamental error of Western thought, which mistakenly favors action over Being because it splits subject from object. The result is the "homelessness" of modern man, characterized by the empty valorization of technology, rationality, and the market, and of knowledge over Being. The latter was clear in philosophy, which since Descartes had held epistemology to be the fundamental problem; this preoccupation with metaphysics led to an overemphasis on action at the expense of Being.

In perhaps the most famous statement in all of his writing, Heidegger declared at the beginning of the letter that "Language is the house of Being." Language – not man, his essence, thought, or action. There was, as Anson Rabinbach and others have pointed out, an odor of self-exculpation about this statement: Nothing as misguided as ethics was appropriate, with its judgment of an individual's acts rather than of Being itself. As Theodor Adorno put it in *The Jargon of Authenticity,* "Language as the House of Being" is an "alibi": Heidegger's approach implied that "the language itself – through its generality and objectivity – already negates the whole man, the particular speaking subject: the first price exacted by language is the essence of the individual ... Whoever stands behind his words, in the way in which these words pretend, is safe from any suspicion about what he is at that very moment

---

[22] See especially Anson Rabinbach's essay on Heidegger's "Letter on Humanism" in *In the Shadow of Catastrophe,* pp. 97–114.

about to do: speak for others in order to palm something off on them."[23] In other words, if language is the house of Being, individual ethics are mere epiphenomena. Indeed, this implication fits well with Heidegger's pre-war writings on conscience, in which he distinguished between a conventional understanding of conscience as an agency which judges us (the agency of guilt) and conscience as "a summons to be what we are authentically: to be ourselves."[24] As Paul Tillich described it, "The call of conscience does not judge anything in particular. Conscience, for Heidegger, rather has to do with a fundamental phenomenon, more profound than any specific judgment about which one might have a so-called bad conscience." This conscience does indeed involve guilt, but here again guilt is understood unconventionally, a sense "over-against the norms and rule by which we are living," rather than a verdict on the ordinary things one might do. To be guilty is thus to be authentic to oneself. This was why Heidegger described conscience as the "silent call to be ourselves." In this light ethical judgment– and the associated inner transformation– seems irrelevant if not debased. The similarity to Benedict's description of Japanese sincerity as "respecting oneself" is striking.

These issues are relevant here in two ways. First, one is struck by the way in which Heidegger's discussion fits within the framework of shame culture– a culture, that is, which refused all acknowledgment and confession as a betrayal of self. Ordinary conscience, for Heidegger, is the external, objective, and rational. But his understanding of conscience as authenticity to self is judged only by oneself; it admits to no external judgments. Where guilt calls one to account for oneself in terms of absolute criteria and to devote oneself to a transformation, Heidegger's conscience as authenticity required "resoluteness." And this resoluteness stemmed entirely from Being. Resoluteness, in Benedict's framework, was a response to the possibility of shame, where guilt called for admission and transformation. Heideggerian conscience was resolutely opposed to transformation, which as the act of an individual is nothing anyway in the house of Being – language, which is greater than any mere speaker.

Second, the claim that Western metaphysics is "forgetfulness of Being" was connected to Heidegger's diagnosis of the West, his proposed treatment for these ills, and his "resoluteness" in the face of the failure of his solutions to triumph. Heidegger, like other thinkers of the so-called

[23] Theodor W. Adorno, *The Jargon of Authenticity*, trans. Knut Tarnowski and Frederic Will (Evanston, Il.: Northwestern University Press, 1973), p. 14.
[24] Paul Tillich, "Heidegger and Jaspers," in Alan M. Olson (ed.), *Heidegger and Jaspers* (Philadelphia: Temple University Press, 1994), p. 23.

"conservative revolution" of the 1920s, was entranced by Nietzsche's nihilism, contrasting it with what they saw as a "half-hearted" nihilism of the West. The history of the West is a history of decay; the only solution was thus a "ruthless nihilism" inspired by Nietzsche, which only Germany could offer. In this light, National Socialism provided the only hope for an alternative to the equally debased liberalism of the West and Communism of the East. The problem was that National Socialism turned out to be only one more half-hearted nihilism. Heidegger's only mistake, therefore, was temporarily misrecognizing National Socialism as a potential rebirth of Being. All that Heidegger admitted in the letter was to have momentarily been seduced by essence, to have slipped into a weaker nihilism from which he very quickly recovered.

Heidegger, of course, was not the only one who saw in National Socialism the hope for renewal after centuries of decadence. Indeed, over many years, Heidegger exchanged ideas and accolades with perhaps the only two other thinkers who achieved the same status in the pantheon of German conservative thought – the writer Ernst Jünger and the legal theorist Carl Schmitt. Heidegger, Jünger, and Schmitt shared not just many aspects of their assessment of National Socialism (first enthusiastic, then claiming – some argue disingenuously – a change of heart) but a similar stance concerning how to confront (or not) the memory of the catastrophe.

Like Heidegger, for instance, Jünger saw in the German catastrophe a mere by-product of the demise of civilization. The implicit message was that nothing as mundane as the responsibility of a particular party was at issue. "We have seen the victims of this war. To their somber ranks all nations add their contingent." "Everyone," Jünger argues, "shared in the guilt, and there is no one who did not stand in need of the healing powers which are to be found in the realm of suffering."[25] For Jünger, "As sons of the earth we are involved in the civil war, in the fratricidal strife." Jünger, like Heidegger, faced the characteristic challenge for Weimar ultra-conservatives, namely that he had been an early enthusiast. What responsibility did one bear whose early sympathies gave succor to the movement? Could one simply disavow one's earlier role? Jünger's famous solution, nearly identical to Heidegger's, was to deny that he was responsible for the ways in which his ideas were taken up. In fact, Jünger argued that as a writer he was a mere observer. All the talk of his responsibility he thus dismissed as misguided. "After the War one bangs on the seismographers. One cannot, however, let the barometer be punished for the typhoon,

---

[25] Ernst Jünger, *The Peace*, trans. Stuart O. Hood (Hinsdale, Ill.: Henry Regnery, 1948), pp. 31–2.

unless one wants to be counted among the primitives." This, then, was his assessment of his role and, by implication, that of his fellow radical conservatives – they were mere diagnosticians.

Carl Schmitt's "silence"

For his part, Schmitt – arrested by the Americans, repeatedly interrogated, denied his library and all the accoutrements of his former fame – took as his motto "the security of silence" (*die Sicherheit des Schweigens*). Despite this, however, Schmitt undertook surreptitious and not-so-surreptitious efforts to delegitimate what he saw as an overwhelming and oppressive culture of guilt, and lamented pathetically his reputational demise. Here indeed was the archetypal example of shame, one railing rabidly against the injustice of lost face, refusing to give an inch on the possibility that one could be in any way culpable. His was also the most aggressive attack against Nuremberg, denazification, and the culture of guilt he saw embodied in both the churches and Jaspers. So when Schmitt referred to the "security of silence," he meant refusing to acknowledge culpability or to accept disgrace, not shutting up about what has happened (though what has happened is largely to him).

The vigor of Schmitt's defense was only partly due to the fact that of the three he was the most burdened, unable to claim convincingly that he had ever truly broken with the regime. Schmitt had been, and continued to be, more thoroughly anti-Semitic than either Jünger or Heidegger, both of whom strenuously disavowed ever having been sympathetic to the racial component of Nazi ideology. Schmitt too argued that his theories did not support anti-Semitism, but he was thoroughly unconvincing (in a 1936 speech, Schmitt had declared that "We need to liberate the German spirit from all Jewish falsifications..."[26]) His post-war diaries, moreover, are rife with the crudest, most despicable individual-level anti-Semitism, by-passing any cover of theoretical complexity.[27]

Schmitt viewed himself as a victim, first of the Nazis (though it was never exactly clear in what way he was their victim, other than that they failed to triumph), and subsequently of the Allies, particularly in the form of his interrogator, Robert Kempner, a Prussian-Jewish émigré who returned to Germany as a prosecutor at Nuremberg. Schmitt expressed

---

[26] Cited in Rolf Wiggershaus, *The Frankfurt School: Its History, Theories, and Political Significance*, trans. Michael Robertson (Cambridge Mass.: MIT Press, 1995), p. 470.
[27] On Schmitt's anti-Semitism, see Raphael Gross, *Carl Schmitt und die Juden: Eine deutsche Rechtslehre* (Frankfurt: Suhrkamp, 2000).

his disgust in his diary not just with the idea of his interrogation, but with the identity of his interrogator:

I have been imprisoned, my most intimate property, my library, has been con- fiscated, and I have been locked up in a cell as a criminal; in short, I have fallen into the hands of this mighty American empire. I was curious about my new masters. But I have until this very day, five long years, not yet once spoken with an American, but only with German Jews, with Herr Loewenstein, Flechtheim and the like, who were not at all new to me but, rather, for a long time well known to me. A peculiar master of the world, these poor modern Yankees, with their ancient Jews.[28]

Indeed, Schmitt had been surprised to have been arrested at all. Throughout his repeated interrogations, he denied any and all grounds for suspicion, including any connection between his own theories of "*Grossraum*," which had inspired National Socialist rhetoric and was responsible for Schmitt's fame under the regime.

In February 1945, Jünger and Schmitt discussed the relevance of the extermination of the Jews – not for the Jews, but for Germany. Both expressed disdain for the horrors, but, again, their primary concern was what this would mean for Germany. Schmitt's pre-war and wartime writings had already ascribed a fearful role to the Jews in generating a particular kind of political accounting. At the end of the war, in a letter to Schmitt, Jünger referred to Josephus Flavius' report of "the obstinacy of the Jews in the siege of Jerusalem." Such attempts only served to wake the beast of Old Testament morality, Jünger wrote, in which the Jews sought to exact terrible revenge. Schmitt's response seems to be that the real reason not to exterminate the Jews was that this would wake the beast again: He quoted Bruno Bauer's line that "in the end, God created the Jews, and if we kill them all, we will suffer the same fate." Later, Schmitt wrote "As God allowed hundreds of thousands of Jews to be killed, he simultaneously saw the revenge that they would take on Germany; and that which he foresees today for the avengers and those demanding restitution, humanity will experience in another unexpected moment."[29]

Indeed, this connected directly to Schmitt's thorough repudiation of "re-education," "denazification," and the "culture of guilt," all of which utterly disgusted him. This had both a theorized and a mundane version. The theorized version came in an essay of the immediate post-war years

---

by Schmitt, entitled "Amnesty and the Power of Forgetting."[30] There Schmitt argued that the nature of war had changed from "a collision between two organized, well disciplined armies" into a seemingly endless fratricidal civil war (*Buergerkrieg*), no longer waged only with military weapons but now with any and all means to undermine one's opponent. This produced a new kind of viciousness that availed itself of particularly despicable tactics:

> Each European people knows today what this means. Each knows not just one, but many fifth columns. The denazification was a cold civil war. The emblem of this civil war consists of treating the others as criminals, murderers, saboteurs, and gangsters. In a terrible sense civil war is a just war because each of the parties sits unconditionally on its rights as on a prize. Each takes revenge in the name of right (pp. 218, 219).

For Schmitt, it was thus a sworn duty to engage in "Frontal struggle against the idea of the just war; open demonstration of its historical, juristic, and moral falsity; its character as an instrument of civil war etc." The correlate of just war is unjust war, whose participants would have to acknowledge their guilt. As a result, no just war means no unjust war, which means no guilt.

The question Schmitt posed was thus how to break what he saw as a cycle of mutual recrimination. The only solution, he argued, was amnesty, which at its core involves a willful forgetting.[31] Implicitly denigrating American gestures to the German population, Schmitt argued that "Amnesty is more than the cigarette that one offers to the disenfranchised in order to prove one's own humanity. The cold civil war is not to be ended so cheaply." Instead, "This word amnesty means forgetting, and not only forgetting but also the strict prohibition against mucking around (*herumzuwuehlen*) in the past and seeking there grounds for further acts of revenge and further demands for redress." Nothing, in Schmitt's opinion, could thus be worse than what the Jews would now extract.

In his post-war diaries, one finds a much less reasoned (for want of a better word) version of the same arguments. Continuing with the theme of the power reversal between Jews and Germans, Schmitt pretended to Tocquevillian insight:

---

[30] Carl Schmitt, "Amnestie oder die Kraft des Vergessens," in Gunter Maschke (ed.), *Staat, Grossraum, Nomos. Arbeiten aus den Jahren 1916–1969* (Berlin: Duncker and Humblot, 1995), pp. 218–21.

[31] The obvious inspiration here, though distorted, was Nietzsche's second *Untimely Meditation, On the Advantages and Disadvantages of History for Life*, in which Nietzsche argued that too much history can be "the gravedigger of the present."

The platform of democratic equality is only the springboard for new inequalities. That is de Tocqueville's real fear. The consequential equality is never real, and only in a single fleeting second true: in the moment in which the old privileges are removed and the new are not yet openly consolidated – that is, in the barely tangible moment of the transformation from the old discriminations to the new, that fabulous interval in which neither the Nazis persecute the Jews, nor the Jews persecute the Nazis.[32]

The Jews, it seems, would emerge as the real winners of the Holocaust, preparing to extract their revenge on Germany.

The diaries (*Ex Captivitate Salus* and *Glossarium*) also expressed Schmitt's disdain for what he felt was expected of him, which he said were "tips for memorial inscriptions in the confessional style." But he did not include himself with the "self-torturers": "If you want to make a confession, go find a priest and do it there." His goal was thus to keep his distance from the current public "spectacle of a brawl between preachers of repentance," referring to public debates about the proper attitude towards the past, particularly within the Protestant Church following the 1945 "Stuttgart Declaration of Guilt." "A good conscience that is expedited by the judiciary," Schmitt stated as a maxim, "is the worst." His most putrid scorn, however, Schmitt reserved for Karl Jaspers, who earned the following ditty: "How his penitential speech offends me / How disgusting are his rotten fish / Now he's gotten where he ought to be: / In the news and on the German telewish."

It was not that Schmitt believed he was trying to evade responsibility, he claimed: He was, he said, "an intellectual adventurer ... I take the risk. I have always paid my bills, and have never played the shirker." And he railed against "most people [who] think taking off a beard is a metamorphosis." "Never complain," he wrote, but also "Injustice is always ever again my lot." The similarity to Heidegger's response to Marcuse that he had nothing in common with those who rushed to repent is striking, though by no means inexplicable, given the on-going correspondence and, to appropriate a term Heidegger used to describe his pre-war relationship to Jaspers, sense of community of battle (*Kampfgemeinschaft*) among Jünger, Schmitt, and Heidegger.

In this light, the assertion of the literary critic Helmut Lethen, discussed at the beginning of this chapter, seems entirely on the mark:

After 1945, Schmitt repeats an attitude that corresponds to the post-World War One Zeitgeist: he does away with elements of the guilt culture – troubled conscience, remorse – and erects once again the artificial realm of a heroic shame culture ... The key concepts of the shame culture are honor and disgrace. After

---

[32] Schmitt, "Amnestie oder die Kraft des Vergessens," pp. 218–19.

World War One the issue was the disgrace of imperial collapse which, according to the rule of male association and bonding, had to be reversed. At issue now for Schmitt is the honor of which he was deprived as a vanquished foe. Everything the Allies undertook with Schmitt ... he [thus] experienced as a shaming ritual.[33]

As Lethen puts it, "In Carl Schmitt's *Glossarium* [the second volume of the diaries], amid the rubble, we see the cool persona's final stand." Lethen argues, however, that the difference between the situation after the First World War and that after the Second World War is that "the idea of a post-World War Two shame culture is a phantasm, with no corresponding public discursive space in which to unfold." My own evaluation, however, is that this conclusion is not entirely warranted. Is it really possible to say that Jaspers' vision predominated? Jaspers certainly did not think so, and the fact remains that Heidegger, Jünger, and Schmitt are today considered more important and interesting figures than Jaspers.

III.   Jaspers, guilt, and national identity

Without the foregoing excursus into the (not so) subterranean world of radical conservatism, one might pass over too easily the monumentality of the task Jaspers undertook. Jaspers was being very specific indeed in *Die Schuldfrage* when he wrote that

A proudly silent bearing may for a short time be a justified mask, to catch one's breath and clear one's head behind it. But it becomes self-deception, and a trap for the other, if it permits us to hide defiantly within ourselves, to bar enlightenment, to elude the grasp of reality. We must guard against evasion. From such a bearing there arises a mood which is discharged in private, safe abuse, a mood of heartless frigidity, rabid indignation and facile distortions, leading to barren self-corrosion. A pride that falsely deems itself masculine, while in fact evading the issue, takes even silence as an act of combat, a final one that remains impotent (p. 11).

Heidegger was obviously at the top of Jaspers' address list here, but Jünger (particularly with regard to masculine pride) and Schmitt were obviously not far behind.

In this light, it is not quite so obvious that Jaspers' vision did indeed represent the official culture of the new state, that the official culture of West Germany would be a guilt culture. The only possibility for reconciling the arguments, then, is to propose that Jaspers' vision triumphed in the long term – though to say this without attending to the ways Jünger, Heidegger, and Schmitt's vision has also persisted is misleading. Either way, the strict ascription of guilt to the Federal Republic, or of guilt to the

---

[33] Lethen, *Cool Conduct*, pp. 172–3.

public and shame to the private, does not hold water. Or, one can note, as I did above, the way in which Jaspers' scheme provided something for everyone.

Conclusion

On the basis of the foregoing narrative, Benedict's implication that guilt is more advanced– and morally superior – to shame in fact seems rather plausible, especially freed of the over-totalizing association of guilt and shame with entire cultures. Who today wouldn't prefer Jaspers over Heidegger, Jünger, and Schmitt? But before coming to this conclusion, it is worth considering that not all distaste for Jaspers' vision came from the right.

In the immediate post-war period, perhaps the most interesting example of this criticism from the left came from Heinrich Bluecher, who was Hannah Arendt's husband.[34] According to Bluecher, "Jaspers' whole ethical purification-babble leads him to solidarity with the German National Community and even with the National Socialists, instead of solidarity with those who have been degraded."[35] For Bluecher, moreover, there is something exculpatory about the generalization involved in "metaphysical guilt," which he viewed as a sort of "original sin." For Bluecher, this makes all guilty before the eyes of God and thus effaces real moral differences in the world: "guilt serves the purpose of extirpating responsibility." As a result, "This whole inner-German and inner-dealing talk of reconciliation of the 'National Community' can only serve the Nazis." Bluecher's position is thus that he does not "give a damn if they'll [the Germans] roast in hell someday or not, as long as they're prepared to do something to dry the tears of the degraded and the humiliated, and to die for freedom." The problem for Bluecher was that this framing of the "guilt question" served "for the vanquished as a way to continue occupying themselves exclusively with themselves..." Bluecher thus characterized Jaspers' "guilt monograph" as a "Christian/pietistic/hypocritical nationalizing piece of twaddle."

Indeed, while Bluecher's analysis is in many respects peremptory (the analysis just quoted was in a letter to his wife), there may be something to it. Jaspers did in fact say little about the victims, focusing instead on what he could contribute to the transformation of the German soul, an entity in

---

[34] In many respects, Arendt seconded her husband's assessment, though her own analysis went in other directions as well.
[35] Lotte Kohler (ed.), *Within Four Walls: The Correspondence between Hannah Arendt and Heinrich Blücher, 1936–1968* (New York: Harcourt, 2000), pp. 84–6.

which, despite all, he still believed. One interesting feature of post-war German discourse was that speakers often denied national identity as a "Nazi" form of argumentation when it was being used against them (e.g. in collective guilt or national character arguments), but were at great pains to reassert it when they saw positive virtues (e.g. the legacies of German humanistic culture or "positive" German values). In this light, Jaspers' argument seems particularly contrived to see national identity only as a positive resource: Like the joke that the oldest lies in German history are that Beethoven was German and Hitler was Austrian. This hypocrisy, of course, is by no means a uniquely German phenomenon: As Ernst Renan points out, nationalism involves a potent combination of remembering and forgetting.

On the surface, then, today we certainly seem to prefer the company of Jaspers to that of Heidegger, Jünger, and Schmitt. Or do we? On the one hand, a sense of pervasive guilt appears to have suffused domestic and international relations, in which a widespread "politics of regret" has encouraged movements for – and gestures of – redress, reparations, apology, reconciliation, as well as accountability of leaders and even of populations for collective crimes. On the other hand, this "politics of regret" is often tempted to the retrogressive pre-occupations about which Nietzsche warned at the end of the nineteenth century, in which too much history can become the "gravedigger of the present." Reactions to the politics of regret include the complaints that the pursuit of reparations is driven by illegitimate motives (e.g. class-action lawyers seeing big fees), that such policies are a "slippery-slope" which threaten to mire us in insoluble conflicts about who is a victim and who a perpetrator and who should pay whom how much (e.g. the case of reparations for slavery in the US), and that the culture of guilt is a substitute for the collapse of any coherent vision of the future.

How, then, does Benedict's framework, in which guilt is an advance over shame, stand up as both an analytical and normative guide? As a fundamental distinction, it operates as hoped – capturing something basic, which is nevertheless more complex in the details: guilt and shame are indeed competing moral postures in German society and elsewhere; guilt has not progressively supplanted shame, nor are its advantages unequivocal. Guilt does indeed contain the potential for wallowing. And confessions can produce a feeling of a burden being lifted, which opens the possibility that one can do it again (since all one needs to do is confess and compensate): in this regard, shame can serve as a stronger barrier. But, in the last analysis, shame does not imply a transformation and the potential for rebirth; while guilt may allow it to happen again, it says explicitly that it won't. Put this way, it is not a choice.

On silence, madness, and lassitude:
     Negotiating the past in post-war West
     Germany[1]

Svenja Goltermann

When the English author, Stephen Spender, went on his journey to
Germany in the summer of 1945 by order of the Allied Control
Commission, he gained a variety of impressions, which, soon after his
return, he published in the form of a travelogue. He had spent several
months in the Rhineland, mostly in bigger cities, the devastation of which
made him shudder. In his report, Spender also spoke repeatedly about the
Germans and their mental state, which was something he tried to decipher.
During one of his forays along the Rhine River, for instance, he met six men
who, apparently in a gloomy mood, were staring at the river in an apathetic
manner. Spender thought that they were former members of the German
army. "The German soldiers now have the soulless ground-down expression as in carved-wood faces of Slav peasants," he explained, before realizing a moment later that he had not come across German POWs, but former
Polish slave labourers. His conversation with these men was brief, where-
upon they relapsed into the "apathetic silence" in which Spender had found
them. He regarded this "apathy" as a mere "surface expression." "Behind
it, there is something much more menacing," he explained, "something
which has happened and left its impression, the fires which burned the cities
of Europe still smouldering in the minds of men. This is a state of mind
which glows beyond despair." Spender added: "I have seen this expression
in the faces of the desperate young men of the demobilized Reichswehr, also
in those of the French repatriated prisoners and in those of other men and
women labelled Displaced Persons."[2]

    Among the many reports that were written by foreign observers follow-
ing journeys through the "destroyed continent,"[3] Spender's observation of
a seemingly apathetic mental condition in those individuals was no isolated

---

[1] The following argument is based on my habilitation thesis *Die Gesellschaft der Überlebenden.
    Kriegsheimkehrer und ihre Gewalterfahrungen im Zweite Weltkrieg* (Munich: Deutsche
    Verlagsanstalt, 2009). References are here only given where necessary.
[2] Stephen Spender, *European Witness* (London: Hamish Hamilton, 1946), pp. 32–5, 32, 35.
[3] Tony Judt, *Geschichte Europas von 1945 bis zur Gegenwart* (Munich: Hanser, 2006), p. 82.

case. Hannah Arendt's widely known "Report from Germany" is another example. She wrote that the "nightmare of destruction and terror" was nowhere felt less than in Germany. German society seemed to be gripped by apathy. In common with other observers, Arendt was convinced that German people were fleeing from reality and with it from their responsibility for the crimes committed in their name. Furthermore, in Germany self-pity was conspicuous, she wrote, and for a considerable time after the war there was a pronounced inclination to blame the occupying powers for the crisis.[4] Two years after the end of the war, no one seemed to know how this situation had come about, and how it had just as suddenly ended. Indeed, according to surveys in 1951, more than fifty percent of Western Germans considered the "Third Reich" to have been the best time of their lives.[5]

Were Germans indifferent to the catastrophe? Historians writing at the time noted repeatedly the supposed excess of silence on the part of the Germans over the mass murder of those persecuted by National Socialism and other war crimes. What these observers saw was profound indifference, amnesia, or repression.[6] But for some time now, scholars have shown that Germans did in fact speak about their own suffering during the war. Thus, it was more precise to speak of "selective memories" and a "rhetoric of victimhood" which dominated the stories of former soldiers, as they did the narratives of other people who bore the scars of war.[7] These studies, however, have focused primarily on public memory construction by analyzing public discourse in the media, the symbolic politics of

---

[4] See Hannah Arendt, "Die Nachwirkungen des Naziregimes – Bericht aus Deutschland," in Hannah Arendt, *In der Gegenwart. Übungen im politischen Denken* II (Munich: Hanser, 2000), pp. 38–63, 39; James Stern, *Die unsichtbaren Trümmer. Eine Reise durch das besetzte Deutschland 1945* (Berlin: Eichborn Verlag, 2004); Saul K. Padover, *Lügendetektor. Vernehmungen im besiegten Deutschland 1944/45* (Frankfurt: Eichborn Verlag, 1999); Dagmar Barnouw, *Ansichten von Deutschland (1945). Krieg und Gewalt in der zeitgenössischen Photographie* (Basel: Stroemfeld, 1997); Richard Bessel, "'Leben nach dem Tod.' Vom Zweiten Weltkrieg zur zweiten Nachkriegszeit," in Bernd Wegner (ed.), *Wie Kriege enden. Wege zum Frieden von der Antike bis zur Gegenwart* (Paderborn: Schöningh, 2002), pp. 239–58.

[5] See Michael Geyer, "Cold War Angst: The Case of West-German Opposition to Rearmament and Nuclear Weapons," in Hanna Schissler (ed.), *The Miracle Years. A Cultural History of West Germany, 1949–1968* (Princeton University Press, 2001), pp. 376–408, 383.

[6] See, for example, Wolfgang Benz, "Postwar Society and National Socialism: Remembrance, Amnesia, Rejection," *Tel Aviver Jahrbuch für deutsche Geschichte* 19 (1990): 1–12. The general assumption about the "repression" of German guilt in postwar society has recently been critically assessed in Anthony D. Kauders, "'Repression' and 'Philo-Semitism' in Postwar Germany," *History and Memory* 15 (2003): 97–122.

[7] See, especially, Robert G. Moeller, *War Stories. The Search for a Usable Past in the Federal Republic of Germany* (Berkeley: University of California Press, 2001).

remembrance, and the public display of memorials. In this way, they have established the extent to which the public memory of the Nazi war and its deadly harvest was socially acceptable and politically useful.[8]

The constraints on what could be remembered *publicly* did not necessarily govern the individual memory of those who lived through the war, and the question as to what extent personal distress had been publicly acknowledged was, however, largely ignored. As I will demonstrate in the first part of this chapter, the 'normality' of post-war Germany was not based upon the suppression of the apocalypse of war and genocide. Indeed, as I hope to show below, death and the dead were constantly present in *individual* memory and imagination in the late 1940s. The understandable desire of many people living in what would become West Germany for reconstruction, social stability, and security was consistent with the persistence of individual memories of deep-seated horrors and tormenting nightmares. As this entire collection of essays shows, silence is not at all synonymous with oblivion. What is unspoken in public can rest among individual people like a blanket on the land. What we need to do is to find ways in which these issues were indirectly addressed. For this purpose, we present the results of research on medical files of psychiatric patients in the post-war years.

The issue here is, however, not the "discovery" of a "trauma" that has recently come to be addressed more and more within public discourse about the post-war era.[9] The concept of trauma as a descriptive and analytical framework is deliberately not applied here, on the grounds of anachronism. In the 1940s this term was hardly ever used, and it was only in the 1980s that it entered the vocabulary of historical study.

It is problematic to read back into the evidence a notion which has influenced later readings of the long-term effects of violence on peoples' lives and suffering.[10] In particular, adopting the framework of "trauma" raises problems as to how to read psychiatric evidence, which we consider in this chapter. In this respect, as Ian Hacking has noted, psychiatry is not only a distinct science but a "science of memory,"[11] that employs

[8] See, among others, Bill Niven (ed.), *Germans as Victims. Remembering the Past in Contemporary Germany* (New York: Palgrave Macmillan, 2006); Sabine Behrenbeck, "Between Pain and Silence. Remembering the Victims of Violence in Germany after 1949," in Richard Bessel and Dirk Schumann (eds.), *Life after Death. Approaches to a cultural and social history of Europe during the 1940s and 1950s* (Washington, DC: Cambridge University Press, 2003), pp. 37–64.

[9] See, among others, Wolfgang Schmidbauer, *"Ich wusste nie, was mit Vater ist." Das Trauma des Krieges* (Reinbek: Rowohlt, 1998).

[10] For a detailed discussion of "trauma" concepts for historical analysis, see Goltermann, *Die Gesellschaft der Überlebenden.*

[11] Ian Hacking, *Multiple Persönlichkeit. Zur Geschichte der Seele in der Moderne* (Munich: Hanser, 1996), ch. 14.

changing concepts and languages of memory.[12] This is one major reason why the concept of "trauma" is a problematic tool for historians. It transports specific notions of how memory works and – in particular – how pain and shocking events are processed in memory.[13] In the words of Allan Young: "Our sense of being a person is not simply shaped by our active memory ... it is also a product of our conception of 'memory'."[14] Instead of starting with a concept like "trauma" and reading the evidence of the time through it, we prefer to study the evidence on its own terms.

The following discussion rests on the assumption that it is important to analyze subjective perceptions and interpretations of events to learn about the time in which they lived. Therefore, this essay will analyze narratives of personal memory composed in the immediate post-war years. These are the "present pasts" of former prisoners of war.

The analysis rests on the evidence of psychiatric files, representing a rarely used reservoir of personal memories and very private confessions, which challenged the accepted mode of speaking about the experience of war and death. Some 450 files of former soldiers born between the years 1897 and 1929 were examined. These records, which cover the years 1945–60, include material on soldiers of different military ranks, who served in varied theatres of war and were imprisoned in different camps. The spectrum of their illnesses was broad. On the whole they were referred to a psychiatrist by a general practitioner who had reached the limits of his diagnostic and therapeutic abilities or through pressure from relatives, who could not cope with the behavior of the men who had returned. Their families described them as unusually withdrawn and unapproachable, but also as nervous and irritable, or as anxious and mistrustful. Hardly anyone suspected that these men suffered from mental illness as a result of the war, least of all the psychiatrists.

Using this material, we turn to the professional reading of suffering. Here, psychiatric evidence shows how practitioners construct patterns of interpretation, having defined both the scope of experiences processed in private life and the degree to which the public expression of suffering was limited in German society after the war. In other words, both the history of post-war experience and the history of war remembrance remain incomplete without attending to contemporary psychiatric readings of extreme experiences. Finally, we address the question as to what extent the public

---

[12] Hacking, *Multiple Persönlichkeit*, p. 93.

[13] In contrast, see Alice Foerster and Birgit Beck, "Post-Traumatic Stress Disorder and World War II: Can a Psychiatric Concept Help Us Understand Postwar Society?," in Bessel and Schumann (eds.), *Life after Death*, pp. 15–35.

[14] Allan Young, *The Harmony of Illusions. Inventing Post-Traumatic Stress Disorder* (Princeton University Press, 1995), p. 4.

imagination of the war and its long-term effects changed fundamentally after the Second World War, informed by such psychiatric readings.[15] By the late 1950s, these interpretations rested on a clear distinction between the lasting mental effects of Nazi persecution on the one hand and the possible effects of action, injury, or imprisonment on war veterans on the other. This distinction also found its way into public memory culture. My claim is that the spectrum of scientifically and publicly acknowledged war-related suffering shaped and changed both the private and public narratives about the war. The fault lines between these narratives did indeed shift, but they never quite disappeared.

I.   The war in their mind: Fragments of personal memory

In analyzing these records, we can see, in the years after 1945, how vivid was the presence of the dead and the war. It surfaces in records written by the patients themselves, and it broke through in bouts of narrative preserved in the records of their conversations with attending physicians. The presence of the dead took shape in the dream-world of the night, and at times the knowledge of the dead also erupted in delusions and hallucinations. Like all dream work, these moments cannot be taken as true readings of lived experience. They are mediated and fictional in character. But they can be read as historical sources because they are part and parcel of violence perceived and in this respect function like "internal mental snapshots," as Reinhart Koselleck has argued with regard to the dreams of the "Third Reich."[16]

To be sure, states of anxiety were not the only form in which the experience of death on a massive scale came to the fore. However, in the first four years after the war, such periods of anxiety were strikingly frequent when compared to the following decade. Of course, it is not surprising that anxiety can be found in psychiatric files: after all, anxiety is an important symptom of specific conditions, for example, with respect to a persecution complex or schizophrenia. Nevertheless, it is wrong to assume that the expressions of anxiety which appear in these sources point only to the state of illness itself. Even in cases of diagnosed schizophrenia, which causes stages of fear-soaked delusion, traces of time-specific references emerge, which indirectly indicate something about

[15] Allan Young, "Suffering and the origins of traumatic memory," in *Daedalus* 125 (1996): 245–60.
[16] Reinhart Koselleck, "Terror und Traum. Methodologische Anmerkungen zu Zeiterfahrungen im Dritten Reich," in Reinhart Koselleck, *Vergangene Zukunft. Zur Semantik geschichtlicher Zeiten*, 2nd edn. (Frankfurt: Fischer, 1992) pp. 278–99, 287.

the experiences out of which they arose. In many cases the circumstances were unambiguously related to the patients' experience of war and National Socialism. We must certainly treat these sources with caution, since they reflect much earlier life experiences as well as those in the recent past. Yet, as "repositories of memory"[17] the anxieties of these men which they articulated following the war always tell us something about the time which had just passed. Used carefully, psychiatric records can tell us about the aftermath of war, and may even disclose images and issues which those outside the medical environment rarely, if ever, discussed.

As Jay Winter notes in the introduction to this volume, liminal figures, such as psychiatric patients, may at times draw away the veil of silence "normal" people construct around difficult events in their lives and in the life of their society (see chapter 1, p. 16). While we must avoid the conceit that the mad see things the sane choose to ignore, it is still the case that the words and dreams of those in psychiatric treatment, and the reports family members offered doctors about their condition, can help decipher codes of what was sayable and unsayable about the past. These records also offer us a glimpse into what went on within the families of returning servicemen.

In many cases the anxiety expressed after the war can be read as a medium for the expression of the soldiers' personal fear of death during the war. "The war ... but you know that ... in the war ... I can't take it any more," cried Alfred S. in his sleep in summer 1949, according to his sister. She also described her brother's recent unusual behavior. For a week he had been speaking "confusedly," although from time to time he was again lucid. She said her brother claimed that "he was a doomed man, he would have to die." At this time he spoke often of the war. He showed, according to his sister, an "indefinite anxiety which got stronger and stronger."[18]

Many such incidents were reported during the post-war period. In a number of cases, distorted speech and fragmentarily recorded dreams show that the past threat of dying in the war continued to follow the former soldiers into the present. They had escaped with their lives, but they could not shake off the closeness of death, about which they spoke in different forms and disturbing ways.

Frequently the anxieties were vague, their precise background difficult to decipher. Often it seems that elements from different times, both

[17] Aleida Assmann, "Funktionsgedächtnis und Speichergedächtnis – Zwei Modi der Erinnerung," in Kristin Platt and Mirhan Dabag (eds.), *Generation und Gedächtnis. Erinnerungen und kollektive Identitäten* (Opladen: Leske und Budrich, 1995), pp. 169–85, quote p. 179.
[18] Hauptarchiv der von Bodelschwinghschen Anstalten Bethel (thereafter HBAB), Bestand Morija, 5054.

during the war and afterwards, mixed in imaginary scenes of anxiety. The case of Rolf S. is a good example.[19] His anxieties, which regularly surfaced without warning, sounded like a distorted echo of different states of emotion dating from and after the war. His peculiar behavior began three years after 1945 – that is, five years after the former soldier had served on the Eastern front. He kept asking 'have the Russians come yet?' Rolf S. felt, as his parents observed, persecuted. Moreover, he repeatedly said that he would have to continue to fight for his family; indeed he had once shouted to them "give us eggs, then we can fight for you." A powerful fear for the safety of his relatives had seized him. He often said "that he had to hang himself in order that his relatives wouldn't have to suffer." The parents repeatedly heard their son say "I must fight, I must fight." At other times they saw how the sounds of passing trains or cars startled him. Rolf S. then "jumped up and kept looking out of the window." He explained to them that he was afraid "that the Russians [had come] to take him away."

These feelings of fear and paranoia were common in the post-war period. The fear of being persecuted, spied upon, denounced, or taken away did not just seize a few individuals after the end of the war; there were sufficient cases to give these fears and rumours a semblance of truth.[20] In the psychiatric files examined here, it is conspicuous that the presence of the occupying armies fuelled these anxieties, and in particular the Red army, even though Soviet troops were not stationed nearby. Rolf S. was terrified that the Russians would come for him. Günter B. also admitted that he had always been worried while at home "that he might be snatched up and brought into the Russian zone of occupation, which is why he was glued to the window and took down the numbers of all cars which passed by."[21] In the cases under review here we can see overwhelming evidence of a panicky fear of being unable to hide from the victorious powers, and the feeling that if one kept one's secret from them longer, one would be more severely punished for the crimes committed under National Socialism. In fact, in search of such leniency, some of these patients had voluntarily handed themselves over to the British or American authorities

---

[19] HBAB, Bestand Morija, 4560.

[20] Anonyma, *Eine Frau in Berlin. Tagebuchaufzeichnungen vom 20. April bis 22. Juni 1945* (Frankfurt: Eichborn Verlag, 2003), 212; Carl Schüddekopf, *Im Kessel. Erzählungen von Stalingrad* (Munich: Piper, 2002), pp. 232–85, esp. 282.

[21] See HBAB, Bestand Morija, 4524. For a more detailed analysis of this case, see Svenja Goltermann, "Languages of Memory. German POWs and their Violent Pasts in Postwar West Germany," in Bob Moore and Barbara Hately-Broad (eds.), *Prisoners of War, Prisoners of Peace: Captivity, Homecoming and Memory in World War II* (Oxford: Berg, 2005), pp. 165–73, 170–1.

to face charges, but wound up being sent home.[22] None presented himself to the Russian occupying forces.

Knowledge of the crimes committed in the East was, it seems, widespread enough to fear punishment from the Russians much more than for those crimes perpetrated by German soldiers in the West. Such was the case for Herbert I., who was well aware of the Red army's penchant for immediate punishment of war criminals.[23] Herbert I. articulated these apprehensions in the course of his denazification proceedings. "Conflict in the filling in of the questionnaire" recorded the doctor in the patient's file under the heading "present illness." He wrote further: "Fear of being delivered to the Russians. The patient travelled from the American to the English occupied zone, presented himself voluntarily to the secret service, [was] set free there after questioning. Suicide attempt with a pocket knife." Herbert I., who had taken on the post of pastor just one year after the end of the war and lived together with his wife and child, could not see any other way out. The reaction of the British had not relieved him of the fear of being handed over to the Russians. He was still consumed by, as he put it to the doctor, "a very terrible fear" of a forthcoming day of judgment.

In contrast to what one would suppose from many of the accounts of the process of denazification, the requirement to fill in a questionnaire on one's actions under National Socialism really did prove to be enough in many cases to provoke a fear so acute that the external appearance of internal stability could discernibly break. Not only the former Nazi elite, who were sent to internment camps, were shocked by the denazification measures;[24] even those who did not seem to bear any serious personal responsibility or guilt for the crimes of the Nazi system found it terrifying. Hopelessness was common. To be sure, such lassitude was related to the fact that the only way to secure a work permit was to complete the denazification process; being in the midst of it was likely to produce anxiety even among those entirely innocent of wrong doing. Personal stability depended in many cases on a notion of occupational continuity and of pride in one's trade or craft. In the absence of opportunities for work, financial need, and the painful experience of losing social status

---

[22] See, for example, HBAB, Bestand Morija, 3885; HBAB, Bestand Morija, 4473, and HBAB, Bestand Morija, 4559; Psychiatrische und Neurologische Klinik Heidelberg, Nr. 47/163.

[23] HBAB, Bestand Morija, 3885.

[24] See, among others, Norbert Frei (ed.), *Hitlers Eliten nach 1945* (Munich: Deutscher Taschenbuch Verlag, 2003); Ulrich Herbert, "Rückkehr in die Bürgerlichkeit? NS-Eliten in der Bundesrepublik," in Bernd Weisbrod (ed.), *Rechtsradikalismus in der politischen Kultur der Bundesrepublik* (Hanover: Hahnsche Buchhandlung, 1995), pp. 157–73; Konrad Jarausch, *Die Umkehr. Deutsche Wandlungen 1945–1995* (Munich: Deutsche Verlagsstalt, 2004).

were the reality for a large part of the West German population. This is of importance because in the fear of material loss and in the distress of social misery, which were fundamentally tied up with the denazification process, the war and the crimes committed reverberated time and again. Flashbacks were absolutely unavoidable: this can be proved with the help of many examples from the medical files. In this way, some memories of events and actions during the war later became frightening through the feeling that one was completely at the mercy of the occupying forces.

In the immediate post-war period, such fears could take on a life of their own. Considered superficially, these fears appeared to be free-floating emotions, without concrete causes. However, that could mean that fears experienced during the war, retrospective anxieties, a simple horror at the crimes for which one might be punished, and a vague worry about the chances of survival broke into it. They all resounded simply like an echo in the general state of fear, which was accompanied by an undercurrent of the knowledge of the countless dead.

This is clear in the case of Gustav N., who had joined the DAF, the Nazi's German Labor Front, in 1939 and was a member of the German territorial army for a short period.[25] Following the defeat, he attempted to commit suicide out of the fear of being punished for the crimes of National Socialism. Even two years later, after he had been released from the internment camp, he was plagued by a strong "internal anxiety and disquiet." The fear of further punishment continued to worry him. In talks with his psychiatrist he just stammered, but slowly it became clear how much he was tormented with the belief that his statements and the evidence he had given about war crimes had "hurt" others. His conversation over the next few days revealed further fears. Above all, one incident was stuck in his mind. This was his own flight to the West as the Russians were "on the march." An overwhelming fear of death descended upon him; but it was not only the nearness of his own death, which had haunted him for some time. He had hidden his own panic from others and at the top of his voice called for steadfastness in the last months of the war. Rather, it was the faces of those he had left behind as he had fled westward; he assumed that these people were now dead, and it was their deaths, which additionally tormented him.

As the files reveal, many others showed an immense unease during the years following the war. This was expressed in a similar way by the mood of disillusionment in post-war Germany which should be regarded as an additional way of coping with the past. But as was the case in the variety of

---

[25] See HBAB, Bestand Morija, 4189.

anxiety states, in the mood of disillusionment different emotions also came to the fore: in some cases, the violence of war had already stripped down idealized self-perceptions prior to total defeat. Many soldiers experienced their own fear unexpectedly; overwhelmed by fright, they became cowards in their own eyes. Others felt a fractured sense of their own ethical integrity; in the light of the fact that they acknowledged their ability to kill another human being, their sense of self had been tremendously shaken. Others again were extremely unsettled by the total defeat of the National Socialist regime, as their own future dreams that had been linked to it were destroyed. In fact, the memory fragments of former POWs often show that for a long time after 1945, nothing remained but complete bewilderment. In these cases, it becomes clear how much of their sense of self rested on their belief in National Socialism; their faith in it was oddly still there. At the same time, though, the same individuals were unable to face the crimes committed by the regime and what those crimes said about who they had been and who they were.

On this critical point, the public by and large remained silent. In complete contrast to the public silence and to external appearances, many former soldiers faced a personal acid test during the post-war period, longing to regain their inner balance. Some attempted to create a different or pseudo identity, hoping this would enable them to live their lives, in spite of the knowledge of the criminal war in which they had fought. It is hardly surprising that many tried to escape judgment or simply ride out the process of denazification by changing their biography.

Simple calculation or deceit was, however, not always the case. In other instances, inventing a new self was motivated by the POW's despair over their personal and family life situation or through learning about the extent of war crimes committed by soldiers just like them. In these invented personal war stories, soldiers tried to create a "different" self, one which could achieve personal rehabilitation. After the end of this murderous war, many soldiers could not achieve this kind of emotional respite, which may have been totally independent from political rehabilitation. The case of Franz F. is a good example. As he confided to his doctor one day, "he really harbored two natures or two souls in his heart," one relentless, the other compassionate. "If put into the same kind of situation again," he insisted, "he would certainly be more compassionate." And he added: "All this did haunt him, but not as a feeling of guilt, he was much too much concerned with real life, and after all, he could always remind himself that he could have been killed himself in this war."[26]

---

[26] HBAB, Bestand Morija, 4749.

Such exercises in self-rationalization were shot through with the nagging memory of past violence. Franz F. eventually took refuge in the imagination of a split identity that would allow him to get on with his life; he hoped memories of violence would disappear at least from parts of his being. Without doubt, in most cases this search for an acceptable idea of one's identity was highly selective: the sufferings of war victims were hardly ever mentioned. Nevertheless, the victims did emerge in these strategies of rationalization, for such attempts to get rid of the past always meant to be faced with the victims of the Nazis as well.

As the medical records show, these issues were not addressed in terms of a general self-victimization or even finding some equality of suffering. On the whole, during the immediate post-war period these personal confrontations with the war usually were not conducted in a framework of victimhood or victim rhetoric. And virtually no one was able to find a degree of certainty regarding his own role in this criminal war. This is probably the main reason for the fragmentary character of soldiers' accounts, even with their next of kin. It was hard for ex-soldiers to confront what seemed to be a caesura, a biographical break, in the story of their lives, and hence their stories rarely were coherent. They did not hold together, and were particularly incongruous in the light of an emerging moral idiom about the Nazis, which framed the range of public speech acts.

The returnees' silence about their violent past was, however, often enforced by women. There was the problem of the non-commensurate nature of soldiers' and civilians' experiences of war. In addition, some women did not realize how deeply the "present pasts" of the war were imbedded within their family relations. This silence – even reticence about speaking – did not necessarily denote an escape from the terror of war or from guilt related to war crimes. More centrally, between the sexes and between generations, there was a difficulty in communication, a sense of strangeness arising out of the war.

If returning soldiers seemed to behave in irritating and difficult ways, it was hard for families to develop the mutual understanding needed for reintegration and the beginning of a sustainable rhythm of everyday life. During the immediate post-war years, family members did not usually identify war experience as a crucial factor accounting for the allegedly strange behavior they perceived in the men who returned from the war. In many such cases, family and friends who were deeply worried about the returnee's state of mind eventually sought the professional advice of a medical expert.

II.   Knowledge and acknowledgement: Psychiatric readings of personal suffering

Many German doctors added their voices to the chorus of commentary about the apparently conspicuous silence, sobriety, or apathy in post-war Germany. In medical journals, psychiatrists shared their impressions of the post-war era in terms that bring to mind Hannah Arendt's observations of the early post-war years. Some psychiatrists spoke of "silence" and also "stoicism", but many expressed their "impression of dull listlessness" among the population they treated.[27]

In the winter of 1945, the American occupation authorities sought out medical opinion regarding the mental state of Berlin's population. In his report, Jürg Zutt, provisional head of the Psychiatric and Neurological Clinic of the Charité Hospital, interpreted silence as a "real expression of [...] human beings surrendering to their inevitable wretched destiny, accepting and handling it." Zutt added this interpretation: "I believe that what we are here experiencing [...] may indeed indicate something more general, i.e.: that the 'human falls silent in his agony.' What we see here is nothing pathological, also no special capacity to endure distress, or unconcern. It is merely the countenance of the suffering human."[28]

Although there were different psychiatric interpretations as to the cause of silence, psychiatrists were in agreement that silence and lassitude were in no way symptoms of an "illness." In particular, they believed that this kind of behavior reflected a passing state of mind which would disappear after a few weeks or months. This interpretation was supported by the prevailing psychiatric assumptions about the extraordinary ability ordinary people had to withstand extreme situations. Long-term mental strains and impairments were, therefore, not to be expected or feared.

This view was not a product of National Socialism,[29] nor was it even limited to German psychiatry. Rather, it traced back to ideas among psychiatrists practicing in Germany and elsewhere in the period of the Great War.[30] Contrary to the long-prevailing belief that this psychiatric point of view had been a mere instrumental understanding of the clinical picture in

---

[27] See, for example, Jürg Zutt, "Über den seelischen Gesundheitszustand der Berliner Bevölkerung in den vergangenen Jahren und heute," *Ärztliche Wochenschrift* 1 (1946): 248–50, 250; Walter von Baeyer, "Zur Statistik und Form der abnormen Erlebnisreaktionen in der Gegenwart," *Der Nervenarzt* 19 (1948): 402–8, 408.

[28] Zutt, "Über den seelischen Gesundheitszustand der Berliner Bevölkerung," p. 250.

[29] See, for example, Christian Pross, *Paying for the Past: The Struggle Over Reparations for Surviving Victims of the Nazi Terror* (Baltimore: Johns Hopkins University Press, 1998).

[30] See, among others, Paul Lerner, *Hysterical Men. War, Psychiatry, and the Politics of Trauma in Germany, 1890–1930* (Ithaca, NY: Cornell University Press, 2003); Mark Micale and

terms of the necessities of war, a variety of empirical research and therapeutic reports during the Great War reinforced the widely held assumption that mental disorders could not be triggered by exogenous stress – provided that no physical damage had occurred to the individual in question.

In the course of the 1914–18 war, psychiatrists interpreted trembling, shaking, and paralysis, as "functional disorders." Since the majority of soldiers did not develop these types of symptoms, psychiatrists assumed that those presenting such symptoms had chosen what they termed a mental "escape into illness." A hereditary cause seemed also plausible among those whose congenital problems were exacerbated by war service.

After the Second World War, these established assumptions underpinned the mainstream of psychiatric thought. It was believed that long-lasting "massive psychogenic manifestations" were rare, both among the civilian population affected by air raids and the soldiers of the *Wehrmacht*. "When the issue is pure survival, one does not have time to be ill," psychiatrist Kurt Beringer reasoned. Like other psychiatrists, he was fully convinced of the functional nature of these disorders. He attributed their absence particularly to the fact that from the 1920s on, war pensions were no longer available. Without pensions, many people could no longer try to add to their profile "the lustre of being victims of war."[31]

Other psychiatrists believed that mental disorders could be traced back to physical exhaustion and to the experience of extreme hunger.[32] Psychiatrists had known of such cases since the First World War. Such an interpretation was, furthermore, supported by specialists in internal medicine, who – in regard to the returning POWs – added the term "hunger disease" or for that matter "dystrophy" to medical expert discussion.[33] Therefore, from the perspective of physicians, it was assumed that the mental states of returnees – and of the German population as a whole – would "normalize" once the food situation had improved.

The transformation of psychiatric knowledge, therefore, shifted only gradually during the post-war era. One could not even speak of a major change in psychiatric discourse before the end of the 1950s. Until then, shifts in psychiatric opinion were cautious and slight. In general, there is

Paul Lerner (eds.), *Traumatic Pasts: History, Psychiatry, and Trauma in the Modern Age, 1870–1930* (Cambridge University Press, 2001); Ben Shephard, *A War of Nerves. Soldiers and Psychiatrists 1914–1994* (London: Jonathan Cape, 2000).

[31] Kurt Beringer, "Über hysterische Reaktionen bei Fliegerangriffen," in Heinrich Kranz (ed.), *Arbeiten zur Psychiatrie, Neurologie und ihren Grenzgebieten* (Heidelberg: Scherer, 1947), pp. 131–8, 136.

[32] Karl Bonhoeffer, "Vergleichende psychopathologische Erfahrungen aus den beiden Weltkriegen," *Der Nervenarzt* 18 (1947): 1–4.

[33] See, for example, Hans Malten, "Heimkehrer," *Medizinische Klinik* 41 (1946): 593–600, 597.

much evidence that the psychiatrists' suspicion of being deliberately or unconsciously deceived by their patients was at the heart of all forms of treatment, and was particularly evident in examinations that required an expert opinion. Former members of the armed forces were entitled to receive war pensions for their medical disabilities, but only when the ailment could be linked to the war or captivity in prisoner-of-war camps. In 1947, regulations regarding compensation for war victims had been approved by the occupying powers. These were turned into law after the West German state came into being, in the form of the Federal Support Law (Bundesversorgungsgesetz, BVG) of December 1950.[34]

Thereafter, there are numerous instances of psychiatrists preparing expert opinions with explicit statements about their suspicion of "false demonstrations of illness" by "pension neurotics." The procedure was clear. Physicians had to come up with a diagnosis; the cause of the illness was rarely evident from the very beginning. Hence, the examination of the patient and the formation of a diagnosis were characterized by a complex negotiation process, affected by the patients' behavior and stories, involving family members as well, and framed by a medical view that former soldiers were not at risk of long-term psychiatric illness.

The clearest example of this give and take is that of Ludwig D., who in 1947 – then aged twenty-six – was hospitalized for a suicide attempt.[35] The attending physician had been informed by the father that his son had become "completely different, extremely boisterous, uncontrolled, and grandiose in gesture and speech," that he had created "dramatic scenes," and – in his father's opinion – "he only felt comfortable as the centre of attention." His son had caused himself to become unpopular everywhere through "his harsh, dominant behavior" and had been especially "abusive" to his relatives. In the opinion of the father, the "suicide attempt" had apparently only "been staged, [...] as a scare tactic."

This information helped the doctor prepare for his first interview with Ludwig. When asked, the former soldier described the relationship to his parents as normal. The psychiatrist asked further questions based on the information he had received from the patient's father. As his remarks in the medical records show, the doctor believed that he did not get "useful answers" from the patient. After a longer session, the psychiatrist wrote: "Preliminary diagnosis: endogenous depression? Reactive depression of a

---

[34] In more detail, see Vera Neumann, *Nicht der Rede wert. Die Privatisierung der Kriegsfolgen in der Bundesrepublik* (Münster: Westfälisches Dampfboot, 1999), pp. 132–4; James M. Diehl, *German Veterans After the Second World War* (Chapel Hill: University of North Carolina Press, 1993).

[35] HBAB, Bestand Morija, 4387. For a more detailed account of this "case," see Goltermann, *Die Gesellschaft der Überlebenden*.

neurotic?" Or was this a case of an "egocentric psychopathic innate nature (with extreme imbalances)," as his handwritten note in the file suggested?

The doctor had trouble dealing with the story Ludwig D. told about his life. While describing his growing nervousness and jumpiness since May 1945, Ludwig apparently remarked abruptly in one of the dialogues, "Do you think that a murderer will strike it lucky in his life? I don't think so." The physician did not understand the remark; "Murderer?" he asked. Ludwig affirmed and explained that – while being in a state of panic – he had suddenly shot and killed a lieutenant in his own unit.

The doctor did not focus on this incident, or consider how it might have triggered a change in Ludwig's comportment. His assumption as to the short-term consequences of this kind of event made him rule it out as insignificant. Instead, he wrote that Ludwig was "tensely clinging" to an "exaggerated feeling of guilt" and "self-lacerating patterns of behavior." The doctor tried to make it clear to Ludwig D. that his behavior as a soldier was absolutely pardonable; such things happened in war. Consequently, the physician called on him to cooperate "in the transformation of his uncontrolled and attention-seeking nature."

Ludwig D. made only one further attempt to return to the story regarding the lieutenant. According to the physician, he asked "in a self-important manner" for a "discussion," during which he insisted that he had told the truth about being responsible for the lieutenant's death. It was "true, completely true," but he had told friends and family members that the lieutenant had been "killed in action before Stalingrad." From then on, he never mentioned the incident again, and according to his doctor, his behavior seemed to improve. Ludwig appeared "ready and willing to take on tasks," but at the same time was also humble in his requests. Above all, in his exchanges with the doctor, he also appeared very "insightful and sensible in regard to his illness." There were doubts in the doctor's mind as to how long he would remain stable, but on balance he seemed capable of "adapting to the current situation in order possibly to continue living his own life."

This physician's approach to psychological disturbances was common and tells us much about the way doctors framed the therapeutic challenge of returning their patients to "normalcy" by silencing their sense of guilt or fear of punishment. The patient had to conform to the doctor's notion of "normal" behavior, and not dwell "unnecessarily" on what he had done in the war. But the case of Ludwig D. also presents a typical dilemma for the physicians who had to render their expert opinions at that time. The suspicion of deception did not vanish before the patients' pattern of behavior adapted to what the doctor considered to be "normal." This is also found in cases in which strange behavior and massive psychological derangement were linked to "dystrophy," consequently to poor nutrition while in Soviet captivity. The problem was these symptoms exceeded the time period that had been granted for convalescence. Though the diagnosis of "dystrophy" temporarily supplied an acceptable manner of speaking about psychological complaints, it was not a diagnostic *passepartout* for being granted war victim pensions. For the entire period of the 1950s, in such cases of doubt, the assumption of a hereditary cause was a fallback position. Cases that seemed difficult were diagnosed as "neurotics" or "psychopaths," hoping for a war pension they did not deserve.

From today's point of view, it is surprising that in the immediate post-war years, many war veterans, as well as their next of kin, meekly accepted the decisions of medical experts that their psychological problems were not attributable to the war or captivity. In some cases, though, objections were voiced and – in contrast to the silent consent – these were often vociferous, chiefly because those affected often looked for help to war victim's associations, and through them, they took legal action. Unmistakably, this protest arose out of the conviction that in fact only the war – and in most cases specifically captivity in a Russian prisoner-of-war camp – was the root cause of mental illness. We can see, however, in these instances too, the need of ex-soldiers to receive official acknowledgement of their afflictions, which could be read as a confirmation of their own "healthy genetics." It was the only way to shed the stigma of congenital mental illness.

This "hereditarian argument," especially popular among returnees from Soviet captivity, may hardly be overestimated as an impulse for opening the psychiatric discussion about the way human beings withstand extreme situations of stress. This is all the more true as some specialists in internal medicine began to adopt a psychosomatic approach, thereby challenging the psychiatrist's interpretive predominance in regard to psychogenic disorders. These experts in internal medicine demanded that the social cause of "illness" be considered more seriously than hitherto.

In fact, with a psychosomatic approach some fundamental methodological changes took shape. This included the revaluation of biographical profiles and subjective modes of perceptions. To the former POWs as well as for a majority of post-war German society, this meant an acknowledgment of the suffering they had experienced. The outcome was that a growing number of people in post-war Germany supported the proponents of psychosomatic thinking.

In the mid 1950s, these issues were contested not only in Germany. Physicians in other European countries were also trying to find explanations for the persistent mental disorders of resistance fighters and deportees. These long-lasting psychological ailments had not been expected in other victim groups either. Thus, foreign physicians confronted their German colleagues through their participation via the German indemnification offices, which were handling compensation payments to victims of Nazi persecution. These doctors asked their German colleagues how acknowledgment of long-term mental afflictions among victims of the Nazis corresponded with their prevailing psychiatric doctrine. For their German colleagues this was a moral challenge.

This pressure by colleagues from abroad was a significant element in the development and implementation of a new psychiatric approach to the mental effects of the Nazi persecution. But establishing a new psychiatric reading of long-lasting mental suffering depended heavily on a whole range of interrelated non-psychiatric impulses and conditions.

Just to give one example. A number of physicians and jurists administering the pension claims of Nazi victims not only shared the view of foreign experts that they must depart from the prevailing psychiatric doctrine; they also saw the legal possibilities for moving away from restrictive compensation practice. In their need to lay down official guidelines for the regulation of claims, it was, therefore, the indemnification authorities who – in the first instance – had to obtain clarification regarding the current state of psychiatric opinion. The broad spectrum of participants in this clarification process consisted – apart from selected medical experts from German universities, jurists, and high officials from various federal ministries; of doctors from abroad, the interested public (in the beginning mostly Jewish pressure groups), and even the Ministry of Foreign Affairs. All of them watched this complex and often highly politically charged negotiation process, in the course of which a new kind of psychiatric approach was defined in Germany.

Considering the time-honored character of established schools of thought, the implementation of a new psychiatric interpretation in Germany took place in a remarkably short period of time. It was only applied to victims of Nazi persecution, though. But in this respect, German psychiatrists went even one step further than many of their colleagues abroad. While in Germany physicians assumed a "change in personality based on experience" (*erlebnisbedingter Persönlichkeitswandel*),[36] which no longer need be linked to physical impairment, many of their foreign colleagues were still tracing back long-term psychological impairment to brain damage. This process, however, was anything but smooth: both the financial fears of official representatives and differing national scientific traditions played a decisive role

---

[36] See, especially, Ulrich Venzlaff, *Die psychoreaktiven Störungen nach entschädigungspflichtigen Ereignissen* (Berlin: Springer, 1958).

in it, presenting obstacles against turning ideas quickly into uniform practices.

To be sure, both moral aspects and political considerations significantly contributed to the shaping of expert opinion in compensation proceedings for Nazi victims. Without doubt, the Federal Republic's precarious status in the Western alliance played a role too. Scientific reasoning with respect to the acknowledgment of mental suffering as a result of persecution, though, addressed these matters only obliquely; but they were still there in the acknowledgment of collective responsibility for the compensation of victims of the Nazi regime who still suffered from mental afflictions.

It is important to emphasize that the implementation of new psychiatric approaches and new forms of diagnosis, had to overcome the resistance of a sizeable part of the medical profession. This opposition at times rested on political grounds. But it was also a dispute about methods. Yes, the chances of state acknowledgment of the mental suffering of Nazi victims improved in the 1960s. But more important were some basic changes in the Federal Indemnification Law and important legal decisions which somewhat eased the restrictive criteria the compensation authorities used in their work. This administrative development made the controversy between psychiatric experts obsolete.

It may have been inevitable that once compensation to Nazi victims was agreed, that other people would come forward with their demands for recognition of their war-related hardships and suffering. Indeed, the boundaries of victimhood were not fixed. They continued to be a matter of dispute. The acknowledgment of long-term war-related mental suffering did not become a generally accepted interpretation, for instance, in war victims' welfare service. Though former POWs asserted the same claims through their associations, the Supreme Court kept the possibility open to restrict the acknowledgment of returnees' mental suffering.

Legal proceedings before social courts, but also psychiatric practice, in particular confirm this. The majority of both jurists and psychiatrists agreed that they had to apply stricter standards to avoid "reactions of desire for war pensions" in German war victims. Contrary to the heated discussion concerning the compensation proceedings of victims of Nazi persecution, psychiatrists, in general, proved much less tolerant in their expert opinions when former POWs claimed war-related mental sufferings. Many psychiatrists even argued that earlier approaches from the First World War concerning the human ability to cope with war experiences had been confirmed after the Second World War. Hence, medical, moral, and judicial reasoning interconnected to generate a rule of thumb, according to which, in the case of war veterans and other victims of war, there was no link between long-term mental disorders and experiences in war and captivity.

III. Negotiating victimhood: German soldiers, the Holocaust, and the media

The slow, partial, but important, transformation of psychiatric knowledge about the mental effects caused by experiences of extreme violence was not without consequences for the public discourse about the Second World War and the effects of the Nazi politics of annihilation. In fact, the media helped broadcast some of the ideas of psychiatrists about the adaptability of human beings and their capacity to withstand violence, and thereby helped frame public narratives about the mental effects of violence. This can be seen both in film and in the print media.

Only for a very brief period after the end of the Second World War – that is, in the mid fifties — was there a time when the longer lasting mental suffering of veterans was openly acknowledged in public media. On the one hand, it can be argued that what were termed the "rubble films" immediately after the war had broached the issue of mental anguish and disorders among former soldiers. Dreams and hallucinations were the cinematic means of expressing this kind of suffering. Wolfgang Staudte's *Murderers Among Us* (*Die Mörder sind unter uns*), made in 1946 and Gerhard Lamprecht's *Irgendwo in Berlin*, produced in the same year, are only the most prominent examples.[37] Some of the moviegoers saw in it, without question, a certain willingness to understand the emotional afflictions of some veterans. On the other hand, *Irgendwo in Berlin* clearly suggests that no unrestrained conversation was possible about soldiers who had suffered in this way. The expectations of society after the Second World War to "normalize" such states of suffering, as transported through early post-war films, stayed very much within the framework of the prevailing psychiatric knowledge in those days. War ends; people recover. If an ex-soldier remained troubled, it was only a reflection of bad character. This is what was communicated by these films and their moralistic reconstruction message. They clearly conveyed a belief in the human powers to overcome the horrors of war; to do so appeared mainly to be a matter of will and persistence.

---

[37] For a general discussion of German post-war films, see Peter Reichel, *Erfundene Erinnerung. Weltkrieg und Judenmord in Film und Theater* (Vienna: Hanser, 2004); Frank Stern, "Film in the 1950s. Passing Images of Guilt and Responsibility," in Schissler (ed.), *The Miracle Years*, pp. 266–80; Heide Fehrenbach, *Cinema in Democratizing Germany. Reconstructing National Identity after Hitler* (Chapel Hill: University of North Carolina Press, 1995).

The cinematic narrative corresponded with the idea the print media developed about our mental abilities to regenerate. Both film and the print media were permeated by the idea that self-healing and self-respect came through work. It could be heard everywhere: You can fight mental suffering if there only is a willingness to work and become healthy. In this respect a renowned paper quoted a hospital director: "They [the bodily injured] quarrel with God, have feelings of helplessness, inferiority and degradation and of being excluded from the circle of the healthy," he declared. But he immediately added: "In most cases the experience of the happy atmosphere around here is enough to rekindle optimism. Those without will are rare; they first need to be forced to acknowledge we want the best for them."[38]

Only in the efforts to secure the return of the last prisoners of war from the Soviet Union after 1953 was there a short period of acknowledgment in the local and nationwide media about the mental consequences of imprisonment. The diagnosis "dystrophy," which located the source of mental changes in severe hunger and resulting bodily damage, turned out to be the accepted language for the abnormalities of this group of returning veterans. After the last of these prisoners had returned from the Soviet Union between 1955 and 1956, this sensitivity for the mental burdens borne by war veterans disappeared almost immediately from public media.

Neither in film nor in nationwide newspapers and journals was there anything to be seen or read on the subject after the 1950s. In war movies of this time, acknowledgment of mental suffering hardly played a role anyway. This was in line with the common assumption that even the hardest war-related afflictions could be overcome through personal exertion and good fortune. This fits in well with the heroic narrative of film in general.[39]

In print media, though, which continued to use psychosomatic approaches in other contexts, we need a different explanation to understand the quick disappearance of war veterans from public discussion. This phenomenon is related to a change in the culture of remembrance that gradually began in West German society with the resumption of the war crimes trials at the end of the 1950s. The changing images of the perpetrators and the victims of the Nazis appear to have blocked the public discussion of the mental burdens of returning soldiers. Since the Eichmann trial, the voices of the survivors as witnesses in the media

---

[38] "Das Tor der guten Hoffnung. Besuch im Hospital der Kriegsversehrten," *Die Zeit* July 11, 1946, p. 2.

[39] Habbo Knoch, *Die Tat als Bild* (Hamburg: Hamburger Edition, 2001).

could not be ignored any longer.[40] The discussion of states of suffering explicable in terms of long-term war-related mental disability focused on the victims of Nazi persecution. Psychiatric knowledge of the long-term mental effects of Nazi persecution then entered the national press,[41] and prepared the ground for the broad acceptance of the need to acknowledge and compensate these surviving victims.[42]

In contrast, there was little room to acknowledge psychological suffering among former German soldiers, if they had been involved in horrible crimes. The media's vehement appeal to the public via the voice of psychiatric experts to finally face up to responsibility for Nazi crimes and, thereby, also recognize the persistent mental suffering of the surviving victims of the Nazis undercut the position of war veterans who claimed long-term mental disability. Addressing the issue of a soldier's possible status as a victim was virtually out of the question. Scientific thinking on the subject was ignored, and the press engaged in what resembled a media offensive to force the reading public to recognize the mental damage Nazi persecution had brought in its wake.

At the same time there occurred a change in public remembrance of the war and the Holocaust. New forms of psychiatric thinking drew on the political and moral impulses of this period to acknowledge the extent to which violence had aftereffects on the lives and the minds of victims. Former soldiers of the *Wehrmacht* did not cross over the boundary between perpetrators and victims. For this reason, their mental suffering never became part of the memory culture of the Second World War in Germany.

IV.   Conclusion

The public memory of Nazi violence dramatically changed in the 1960s and after. The victims had finally arrived. On the other hand, the story of former soldiers, long-term imprisonment remained in the realm of private and family memory. The transformation of psychiatric knowledge, nevertheless, provided them with a way to integrate their divergent, personal memories through the language of psychology. Altogether, a new way of interpreting biographical processes and contexts of experience appeared

---

[40] Annette Wieviorka, *The Era of the Witness* (Ithaca: Cornell University Press, 2006).

[41] See, for example, "Angeklagt ist die Gesellschaft," *Süddeutsche Zeitung*, May 30–June 1, 1961, p. 19; Das Dilemma der Seelenärzte. "Ein Kongreß wie alle anderen wurde in die Wirklichkeit zurückgestoßen," *Die Zeit*, June 2, 1961, p. 12; "Im tiefsten Schatten der Vergangenheit," *Die Zeit*, August 11, 1961, p. 29.

[42] "Im tiefsten Schatten der Vergangenheit," *Die Zeit*, August 11, 1961, p. 29; "KZ-Syndrom. Quälende Träume," *Der Spiegel* 18, 1964, pp. 96–8.

which was available to anyone. This was in line with the spreading notion throughout society that the individual was socially constructed, rather than bounded by his hereditary predisposition. Consequently, a new kind of respect for subjective human experience emerged, as can also be observed in the humanities and in public discourse alike.

Only in this context could painful wartime experiences, which were past but yet present, find a publicly accepted language. The "trauma industry" generalized the story.[43] And yet the limits of victimhood were still apparent. Those who fought for the Nazis could not be equated with those whom they imprisoned, brutalized, and killed. The result has been a selective and shifting array of images of the suffering war brings about, one which acknowledges some of war's victims – those deemed innocent – and excludes and silences others.

---

[43] Carol Tavris, "Just Deal with it," *Times Literary Supplement*, August 15, 2003, p. 10.

Part III

Africa

6 Silences on state violence during the Algerian War of Independence: France and Algeria, 1962–2007

Raphaëlle Branche and Jim House

This chapter examines two aspects of colonial violence that have come to occupy a significant place in political, media and intellectual debate on the Algerian War of Independence (1954–62) since the late 1990s in France. The first is torture practised by the French military against Algerians in this period. The second is the 17 October 1961 police repression of Algerian nationalist demonstrations in Paris, during which many dozens were killed. Although these events were both state crimes that the French authorities denied, and were committed during a colonial war the existence of which the French state refused to admit, this chapter will show the different afterlives of these two events. Such differences stem from the presence or absence of individuals and groups willing to speak out about such violence, and the political and wider social context in which such voices could or could not be publicly heard.

Our analysis focuses on the main actors of this violence: both those who suffered violence – the victims – and the perpetrators. However, we do not use the terms 'victim' and 'perpetrator' unquestioningly. Our discussion charts the complex articulation between individual and social silence and/or forgetting shown by these groups over the decades since 1962, and the various strategies individuals and groups have adopted in order to deal with this past. Our aim is to explore the processes determining the forms and levels of silence regarding both torture and the brutal events of October 1961, and how and why such silences can be transcended, when, and by whom. To do so, we adopt Luisa Passerini's suggestion that 'it is constitutive of the definition of a silence to find out its limits, its context, and its reference: in respect to whom and what is it a silence?'.[1]

---

[1] 'Memories between silence and oblivion', in Katherine Hodgkin and Susannah Radstone (eds.), *Contested pasts: the politics of memory* (London and New York: Routledge, 2003), pp. 238–54, p. 249.

Memory and silence, we argue, are multi-layered at both the social and the individual level.[2] In turn, the social conditions in which written and oral testimony are produced strongly influence the nature of the questions asked, the responses given, and the different uses which these testimonies serve (academic, political, etc.). Political and social developments in Algeria and in France, and the shifting diplomatic relations between the two countries, provide the essential backdrop to our analyses of these questions.

However, before addressing each case individually, it is important to examine the longer-term historical context in which such colonial state violence occurred. While violence – both symbolic and physical – was by no means the only dynamic used by colonialism, it was nevertheless an ever-present aspect of colonial governance. Physical violence was used to discourage overt anti-colonial resistance, and whenever colonial hegemony was most directly and publicly threatened, levels of violence grew to extreme and punitive levels. Indeed, the complex long-term processes of what has been termed the dehumanisation of Algerians facilitated such violence and indifference to it.[3]

However, in metropolitan France, sectors of opinion could and did express political or moral outrage about colonial violence. Consequently, colonial governance aimed to hide from metropolitan French public opinion the violence inherent in its functioning. The authorities therefore censored those who denounced the repression of anti-colonial resistance in order to render socially and politically inaudible and invisible the violence the state deployed in Algeria. When violence could not be entirely occluded, the state sought to provide a 'plausible' political rationale for it, and to discredit those who opposed its use.[4]

The effects of such policies were felt well after the war, as generations of French people continued to embrace or nostalgically reconstruct their colonial past. Many had been unaware of the extreme levels of violence (and their political and military coordination); others had accepted the justification for such violence offered by the French authorities. After 1962, the French state sought to prolong attempts to impose silence on its colonial violence through amnesties, censorship and denial.[5] Colonial

[2] See James Fentress and Chris Wickham, *Social memory* (Oxford: Blackwell, 1992); Paul Ricœur, *La mémoire, l'histoire, l'oubli* (Paris: Seuil, 2000).

[3] Yves Bénot, *Massacres coloniaux 1944–1950: La IVè République et la mise au pas des colonies françaises* (Paris: La Découverte, 2005); Sidi Mohammed Barkat, *Le corps d'exception: les artifices du pouvoir colonial et la destruction de la vie* (Paris: Editions Amsterdam, 2005).

[4] Raphaëlle Branche, *La torture et l'armée pendant la guerre d'Algérie, 1954–1962* (Paris: Gallimard, 2001); Jim House and Neil MacMaster, *Paris 1961. Algerians, state terror, and memory* (Oxford University Press, 2006).

[5] Stéphane Gacon, *L'amnistie: de la Commune à la guerre d'Algérie* (Paris: Seuil, 2002).

governance was therefore much concerned with the manipulation of memory and silence.

For Algerian nationalists, on the other hand, such colonial violence was made as visible as possible to international opinion. However, we shall see that after the war, the official narrative of the National Liberation Front (*FLN, Front de libération nationale*) in power in Algeria proved highly selective with respect to which aspects of colonial violence to commemorate.[6]

During the war, the French security forces used torture on a very large scale not only to fight against the nationalists, but also to compensate for their inability to convince the Algerian people that they should stay 'French'. In this way, the population would not encourage, protect or support the nationalists. Torture was, in essence, an everyday form of violence employed throughout Algeria for many years by French troops who were ordered to use methods which they understood as constituting torture in their interrogations. Although impossible to count, the number of victims of torture was numerous, possibly hundreds of thousands. They were civilians and fighters indistinctly called 'rebels'. Resorting to violence was routine and perpetrated far from foreign eyes or media attention and denied by the French state.[7]

While the French state also denied the existence of the 17 October 1961 massacre, the nature of this violence was in many respects different. This repression constituted the largest massacre perpetrated in France during the Algerian War of Independence. Around 30,000 Algerian demonstrators protesting the curfew imposed on them by the prefect of the Paris police, Maurice Papon, at the beginning of October 1961, were confronted by the police. The result of these clashes was many deaths that night and probably one thousand injured.[8] Here we have extreme violence centring upon one day (17 October 1961) in the French capital, involving the deaths of dozens of unarmed civilians in a few hours. Notwithstanding considerable controversy about the numbers killed, this was an event immediately reported by the press and known outside France via the international press.[9]

---

[6] Gilles Manceron and Hassan Remaoun, *D'une rive à l'autre: la guerre d'Algérie de la mémoire à l'histoire* (Paris: Syros, 1993).

[7] Branche, *La torture et l'armée*, ch. 4.

[8] Police violence continued for several days after 17 October, in particular in the stadia used to house the thousands of Algerians detained during the demonstrations. The demonstrations themselves were also protests over the longer-term violence to which Algerians had been subjected. In this chapter 'October 1961' refers to the violence of that wider period in addition to that of 17 October. However, '17 October 1961' will be used to refer specifically to the repression of the demonstrations and the killings which followed them.

[9] House and MacMaster, *Paris 1961*, chs. 5–9.

Now, fifty years later, there have been calls for reparations or the symbolic recognition of two sets of crimes – the systematic torture of hundreds of thousands of people in Algeria on the one hand, and on the other, the killing by police of many Algerian protesters in Paris.

This chapter seeks to answer a number of questions in relation to both examples of violence. Why did the subject of torture in Algeria and police killings of protesters in Paris become largely marginal to discussions of this period in both France and Algeria? And why has the October 1961 violence, more than that of torture, emerged as a central political and social question since the late 1990s?

In this chapter we argue that the key to this unequal resurfacing of the past lies in the way in which, beginning in the 1980s, Algerians and their descendants of several generations have come together to create shared memories and a shared but not identical inter-generational demand for commemoration of the victims of the October 1961 events. These groups have refused to accept French public silence on 17 October 1961 and have made specific claims on the French state to recognise and acknowledge what happened on that day. In contrast, discussions of torture during the Algerian war have emerged in different ways, in part reflecting the foreign policy priorities of the Algerian government, whose interests were not the same as those of the survivors of torture and their families.

Torture

French soldiers first set foot on the coast of North Africa in 1830. Thereafter Algeria became a very specific territory within the French empire. It was considered an integral part of France and administratively divided into departments. Although theoretically Algeria was not a colony, it was nonetheless colonised by European migrants that formed a non-native population of around one million by 1954. From a very general point of view, this population came under French common law, whereas the natives came under a specific legal status linked to their position as 'French-Muslims'. This legal and status inequality was mitigated after the Second World War but remained a guiding principle enabling there to be a clear distinction between French citizens and French-Muslims.

Before 1954, the police used torture in Algeria, but after 1954, with recourse to the army, its use became systematic and routine.[10] People

---

[10] Pierre Vidal-Naquet, *La raison d'État* (Paris: Minuit, 1962) and *La torture dans la République: essai d'histoire et de politique contemporaines, 1954–1962* (Paris: Minuit, 1972).

were tortured indiscriminately in towns and in the mountains, during active operations or back in barracks. Those tortured were military prisoners – fighters in the Algerian independence movement – but much more often civilians suspected of providing the 'rebels' with supplies and money, or engaging in political organisation and mobilisation. Some Algerians were tortured immediately after their arrest, while others – or the same ones – languished in captivity for a period before being subjected to torture. Professional soldiers as well as conscripts were the perpetrators.

On the one hand, the *FLN* would denounce torture when it fitted with one of its international campaigns for support against France in the war. The *FLN* therefore published some accounts of victims of torture, especially those collected by activist lawyers. On the other hand, the French public was occasionally informed about torture by a few newspapers that obtained information from soldiers or officials. Nevertheless, for French public opinion in general, torture was only limited (not general) and, above all, it was inflicted on more-or-less guilty people.

It is important to note that torture was not authorised. It remained an illegal form of violence, forbidden to all state agents and soldiers. However, insidiously, it also became a justified and rationalised form of violence. As soldiers were under pressure to view the search for information as their greatest priority, torture, rarely explicitly recommended but often quietly suggested, was one way of obtaining it. At the same time, torture had the remarkable effect of terrorising entire groups to which the victim belonged, whether family, village or political.

An act of violence inflicted by soldiers, under the command of a superior, torture appeared to be subject to certain rules, and drew on a relatively limited range of violent acts. Apart from systematic beatings, electric shock was undeniably the most widely practised torture method.[11]

Though torture was forbidden and illegal, the reality was that it was inflicted with the knowledge of all levels of command and that it went unpunished. If official texts condemned it,[12] police and military practice itself allowed and nurtured it, without any direct opposition from the high

---

[11] This is one of the most important characteristics of the French use of torture in Algeria. On the specificities of torture in different political contexts, see Darius Rejali, *Torture and Democracy* (Princeton and Oxford, Princeton University Press, 2007).

[12] See for example the directive in the Service historique de la défense (SHD) by General Lorillot, Commander in Chief in Algeria (31 January 1956): 'Depuis le début de la rébellion [...] les sévices de toute sorte sur les personnes et les exactions sur les biens sont formellement interdits' ('Since the start of the conflict, physical abuse and violence against property have been formally prohibited') (SHD, 1R 296*).

command or the broader political apparatus. The logic of war appeared to justify torture; thus, it would have been 'illogical' to punish it.[13]

In fact, only three trials took place during the entire war. Conscripts were only involved in the last trial held for causing death under torture. It concluded with the acquittal of the three accused men, despite the fact that they admitted their involvement. The truth is that the soldiers who carried out torture committed it in the context of what they understood to be their duties.

The French government arranged for soldiers' immunity from prosecution at the end of the war. It was part of the cease-fire agreement that those who had committed crimes ('actes' is the French word frequently used) during the war were to receive amnesty from both sides. This supposedly balanced effect was a distorted one, since about 200 people had already been executed for their participation in the Algerian fight for independence and tens of thousands of Algerians had been found guilty and/or imprisoned for years.[14] However, on the French side, practically no one was prosecuted, despite the large numbers involved in torture. Yet the *FLN* negotiators still signed the cease-fire agreement: with this double amnesty, they, along with the French, became responsible for the subsequent and enduring silence on the subject of torture after the war.

Things then went in different ways in Algeria and in France. French opinion was not particularly interested in the war and especially in its darkest aspects. Pierre Vidal-Naquet published a very important book on the subject, called *Torture: A Cancer for Democracy*, in English and Italian but no French publisher took it before the 1970s.[15]

However, for Algerians, torture did not disappear. The fight for power led very rapidly to the repetition of torture by the new regime against political opponents. Torture did not become a matter of the past: it remained a political and topical subject. Moreover, Algeria's relationship with France was dominated by the negotiation of economic and diplomatic cooperation; in this context painful memories served no useful purpose. Official history in Algeria magnified the struggle for independence (the 'war of liberation'), and tried to consider the colonial past as a parenthesis, an insignificant event in the great story of the Algerian people. Colonial violence was hardly mentioned; attention was drawn instead to

---

[13] After General Lorillot, General Salan adopted a much looser interpretation of legality. Acts of torture were regularly practised under his command without being repressed. On this central question of law and war in Algeria, especially regarding the question of torture, see Vidal-Naquet, *La raison d'État* and Branche, *La torture et l'armée*.

[14] Sylvie Thénault, *Une drôle de justice: les magistrats dans la guerre d'Algérie* (Paris: La Découverte, 2001).

[15] Raphaëlle Branche, *La guerre d'Algérie: une histoire apaisée?* (Paris: Le Seuil, 2005).

the victims who were glorified, especially when they were dead and called '*chuhadā*", or martyrs.

A film encapsulated this *modus vivendi*. *The Battle of Algiers* was made by Gillo Pontecorvo, an Italian filmmaker, with the support of Yacef Saadi, a powerful Algerian nationalist who was the former head of the military branch of the *FLN* in Algiers in 1957 and director of the first national film production company in Algeria ('Casbah Films'). The 'people of the Casbah' were celebrated as the main protagonists of the struggle against French colonialism and especially French paratroopers who were engaged in what they called a counter-revolutionary struggle, leading to systematic torture when they caught someone. Women committing terrorist attacks personified these 'people of the Casbah', and the film begins with a man being tortured and then forced to show the paratroopers a place where a man, a woman and a boy are hiding. These three were killed rather than given the option to surrender. The film gained a large international audience and won the Golden Lion award at the Venice festival in 1966. The French representatives at the festival walked out. Censored in France until 1970, the film was then banned from public screenings because of the threat to public order it purportedly represented.

Nevertheless, Pontecorvo's film helped rekindle the debate on torture that had begun during the so-called 'Battle of Algiers' itself, in 1957. This debate involved moral judgments and human rights being opposed to military efficiency and the rationality of state security. Even after France's defeat, high-ranking French officers still used the argument of rationality and necessity to justify the use of torture.[16] The conscripts, rank-and-file soldiers and the victims kept silent until at least the end of the 1970s. Pierre Vidal-Naquet, who was a leader in denouncing torture during the war, published two books on these crimes.[17] He raised the question of the responsibility of the Republic and the French government for torture, but no political movement emerged to press his claims.

After 1964, France and Algeria tried to normalise their relations. Migration from Algeria to France represented the main point of tension between the two countries during the 1960s and the beginning of the 1970s. The French government tried to heal the civil wounds of the war. French veterans were recognised as such. The approximately one million French repatriates from Algeria were given compensation, and another amnesty aimed to put an end to the claims of those who fought for 'French

[16] General Jacques Massu, *La vraie bataille d'Alger* (Paris: Plon, 1971).
[17] Vidal-Naquet, *La torture dans la République*, and Pierre Vidal-Naquet, *Les crimes de l'armée française* (Paris: Maspero, 1975).

Algeria'. However, the issue of torture and of state violence still surfaced, in roughly ten-year intervals.

Yet, something different in degree and in kind took place from 2000 onwards. In June 2000, a few days after Algerian President Bouteflika's official visit to France and his very provocative speech about the Algerians who served as auxiliaries in the French army during the war, the testimony of Louisa Ighilahriz, an Algerian female victim of torture, appeared on the front page of the newspaper, *Le Monde*. She had been tortured and raped by French soldiers in Algiers and then rescued and protected by a French military doctor. The newspaper henceforth led a campaign for the truth about torture during the French–Algerian war. For months, it published something on the subject daily, keeping the government and the deputies under pressure. In October 2000, the communist newspaper *L'Humanité* published an appeal by well-known personalities such as Pierre Vidal-Naquet, and this became known as the 'Appeal of the Twelve'. Their demand was that the French state recognise its responsibility for the practice of torture. The highest authorities of the French state continued to deny that there had been massive recourse to torture and continued to assert that its incidence had been the exception rather than the rule.

That position became untenable when attention turned to a general commanding a unit which carried out summary executions and torture during the war. As a member of the special services, Paul Aussaresses had remained silent about the war, but decided to break this silence and to admit the facts. He could not be prosecuted thanks to amnesty provisions, but he was then generally criticised. Perceived as cynical, as a cold monster and perfect criminal, he was repulsive to many people who through him discovered the reality of torture and summary executions during the war. However, most of all, he was the ideal incarnation of a torturer as an exception within an untainted army. Instead of taking a political stand on the issue, Prime Minister Lionel Jospin personally condemned this man and his acts. The then French president, Jacques Chirac, chose to withdraw the Legion of Honour that Paul Aussaresses had received for his actions during the Second World War.

The controversy then appeared in the courts. General Aussaresses was prosecuted not for what he did (the amnesty prevented it). Instead, he was taken to court for what he said in his memoirs published in 2001,[18] and convicted. Some other trials took place, always libel suits. People were prosecuted for what they said (was it apologetic? slanderous? etc.). In this

---

[18] Paul Aussaresses, *Services spéciaux, Algérie 1955–1957* (Paris: Perrin, 2001).

context old arguments about torture were revived. However, the validity or necessity of the recourse to torture itself was not always questioned.

Torture, presented as a weapon against terrorism and appalling enemies, was even justified by some officers in the very favourable context of the post-9/11 war on 'terror'. France, like other Western countries, experienced a kind of political and moral regression about torture.[19] This regression was also at work at a cognitive level. The issue was not about the extension of torture or the political implications of this violence being perpetrated by agents of the state but, instead, about the efficiency of the methods used. Even some former interpretations – such as the *FLN* being part of a communist plot against the West – gained new currency.

Given that France had lost Algeria, the efficiency of torture could be questioned. However, from a political point of view, the outcome of such debates was uncertain, and remains so. In order to understand why, we need to ask who – beyond some intellectuals and newspapers – could have brought the question of torture to public and/or political attention. At least two groups could have played this role: the soldiers – the perpetrators – and their victims. What therefore happened to silence them?

Since the beginning of the 1990s, French veterans have gained influence in relation to the state. Thanks to their lobbying, a decree recognised the syndrome of post-traumatic stress disorder (PTSD) for soldiers who had served in Algeria.[20] Officially, then, they could be considered as victims. From this date onward, this ambiguous status could become part of their social identity. They used it to gain confidence and speak up. These men's autobiographical texts often showed these characteristics, with authors torn between their convictions and their duties, their feelings and their comrades, and so on. From 1998 onward, we see a marked increase in autobiographical texts written by former conscripts: *Telle fut ma guerre d'Algérie*,[21] *Ma guerre d'Algérie*,[22] *Les djebels de l'illusion: récit d'un appelé de la guerre d'Algérie*,[23] *La villa Susini: tortures en Algérie, un appelé parle*,[24] *En Algérie: la guerre d'un jeune appelé forézien*,[25] *Algérie: mes trente mois*,[26] and so on. These texts insist on their author's specificity: *my war has to be told* as if the general narrative was not satisfactory, whether

---

[19] See Rejali, *Torture and Democracy*.
[20] French designations do not literally speak of PTSD. The idea is nonetheless that of imputing causality of later psychiatric disorders to events that happened during the war.
[21] Jean Moriot (self-published, 2001).
[22] Bernard Gerland (Villeurbanne: Éditions Golias, 2001).
[23] Michel Leribel (Montpellier: Artistes en Languedoc, 2001).
[24] Henri Pouillot (Paris: Éditions Tirésias, 2000).
[25] Jean Baudou (Montbrison: Village de Forez, 1998).
[26] Maxime Marsollier (self-published, 1998).

emanating from former officers, the veterans' associations or officials. These authors condemn violence, but always present this violence as perpetrated by someone other than the author, and they generally avoid the issue of personal involvement in the violence. There are also some memoirs with a self-denigrating or generally disparaging tone, sometimes expressed with irony.

After 2000, some testimonies surfaced in French newspapers and on television. The most important was a documentary lasting more than three hours called *The Intimate Enemy*. It was produced by a public channel, broadcast at prime time for two successive nights, and the last part was followed by a debate.[27] The documentary aimed to show the intimate face of perpetrators: several ex-conscripts gave interviews about violence they had witnessed or, more rarely, practised. Unknown to public opinion, these faces contrasted with that of General Aussaresses, even if he was, of course, part of the film. There were tales of atrocities inflicted on all sorts of victims, but the focus was on the perpetrators who were looked upon with either compassion or disgust.

This documentary was a sign of the confusion evident among political authorities in 2002. Indeed this film was *the* film broadcast on public television in March to mark the fortieth anniversary of the cease-fire. The film constituted a strange and indirect official sanction of the end of some aspects of silence on the issue of torture, which was once more associated with personal behaviour and not policies formulated at the highest levels. It was also a strange way of commemorating the war, which could not be reduced to torture, especially if torture was not related to the wider political context in which it had been long practised.

The veterans' associations, which could have addressed claims for recognition or even regret to the state, felt very ill at ease with all the public interest in the subject. They kept to the line that torture was exceptional or insisted on the fact that the nature of the war should not be reduced to this violence. They even encouraged their members to remain silent on the issue.

The possibility of being prosecuted for their writings may have led those veterans who had initially been willing to talk, to keep silent, or, at least, to keep their statements within private and family circles: their grandchildren were beginning to ask them questions. However, public opinion and public debate missed these new narratives, which could have served as a stronger means of addressing the state on this dark part of French history, perpetrated far from French eyes, across the Mediterranean Sea.

---

[27] Patrick Rotman, *L'ennemi intime*, broadcast on France 3 (national television channel) in March 2002.

Another group could have carried forward the claim to be heard and to be recognised: the victims. Although one of them stood up and spoke out in 2000, they were not sought out by the media, and the Algerian state made no real attempt to represent them. During the war, very few Algerian victims had been able to bring their cases to court or before public opinion. After the war and the amnesty, the *FLN* veterans who had been recognised as such gained some benefits from the Algerian state. However, Algerian associations organised by the Algerian state in this so-called 'Democratic and Popular Republic' never sought any compensation from the French state. The good health of French-Algerian relations came before the victims of torture and other violence.[28]

At the end of the 1980s, the Algerians gained some liberties: new associations and newspapers appeared. Notwithstanding these developments, the civil war from 1992 onwards led Algerians to focus on the present and not on the past. Intellectuals were assassinated; others sought refuge in France or elsewhere. Apart from these targeted killings, massacres took place in several localities, some even not far from Algiers. State repression was terrible: torture, summary executions and disappearances were commonly used by the Algerian forces officially fighting against terrorists or armed Islamist groups. Some voices from inside spoke out to denounce these methods. They found some echoes outside Algeria, but France mostly shared the official Algerian interpretation of what was happening across the Mediterranean, given that some terrorist attacks also targeted France.[29]

When the debate about the use of torture during the French–Algerian war surfaced in France, some Algerian media reported it, but the Algerian authorities themselves kept silent. The treaty they were negotiating with the European Union was worth this silence. Above all, the issue of torture and state terror was too topical for the Algerian people and then too risky for their state. Nonetheless, a debate did take place in Algeria about the colonial war. A few personalities focused on the biographies of the higher ranks of the Algerian army: some of the most important had been former French officers before they deserted to join the Algerian National Liberation Army. Their strategy and tactics during the civil war of the

---

[28] From the French point of view, the same applies to the Algerian attitude towards the *harkis* (Algerians having served in French security forces) and their families (including the murder of thousands of *harkis* after Algerian independence), the kidnapping of French European citizens during the war, or the confiscation of the so-called 'vacant assets' of the European settlers who left Algerian soil en masse in 1962–3.

[29] Luis Martinez, *La guerre civile en Algérie, 1990–1998*. (Paris: Éditions Karthala, 1998). Mohamed Benrabah, Abdenour Jellouli, Nabile Farès et al., *Les violences en Algérie* (Paris: O. Jacob, 1998).

1990s were linked to this training. However, the French army was not accused. Evoking the repressive methods of French colonial governance was simply a means to point the finger at the Algerian generals and politicians in charge of the war.[30]

In this case, silence about the past was the consequence of an immediate emergency: Algeria had to deal with the violence of the 1990s. President Bouteflika organised an amnesty[31] to bring about what he called 'civil Concordia' and then 'Peace and National Reconciliation'. Consequently, once again agents of the state received protection for what they had done.

In France, it was finally ex-conscript soldiers who took the ambiguous place of the victims. The former soldiers became victims of a misguided state policy that had sent them to fight an unwinnable war in which they were sometimes forced to use torture, and were themselves sometimes killed or maimed. The Algerian victims of these soldiers are not organised within associations, and have not lobbied in Algeria or in France for the French government to recognise the responsibility of French authorities for the use of such methods or the conduct of the war.

October 1961

As we have already seen, the French press and anti-colonial activists gave considerable coverage to the repression of 17 October 1961, and collected many, often anonymous oral testimonies of Algerians who were subjected to police violence. These testimonies, some of them from legal depositions, fed into an anti-colonial narrative denouncing such violence.[32]

However, testimony given by those Algerians who suffered violence soon sank from view for several reasons. In addition to the French official cover-up, the French left, already divided due to the Cold War, was also deeply split on the question of Algerian independence and therefore did not organise mass, unified protests after 17 October.

Furthermore, the political context also shifted rapidly away from police violence against Algerians to related but separate police violence against French anti-fascist demonstrators. Nine protesters died at the Charonne

---

[30] See for example the testimony of Habib Souaïdia and the accusation targeting Khaled Nezzar. Habib Souaïdia, *La sale guerre: le témoignage d'un ancien officier des Forces spéciales de l'armée algérienne* (Paris: Éditions la Découverte, 2001). Between 2000 and 2004, General Nezzar published one book every year to answer his critics.

[31] Some crimes remain excluded from this amnesty. See Martin Evans and John Phillips, *Algeria. Anger of the dispossessed* (New Haven and London: Yale University Press, 2007), pp. 262–9.

[32] Paulette Péju, 'Ratonnades à Paris', in *Les harkis à Paris précédé de Ratonnades à Paris* (Paris: La Découverte, 2000 [1961]).

metro station in Paris on 8 February 1962, an event that was to provoke more unified protests from the French left than the incidents of 17 October, and the Charonne killings had greater memorial resonance with the French public.[33]

On the Algerian side, the *FLN* leadership was unwilling to allow the events of 17 October 1961 to compromise its negotiations with the French state. Infighting within the Algerian national movement over the next year led to the marginalisation of the leaders of the French *FLN* Federation that had organised the 17 October 1961 demonstrations.[34]

This silencing on the Algerian side led to the disappearance of the written testimonies of many hundreds of Algerians who, at the instigation of the *FLN*, had recorded their experiences of 17–20 October 1961 in the weeks immediately following. These reports provide historians with a useful alternative version of 17 October to that of the official cover-up, and serve as a useful complement to oral testimonies by Algerians collected in the 1980s and 1990s. Such reports provide graphic details of police violence – often by Algerians injured during the protests. These testimonies also show a remarkably balanced assessment of the range of French public reactions to the demonstrators – from violent hostility to help and medical support.[35]

With a few exceptions, such as Jacques Panijel's underground militant film *Octobre à Paris* ('October in Paris', 1962), the period 1962–68 was marked by public silence regarding October 1961 in both France and Algeria.[36] Few in either country were interested in hearing what Algerians had to say. Algerians' voices were politically illegitimate for a number of reasons. The Gaullists remained in power, and, as we saw with the torture question, diplomatic relations and immigration policy between France and Algeria dictated strategic mutual silence at an official level. Furthermore, many in Algeria viewed Algerians in France as having experienced a lesser degree of suffering than those Algerians who fought

---

[33] Alain Dewerpe, *Charonne 8 février 1962. Anthropologie historique d'un massacre d'État* (Paris: Gallimard, 2006).

[34] House and MacMaster, *Paris 1961*, chs. 8 and 9.

[35] The Archives of the Paris Préfecture de Police (file H1B35) contain some of these reports, seized by police in November 1961. These and other *FLN* reports have been used by Linda Amiri, *Les fantômes du 17 octobre* (Paris: Éditions Mémoire-Génériques, 2001), and *La Bataille de France: la guerre d'Algérie en Métropole* (Paris: Laffont, 2004). On the use of written and oral testimony by historians investigating the October 1961 events, see the exchange between Jean-Paul Brunet ('Police Violence in Paris, October 1961: historical sources, methods, and conclusions') and Jim House and Neil MacMaster ('Time to move on: a reply to Jean-Paul Brunet') in *The Historical Journal*, LI, 1 (March 2008), pp. 195–214.

[36] Panijel shot his film immediately after the 17 October 1961 repression with the collaboration of the *FLN* in Paris.

or endured the war in Algeria. Official Algerian memory celebrated the role of the rural rather than urban actors of the war, those in Algeria rather than in France, and the actions of soldiers and bombers rather than street demonstrators. These developments combined to leave Algerians in France caught in a sort of discursive and memorial 'no-man's-land' after 1962.

Many additional factors explain why Algerians kept publicly silent during this period, and in many instances, remain silent today. Algerians in Paris suffered kidnappings, torture and other forms of intimidation by the Algerian police auxiliaries (*harkis*) and much repression at the hands of the other police units under the command of Paris prefect of police Maurice Papon. In this respect, 17 October 1961 served to 'reveal' to sectors of French public opinion the longer-term pattern of security force violence against Algerians that had been going on for years. For many Algerians, police violence induced a coercive fear that four decades have not dispelled, and colonial-style police surveillance in Paris continued well into the 1970s.[37] As in Algeria, however, the war in France was very complex, involving internecine violence and *FLN* assassinations of 'reluctant supporters', turning it into a war which threatened the personal safety of everyone involved.

Understandably, many Algerians therefore wanted to 'move on' after the war, and to improve their socio-economic conditions. Algerian parents often sought to protect their children from knowledge of the violence they had suffered during the war, deliberately not transmitting these experiences. Silence for Algerians was thus not forgetting, but such a strategy made the transmission of family memories difficult or impossible. Moreover, given the indiscriminate nature of police violence, coming forward individually to speak out could have been viewed as selfish. Additionally, Algerian migrants seldom recounted the sufferings of exile in France.[38]

Revisiting the war by speaking out about it would also have opened a sensitive question for Algerians in France. Why had they stayed in the country of the former coloniser, where anti-Algerian racism remained ever present? In the 1960s and 1970s, many Algerians therefore retreated into a 'strategic silence' as a way of negotiating their sense of past, present

---

[37] Jim House, 'Contrôle, encadrement, surveillance et répression des migrations coloniales: une décolonisation difficile (1956–1970)', *Bulletin de l'Institut d'Histoire du temps présent*, 83 (premier trimestre 2004), pp. 111–27.

[38] Abdelmalek Sayad, *L'Immigration ou les paradoxes de l'altérité* (Brussels: de Boeck Wesmael, 1991); *La Double absence: des illusions de l'émigré aux souffrances de l'immigré* (Paris: Seuil, 1999).

and future, as they viewed their status in France as provisional, preparing an eventual (but often mythical) return to Algeria.[39]

The silence of Algerians was therefore a reflection of war memories and migrant memories, in a political, social and cultural context that was seldom conducive to speaking out within a family or public context, and in which no campaigning groups sought to seek out, collect, preserve and disseminate their testimonies. Just as a congruence of factors had ensured the rapid loss of public engagement with the events of October 1961, so there was a variety of reasons for Algerian public silence in France.

Yet when the Algerian state did officially recognise the events of 17 October 1961 in 1968, making 17 October 'National Emigration Day', it was in order to celebrate the 'Martyrs of the Revolution' and to stress the attachment and political 'loyalty' of the Algerian emigrant community in France, many of whom were opposed to President Boumediene, who was in office from 1965 to 1978. During the years 1968–1971, the annual commemorative ceremonies held in both Algeria and in the migrant community in France received high official visibility. However, the Algerian state was not interested in spreading awareness of October 1961 to a wider French public. The Algerian state's official association for Algerians in France – the *Amicale* – organised numerous commemorative events in France, and collected Algerian testimonies of the October 1961 violence in print and on film. These testimonies fed into a 'heroic narrative' claiming that many hundreds of Algerians had died in October 1961 as part of the struggle to cast off the colonialist yoke.[40]

Yet many Algerians could not identify with the image such commemorative rhetoric portrayed and felt disappointed that independence had not provided the economic and political opportunities for which they had hoped. Similar to the limits on discussions of torture, there was thus not total silence about October 1961 during the 1960s and 1970s, but rather a muted reaction. With respect to French society, the official Algerian commemoration of these events was socially and politically invisible.

Despite all of these highly constricting factors, including the way official Algerian representatives sought to monopolise the story of October 1961, several key, but politically and socially marginal groups, recorded and preserved their own memories of the events of 17 October. A minority of former *FLN* activists had deliberately chosen to transmit their memories of the war to their children. Additionally, many key French former anti-colonial activists such as Jacques Panijel and François Maspero had first-hand knowledge of the 17 October 1961 demonstrations (if not the worst

---

[39] House and MacMaster, *Paris 1961*, ch. 10.
[40] See the *Amicale*'s publication *L'Algérien en Europe* each October during this period.

examples of police violence). Such activists maintained informal networks that to this day have kept alive public discussions of the war. The Maoist and Trotskyist left used the remembrance of 17 October to remind the French Communist Party of its lacklustre reactions to the violence. In their more organised forms (e.g. the Maoist-leaning Arab Worker's Movement, 1972–7), these groups articulated counter-memories in relation to the Algerian *Amicale* and Algerian state.

These different left-wing actors in the period after the student and worker protests of May 1968 provided the context in which young people of Algerian migrant origin, usually born in France, started to become sensitised to questions arising out of the war of independence, and to the violence experienced by their parents.

It was therefore the *descendants* of those having experienced the October 1961 violence that became by the 1980s the key spokespeople and memory transmitters of the story of that set of crimes. The victims still found speaking out extremely difficult, and many remained silent within their families. These young activists, commonly known as 'Beurs',[41] mobilised the story of October 1961 within the context of their struggle to achieve an autonomous collective political identity in French society away from the mainstream French left and the *Amicale*. However, these activists found it difficult to construct a political 'space' precisely because of their marginalised status. Young memory activists framed the October 1961 violence within a discourse of anti-racism, arguing that the origins of anti-Algerian racism in the 1980s lay in the colonial racism and violence experienced by their parents during the Algerian war. In particular, they highlighted the alleged impunity of the police for acts of often lethal violence (commonly termed *bavures*), mostly committed against young people who came from groups suffering from racism.[42] Counter-cultural organisations such as *Sans frontières* ('Without Borders', 1979–85) also underlined the need for greater memory transmission within the Algerian migrant communities and questioned the way in which most French people had forgotten, or were unaware of, the October 1961 repression.

The 1980s therefore saw the descendants of Algerian migrants emerge as significant new carriers of the memories and narratives of October 1961. Some of the activists – Farid Aïchoune was one – had been very young in 1961, but many were older. This situation raised important questions regarding 'post-memory' or the re-presentation of the past by later generations, as well as about the political function of

---

[41] The term is slang for 'Arab'.
[42] Jim House, 'Antiracist memories: the case of 17 October 1961 in historical perspective', *Modern and Contemporary France*, IX, 3 (2001), pp. 355–68.

re-representation when activists made claims to 'speak for' their parents' generations.[43] There were also problems imbedded in their framing of October 1961 within an anti-racist paradigm.

Simultaneously, however, some older Algerian migrants hoped that creating a political debate in France on October 1961 would have repercussions in Algeria and force a wider recognition of the role of the French *FLN* Federation that had been politically marginalised in 1962 during the power struggles for leadership of the newly independent state. Thus, older and younger generations within the Algerian communities could invest different symbolic meanings in the same event, a situation that continues today. Both migrants and their descendants, however, saw the repression in Algiers in 1988 – when security forces opened fire on unarmed demonstrators – as an event echoing 17 October 1961 through the same disregard for legitimate protest, the same indiscriminate levels of violence, and the same judicial impunity of those who carried out the repression.[44] This set of parallels between 1961 and 1988 showed what Paul A. Silverstein calls the 'transpolitical space' that existed between France and Algeria.[45]

From the 1991 commemorations onwards, there was a new turn in the work of memory activists regarding October 1961. Rather than October 1961 fulfilling a mostly 'internal' function within the Algerian and wider Maghribi communities, dedicated multi-ethnic associations such as *Au nom de la mémoire* ('In Memory's Name', *ANM*), along with established anti-racist and human rights groups, began to formulate demands on the French state for symbolic (as opposed to financial) reparations, justice and truth. Such demands centred upon the recognition of the reality and scale of the massacre and the responsibilities for it, access to official police and judicial archives in order to increase social knowledge of the period, and the placing of the events of October 1961 on state school history curricula. These demands were couched within a human rights discourse and can be understood within wider social processes affecting the centrality of 'memory', commemoration and the mobilisation of the past in contemporary French society.[46]

---

[43] Christine Polac, 'Quand "les immigrés" prennent la parole', in Pascal Perrineau (ed.), *L'Engagement politique: déclin ou mutation?* (Paris: Presses de la FNSP, 1994), pp. 359–86.
[44] Abdel Aïssou (ed.), *Octobre à Alger* (Paris: Seuil, 1988).
[45] *Algeria in France: transpolitics, race and nation* (Bloomington and Indianapolis: Indiana University Press, 2004).
[46] Emmanuel Kattan, *Penser le devoir de mémoire* (Paris: Presses Universitaires de France, 2002); Sandrine Lefranc, *Politiques du pardon* (Paris: Presses Universitaires de France, 2002).

In order to press their case, campaigning groups sought out written and oral testimony, and used studies,[47] documentary films[48] and fiction.[49] However, leaving silence behind was easier for some groups than others, since these various initiatives featured far more French than Algerian interviewees, and the Algerians who did appear were often high-ranking former *FLN* leaders rather than 'ordinary' Algerians. Since the aim of much of this work was to prove the existence of a massacre on 17 October 1961 in the light of persistent official French denials, the overarching narrative within which the interview questions were often set concentrated as much on the perpetrators as on the victims, at times and unwittingly tending to conceal the complexity of their experiences.

Simultaneously, some relatively low-ranking former police officers did come forward to explain (rather than justify) police attitudes towards Algerians and the nature of police violence in October 1961.[50] However, few new critical voices amongst former police officers have been heard since the early 1990s. The silence of those who served in the Paris police and other security force units in 1961, with a few exceptions, remains largely in place today.

While memory activism concerning October 1961 certainly spread out from Algerian migrant groups and the far left to wider sectors of French society, there was little evidence that October 1961 could find a place within national French consciousness during the early 1990s. In the absence of any concerted debates on the colonial past and colonial violence in particular, there were few frameworks within which to 'ground' such memories. In addition, neither the mainstream French right nor left had much to gain politically from being more open about October 1961. There was some progress on this issue in Algeria in the early 1990s, but as in the case of torture, the quasi civil war in Algeria turned public attention to present and wartime events in Algeria, rather than in France.[51]

A further element in the activists' repertoire came from another source. Starting in the 1980s, France has been confronted with another aspect of its painful recent past. Trials began, indicting former Nazis or French officials with having tortured, killed or carried out round-ups and

---

[47] Michel Levine, *Les ratonnades d'octobre: un meurtre collectif à Paris en 1961* (Paris: Ramsay, 1985); Jean-Luc Einaudi, *La bataille de Paris. 17 octobre 1961* (Paris: Seuil, 1991); Anne Tristan, *Le silence du fleuve* (Bezons: Au nom de la mémoire, 1991).

[48] Alan Hayling and Philip Brooks, *Drowning by bullets* (1992), and Mehdi Lallaoui and Agnès Denis, *Le silence du fleuve* (1991).

[49] Didier Daeninckx, *Meurtres pour mémoire* (Paris: Gallimard, 1984).

[50] See Einaudi, *La bataille de Paris*, and his later book, *Octobre 1961. Un massacre à Paris* (Paris: Fayard, 2001).

[51] Benjamin Stora, *La guerre invisible: Algérie, années 90* (Paris: Presses de Sciences-Po, 2001).

deportations of Jews and resistance leaders during the Occupation. Tolerance of impunity was weakening, and the past was increasingly scrutinised with a judicial eye searching for crimes, especially crimes against humanity.

Indeed, the key 'tipping point' in political terms regarding October 1961 came from two highly symbolic trials: Papon (1997–8) and Papon–Einaudi (1999). The first trial was essentially concerned with Vichy crimes, since it focused on Papon's role as general-secretary of the Gironde prefecture and his role in the round-up and deportation of Jews. However, campaigners used the proceedings, and the media attention they attracted, to highlight Papon's repressive career in Algeria and Paris.[52] In 1999, Papon unsuccessfully sued the researcher Jean-Luc Einaudi for having accused him of direct responsibility for the 17 October massacre.[53] Here the courts played a role, albeit a problematic one, which the state had largely abandoned. During the Papon–Einaudi trial, for the first time Algerians gave written and oral testimony in court of their experiences of the violence perpetrated by police, who were acting under the authority of Maurice Papon on 17 October 1961.

These two trials had several important outcomes. First, by revealing the punitive violence exacted by police on 17 October, these testimonies gave credence to the campaigning groups' position that a 'massacre' had occurred and hence brought into question the official version of October 1961. The trial therefore finally validated the testimonies of Algerians whom many politicians had ignored for years. Secondly, after much controversy, the left-wing Jospin government granted access to the police and judicial archives, enabling scholars to investigate these events in rigorous ways heretofore impossible. Thirdly, the October 1961 violence gained both national and international media visibility, buoyed by further publications and appeals by campaigning groups. Some students began to learn of October 1961 in the classroom.

This greater awareness in turn inspired a further wave of history work and memory work, often (but not exclusively) undertaken by descendants of Algerian migrants. These individuals and groups took advantage of the greater willingness of some Algerians publicly to speak out. These Algerians were typically the most fluent in French, most socio-economically integrated and most politicised, and were able to convey effectively their experience and knowledge of October 1961 and more generally of the war of independence. In turn, this greater publicity

---

[52] Richard J. Golsan (ed.), *The Papon affair: memory and justice on trial* (London: Routledge, 2000).
[53] Einaudi, *Octobre 1961*, pp. 40–57.

encouraged other Algerians to abandon their former silence. Here was a rich dynamic of inter-generational memories. Finally, because of the Papon–Einaudi trial, and in anticipation of the 2001 commemorations, campaigners sought – ultimately unsuccessfully – to have the 17 October 1961 repression deemed a 'crime against humanity', in order to circumvent the existing amnesty legislation.[54]

The development of campaigning groups such as *ANM* and *Le 17 octobre contre l'oubli* ('17 October against forgetting', created in 1999) that have mounted political initiatives supported by a wide range of left-wing groups therefore marks a contrast with the way the torture question has been treated in public memory. As with the emergence of 'Beur'-led campaigning in the 1980s, this was another key reason – along with the trials – explaining the emergence of public interest in October 1961 in France. However, as with the question of torture, some of the specific demands – in particular that of official French recognition of what happened – proved unsuccessful during the 1997–2002 left-wing government and under the right-wing administrations (since 2002) still tied to Gaullist legacies. Since 2001, political recognition of the repression has devolved to the local level, in particular the Paris suburbs, where local councillors who are descendants of Algerian migrants have often played a key role in tapping into grass-roots associations and networks to pressure left-wing councils. In Paris, the commemorative plaque on the Pont Saint-Michel over the Seine, voted for by Paris City Council in 2001, marked the inscription of October 1961 into public space, but this did not constitute official recognition on the national level. Moreover, in order to avoid further political divisions, the plaque's wording was relatively consensual, only admitting that 'bloody repression' had occurred (rather than a 'massacre'), and studiously avoiding any mention of who had carried out the killings.

However, more generally after 2002, with the right in power, there developed a political 'backlash' against the perceived gains made by the 'neo-anti-colonialist' left during the 1997–2002 period in forcing the question of colonial violence onto the political and media agenda. Former Gaullist politicians, civil servants and key senior members of the metropolitan administration in 1958–62 have been forthright in their criticism of left-wing memory activism and its search for truth, and at times open in their highly visible public support for Papon. Such individuals attempt to minimise the responsibility of civil servants or police officers by pointing out that these men were applying Gaullist policy.

---

[54] Olivier Le Cour Grandmaison (ed.), *Le 17 octobre 1961: un crime d'Etat à Paris* (Paris: La Dispute, 2001).

However, by calling for an examination of the role of politicians in granting relative autonomy to repressive agencies – and hence seeking a discussion of the political responsibilities for such violence – these voices paradoxically argue, from a different perspective, for the opening of a debate on political responsibilities that their political opponents also seek to address.[55]

There is therefore no linear narrative regarding how politics frames silence or liberates voices from its hold. In Algeria, the period 1988–92 provided the chance for a more pluralistic debate on the war of independence – a debate soon cut short by the terrible internecine violence that ensued. Similarly, we have seen that in France, the political context altered after 2002 to provide less favourable institutional conditions within which to address some wartime legacies. The balance shifted to other competing memories of the war, notably those of the former European settlers in Algeria (*pieds-noirs*) and the *harkis*. In Algeria, the role of the former French *FLN* Federation remains problematic, but is less marginalised than previously, providing a context in which October 1961 can be discussed. It is important to note, though, that this event has never occupied the same place in the social memories of Algerians in Algeria as it has done in France.

Conclusion

With no group strong enough to speak for Algerian victims, there was and is little reason for the French government to accept responsibility for the widespread use of torture in the Algerian war of 1954–62. However, there is a palpable difference between silence and forgetting. The history of torture in Algeria is no longer occluded. Slowly but surely, French people can discover the truth. The official archives are not completely closed, and historians can undertake research. Silence is not eternal, and as the rest of this book shows, it is rarely permanent.

With respect to the events of October 1961, a critical threshold of openness had been passed by 2002. Growing awareness (seen during the wide-scale 2001 commemorations), political campaigning and historical publications combined to ensure that this episode of state violence will not 'disappear' a second time. Campaigning groups have ensured the visibility and social 'audibility' of the October 1961 repression and of the Algerians who experienced it. Here is a marked shift from the 1960s.

---

[55] See the depositions of Pierre Messmer, Pierre Somveille, Raymond Montaner and Maurice Papon during the latter's libel case against the researcher Jean-Luc Einaudi (see *Libération*, 6 February 1999, and *Le Monde*, 7–8 February 1999).

Reassured that more people believe their stories, and solicited by the media, researchers, campaigners, teachers and family members, more and more Algerians are speaking out to provide evidence of their painful experiences during the war in France. These testimonies are readily available on the internet, and in books and documentaries. Approaching retirement or in their retirement years, they feel the need to transmit their past experiences. Here is an additional factor explaining the departure some Algerians have taken from previous personal or public silence on October 1961. We see here the way in which individual and social silence and memories are linked, and we can begin to measure the impact of the national debate regarding the killings of October 1961 on the familial, local and associative-level forms through which memories are expressed and transmitted.[56]

Campaigning groups rely on the voices of this dwindling number of former demonstrators on 17 October 1961, whose relationship with their wartime past, and willingness or otherwise to speak out, are influenced by their status, their attitudes towards the regime in France and in Algeria, and the way they see their place in society. In contrast, many Algerians – the vast majority – remain silent about October 1961 and torture, and will probably do so until they die.

In addition, many of the published testimonies, and research interviews we have conducted, suggest that Algerians rarely represent or define themselves as 'victims', even if, as we have already seen, this was the narrative within which such testimonies had initially been solicited, i.e. to show the guilt of the perpetrators. Furthermore, now that this official version of October 1961 has lost much of its popular credence, there are signs of a qualitative shift, away from the counter-narrative status of earlier testimony. Algerians' testimonies are increasingly forthcoming on wider themes such as wartime experiences, migrant trajectories and the social and local histories of the period.

With the passing of time, certain themes have arguably become less difficult to talk about, socially and culturally speaking. For example, it is easier today than in the 1960s for Algerians to state that they ran away from the demonstrations in order to save their lives, that they pretended to be Italians, not Algerians when stopped by police, or that, hiding in Paris bars they ordered alcohol (against *FLN* rules) to avoid being singled out as 'Algerian' and hence risk violence.[57] Nothing of the kind has emerged about torture yet.

---

[56] House and MacMaster, *Paris 1961*, ch. 12.
[57] Interviews (Jim House) with Belkacem S., an Algerian demonstrator on 17 October 1961 (Sarcelles, 16 April and 5 December 2005).

This chapter has highlighted the importance of the emergence of campaigning groups and new memory activists who inject dynamism into the efforts to force public and/or official recognition of the reality of state violence in the context of past colonial conflicts. Given the momentum of the campaigns about October 1961 – in contrast to those on torture – it is evident that there has been movement away from the cultivation of silence about and at the heart of colonial governance. But with respect to the phenomenon of torture during the Algerian war, silence (and not forgetting) still echoes like a bell.

Ruth Ginio

In his short story 'Fahavalo,'[1] the Malagasy author Jean-Luc Raharimanana tells of his 1994 encounter with an old man who stands on a beach and stones a dead dog. A local resident explains to the author that the old man had lost his mind after having witnessed a massacre in his village during the suppression of the Malagasy insurrection in November 1947. The perpetrators were black colonial soldiers. Afterwards dogs devoured the unburied villagers' bodies. Unable to forget the moment, the man kept stoning dogs whenever he saw them.

Throughout the massacre, this man kept silent. Forty-seven years later, the madman was still silent, expressing his memories of the crime he had witnessed through gestures rather than in words. Silence, as the story's narrator puts it, sometimes calms the soul but the tongue naturally hates its weight. Silence is heavy; it is substantial. It is this substance which the narrator presents to us, the readers, in his account of the apparently irrational, but deeply expressive image of the stoning of a dead dog.[2]

This dialogue between words and their absence, with both doing the work of remembrance, is a central theme in this book. Raharimanana's story enables us to glimpse elements of a certain African silence – the one pertaining to the exercise of force and colonial brutality in Sub-Saharan Africa. Moreover, it also deals with another silence that is related directly to the subject of this chapter: the participation of African soldiers, known as the *tirailleurs sénégalais*, in the repression of the Malagasy insurrection in 1947.[3]

This chapter examines some African silences by considering the selective historical narrative of the relationship between France and its ex-colony Senegal, with special reference to the service of the *tirailleurs sénégalais* in the French army during the colonial period. My argument

---

[1] Jean-Luc Raharimanana, 'Fahavalo', in Adele King (ed.), *From Africa: New Francophone Stories* (Lincoln, Neb. and London: University of Nebraska Press, 2004), pp. 93–6. *Fahavalo* means enemy. The French used this term between 1896 and 1948 to designate insurgents.
[2] Raharimanana, 'Fahavalo', p. 94.   [3] Raharimanana, 'Fahavalo', p. 95.

is that silence is part and parcel of remembrance. I use the case of the *tirailleurs sénégalais* to illustrate how Africans have fostered their own silences regarding the colonial past. These silences, like all others, have boundaries that shift over time and can on occasion be broken.

As noted in chapter 1, this volume goes beyond the tendentious view of silence as negative and the speech act as positive. In the following analysis there is no fixed moral value attached to each. Rather, I use remembrance of the *tirailleurs* to uncover the process of the construction, transformation and occasional breach of silences about the past, silences framed and preserved by white and black alike. When former colonial subjects frame silences about their own past, their aim is less likely to be calming the soul, than shaping a usable past which conforms to perceived strategic necessities in the present. Political silences of this kind happen in almost all post-colonial settings, since there were those of the same race or ethnic group who did the dark work of maintaining order, power and domination. This co-exploitation implicated blacks in crimes committed against other blacks, a subject of deep discomfort in the post-colonial period. Silence is a useful strategy for negotiating this difficulty, which informs stories and lacunae about the French African empire. But as in other chapters of this book, silence is not uniform nor absolute. Speech acts are selective, to be sure, but so are silences, especially those which describe the ugliness of a colonial past in which black soldiers broke the protests of black men and women struggling against their French masters. The men in uniform were therefore in a liminal position, half way between the subjugated and the subjugators. The story of their lives and fate both during the two world wars and in the years of decolonisation is redolent with silences, with selective occlusions and exaggerations related to the needs of today more than the events of yesterday.

The structure of this chapter is as follows: I start with a brief survey of the African soldiers' recruitment into the French army. I then examine two contemporary groups of Africans living in France. First I discuss how undocumented African immigrants in France known as the *sans papiers* ('those without documents') use the commemoration of the African soldiers who fought in the two world wars for their own political ends, and in the process produce certain silences regarding other facets of the colonial past. I then examine the silences produced by French Africans in France – meaning African and North African immigrants who hold French citizenship and identify themselves as no less French than African. Next, I turn to discuss silences that are imbedded in the official commemoration of African colonial soldiers in Senegal. We find that different motivations and circumstances create similar selection processes in the soldiers' commemoration in France and in its ex-colony, Senegal.

It should be emphasised, though, that the use of the term 'African' does not imply that the very same kinds of silences are produced in other African countries from which the *tirailleurs* were recruited. Senegal has its own kind of post-colonial relations with France that encourages a certain official image of the colonial past that is not necessarily valid for other African countries. Through the example of the commemoration of a *tirailleurs*' revolt (one that occurred in Thiaroye near Dakar in 1944), I consider the shifting boundaries of what can and cannot be said.

This chapter focuses on the silences produced by the ex-colonised. Obviously, ex-colonisers often attempt to keep certain aspects of their colonial enterprise in the dark. In February 2005, the French government introduced legislation to encourage teachers and scholars to present 'positive' features of the country's colonial past. For instance, it ruled that 'school curricula [must] recognise in particular the positive role of France's overseas presence'.[4] As will be demonstrated in this chapter, the ex-colonisers were not the only participants in the establishment of appropriate silences. Africans also produced their own silences regarding the colonial past. Curiously, French and African silences at times even converged.

African colonial soldiers in the service of France

In 1857, the French recruited throughout French Sub-Saharan Africa the first battalion of African military corps and named it the *tirailleurs sénégalais*.[5] At that time, there was no intention of dispatching them in Europe. However, with the rise of international tensions in Europe before the First World War the idea circulated in France of using African troops within Europe, primarily against Germany. A major promoter of this idea was General Charles Mangin, who maintained in a book he had published in 1910, *La Force noire*, that the falling birth rate in France made the recruitment of African soldiers a necessity.[6] Thus, African soldiers were recruited to fight in Europe, especially after 1916, when French casualties mounted rapidly and following the disastrous 1917 Chemin des Dames offensive, which precipitated mutiny. Some 134,000 *tirailleurs* served in the trenches of the Great War and formed 1.6 per cent of the entire French

---

[4] www.assemblee-nationale.fr/12/dossiers/rapatries.asp.
[5] Myron Echenberg, *Colonial Conscripts: The Tirailleurs Sénégalais in French West Africa, 1857–1960* (Portsmouth, NH: Heinemann, 1991), pp. 7–8.
[6] Jean-Yves Le Naour, *La Honte Noire – L'Allemagne et les Troupes Coloniales Françaises, 1914–1945* (Paris: Hachette, 2004), pp. 16–18.

army. Nearly 30,000 of these African soldiers lost their lives on active service.[7]

In the interwar era African soldiers played a key role in the continental defence of France, and some were deployed during the occupation of the Rhineland, a decision referred to by the Germans as '*der Schwarze Schande*'.[8] Between the outbreak of the Second World War in September 1939 and the fall of France in 1940, about 100,000 soldiers from French West Africa were conscripted into the French army. In 1942 and 1945, a further 100,000 soldiers from West and Central Africa were members of Allied units.[9]

After the Second World War, African colonial soldiers participated in France's wars of decolonisation in Madagascar, Indochina and in the eight-year-long Algerian war. Following the end of French colonial rule in Sub-Saharan Africa in 1960, the units of the *tirailleurs sénégalais* were gradually integrated into the national armies of the new African states.

African silences in France

The African presence in France was enhanced by the recruitment of African soldiers to fight in Europe during the First World War. At the same time, the French government encouraged the immigration of African workers to substitute for French workers who were sent to the trenches. While most of the soldiers and workers were sent back to the colonies after the war, some were allowed to stay. French dependency on African manpower goes back to this period. In the years that followed, African immigrants kept arriving from the French colonies, seeking work and improved living conditions.[10]

During the years of decolonisation, and especially following the Algerian war, a large number of immigrants from France's ex-colonies arrived in France. This massive immigration that continues to this day led to social problems due to the exclusion of and discrimination against a growing number of immigrants and their descendants. Many immigrants

---

[7] Le Naour, *La Honte*, pp. 18–21.

[8] Marc Michel, *Les Africains et la Grand Guerre – L'appel à l'Afrique (1914–1918)* (Paris: Karthala, 2003), p. 234. On the occupation of the Rhineland and the French deployment of colonial troops, see Keith L. Nelson, 'The "Black Horror on the Rhine": Race as a Factor in Post-World War I Diplomacy', *The Journal of Modern History*, 42:4 (1970), pp. 606–27.

[9] Echenberg, *Colonial Conscripts*, p. 88.

[10] On African workers' immigration to France see Tyler Stovall, 'National Identity and Shifting Imperial Frontiers: Whiteness and the Exclusion of Colonial Labor after World War I', *Representations*, 84 (2004), pp. 52–72.

today, who live under harsh conditions and on the margins of the big cities, express resentment toward the French government and feel alienated from French society.

In October 2005, riots erupted in the predominantly immigrant suburbs around Paris, later spreading throughout the country. The anger of the protesters was mainly expressed through the torching of cars. Several months later, the daily *Le Monde* announced, on its front page, the government's decision to construct a memorial for the Muslim soldiers who had died at Verdun during the First World War. Under the headline, 'Les combattants musulmans de 14–18 vont avoir leur mémorial', the newspaper printed a caricature showing an African soldier standing on a memorial bust under the French flag overlooking German burned military vehicles while exclaiming: 'Ah! I remember! We used to burn cars!'[11]

Figure 7.1 A caricature by Plantu, printed in *Le Monde*, 22 February 2006.

[11] *Le Monde*, 22 February 2006, p. 1.

This caricature locates the current tribulations of French society with the commemoration of African soldiers. The massive immigrant population living within France, and the debate over the place of Islam within French society, were understood in the context of African participation in the two world wars. Immigrants reminded France of its colonial past and exploited it for their aims. Indeed, the call to remember African colonial soldiers' sacrifice was linked to the demand for immigrants' equal rights in France today. One of the main themes was defined as the 'blood debt' (*dette de sang*). The *sans-papiers* claimed that France remained indebted to them because their forefathers had fought in the two world wars and contributed to its liberation from Nazi Germany.[12] This is probably what led them to choose major anniversaries of events in the Second World War for their protests. For example, the municipal theatre of the city of Poitiers was occupied by protesters on 8 May 2005 (the sixtieth anniversary of the end of the war in Europe) who demanded the regularisation of immigrants' status.[13] Thus, African immigrants in France demand better treatment in light of an image of the colonial past characterised by a brotherhood-in-arms as well as shared glory and sacrifices. These images carry more than a few silences about that past.

What kind of silences, then, can be identified here? To call attention to the way Africans have earned a place within France, the story of shared sacrifice has to be simplified and disseminated. Up front are heroic images of African soldiers who contributed to the salvation of France; at the margins or out of sight are aspects of the soldiers' past that do not conform to this message. Who and what gets left out? First, only the soldiers who fought in the two world wars are commemorated, while those who fought in France's colonial wars are ignored. The aim of focusing on the world wars is to demonstrate the contribution of the soldiers to France as a nation and not to France as a colonial power.

This is both a general problem and a specifically African one. Antoine Prost, who himself was a soldier in the Algerian war, has shown how difficult it has been to construct a commemorative narrative of that war for French-born soldiers. Some of them saw the war as illegitimate. 'Soldiers without victory, without good causes, and without enthusiasm cannot become positive figures.'[14] This is even more evident in the case of Africans who fought alongside French men in colonial wars. The fact that

[12] Gregory Mann, 'Immigrants and Arguments in France and West Africa', *Comparative Studies in Society and History*, 45:2 (2003), p. 362.

[13] *Agence France Press*, 28 August 2004.

[14] Antoine Prost, 'The Algerian war in French collective memory', in Emmanuel Sivan and Jay Winter (eds.), *War and Remembrance in the Twentieth Century* (Cambridge University Press, 1999), pp. 171–2.

these soldiers fought ostensibly against their 'own people' – although Sub-Saharan Africans and Algerians are definitely not the same people – makes them unsuitable for commemoration. Those who do not symbolise or embody a story with an accepted moral message are bound to be ignored.

Another silence pertains to the French methods of recruitment in the colonies. Many soldiers were recruited by force, often brutally, and this story does not fit into the heroic narrative; silence is its destination. If the soldiers are to be presented as heroes, they cannot at the same time be presented as victims of forced mobilisation and of colonialism.[15] The only kind of victimhood the *sans papiers* refer to is that inflicted by the Germans during the two world wars. The French sin towards the memory of these African soldiers is their current ingratitude, reflected in their treatment of these soldiers' putative descendants – the undocumented African immigrants of today. But of course, not all of the Africans living in France are undocumented immigrants. Many of them hold French citizenship and were even born in France. Some, undoubtedly, feel no less French than African. It is to this group that I now turn. I would like to discuss the narrative produced by two French Africans, a filmmaker and an author, regarding the remembrance of the *tirailleurs*.

Rachid Bouchareb's film *Indigènes* (2006) drew French public attention to the sacrifices of North African soldiers during the liberation of France in 1944 and 1945. Bouchareb, born in France to North African immigrants, testifies he feels 'very French'. His proclaimed aim is 'to tell this little-known chapter of French history because we are part of it'.[16] The film tells the story of four Moroccan soldiers who fought in the Second World War, all but one of whom were killed in a bloody battle in an Alsatian village in 1945. In the last scene, sixty years later, the sole survivor is seen returning to his tiny apartment in a shabby suburb of Paris from a visit to the cemetery where his Moroccan and French comrades are buried.[17] This scene juxtaposes the soldiers' heroic past with the miserable living conditions of immigrants in France today.

---

[15] On the recruitment methods of African soldiers see for example Vincent Joly, 'La mobilization au Soudan en 1939–1940,' *Revue française d'histoire d'outre-mer*, 73:272 (1986), pp. 281–302. In interviews that Joe Lunn conducted between 1976 and 2001, stories of forced recruitment are abundant. For instance, Sara Ndiaye told him of his father's decision to send him rather than his older brother who contributed more to the welfare of the family. Souan Gor Diatta recalls the attempts of his fellow villagers to resist recruitment, and many of the veterans equate the voyage to France with the trans-Atlantic transport of slaves to the New World. Joe Lunn, *Memoirs of the Maelstrom: A Senegalese Oral History of the First World War* (Portsmouth, NH: Heinemann, 1999), pp. 33–51.

[16] http://cineuropa.org/interview.aspx?documentID=64764.

[17] Rachid Bouchareb (dir.), *Indigènes* (France, Algeria and Morocco, 2006, 123 mins.).

Here again, the aim is to present the soldiers as heroes who belong to the French national story. Bouchareb does not ignore cases of discrimination in the past. In one scene the African soldiers do not receive tomatoes during mealtime, as these are reserved for French soldiers. However, this kind of discrimination is presented as coming from higher military authorities who see the African soldiers as *indigènes* (natives) unlike their French sergeant who prefers to call them *hommes* (men). The film, once more, focuses on the Second World War and is silent regarding the recruitment methods the French used in North Africa. Although it begins with a scene of recruitment, all the recruits volunteer to join the army. Some do it for money, others for hope of being respected and rewarded, but none is compelled to join up.

Bouchareb's film targets two major audiences. First and foremost, those immigrants and their descendants who are French by citizenship but do not feel integrated within French society. Secondly, it targets the French general public, whom Bouchareb sees as ignorant of the colonial subjects' contribution to the liberation of France. Here too, the emphasis is on a shared past of sacrifice and glory, and forced recruitment is ignored yet again.

Another French African contribution to the discussion of the colonial soldiers is a series of illustrated storybooks titled *La Patrouille du Caporal Samba* (The Patrol of Corporal Samba). The author, Fayez Samb (the eponymous hero of the series), lives in France and is a son of a *tirailleur* from Senegal and a French mother. To date, three booklets have been published (2003, 2004 and 2007). The first, *Les Tirailleurs Sénégalais à Lyons*, tells the story of the capture and massacre of African soldiers by the Germans in June 1940 in the village of Chasseley near Lyons.[18] The second booklet, *Le Naufrage de l'Africa*,[19] features the 1920 tragedy of the ship *L'Afrique*, which sank en route home; a large number of African soldiers drowned in the incident.[20] The third, *Le Tirailleur de Vosges*, pays homage to a Guinean *tirailleur* who was active in the French resistance movement during the Second World War and was executed by the Germans in 1943.[21]

Samb's three booklets focus again on the two world wars, and especially on the second. He emphasises the integration of the *tirailleurs* into French military history in the first booklet, by citing Rimbaud's poem,

---

[18] Fayez Samb, *Tirailleurs Sénégalais à Lyon* (Paris: L'Harmattan, 2003).
[19] According to the author, he used the name 'Africa' and not 'Afrique' because he did not want to sound 'Afro-pessimist'.
[20] Fayez Samb, *Le Naufrage de l'Africa* (Paris: L'Harmattan, 2004).
[21] Fayez Samb, *Le Tirailleur de Vosges* (Paris: L'Harmattan, 2007).

'Le Dormeur du Val' (1870). Under an image of a *tirailleur* lying on the ground with his rifle beside him, Samb inserted the poem's famous line: 'Il dort dans le soleil, la main sur sa poitrine. Tranquille ... Il a deux trous rouges au côté droit' (He sleeps in the sun, hand on his chest. Tranquil ... He has two red holes on his right side).[22] The use of this line (written following the Franco-Prussian War and emphasising the evil of wars in general) in relation to African soldiers, clarifies how the author wishes to remember the *tirailleurs* – as part of the French nation and as its heroes, not its victims.

Samb touches on the issue of recruitment and the African resistance to fight for France. The story of the massacre in Chasselay opens with several recruits refusing to go to France by simply stating the word 'no'. One of them explains his refusal in broken French (associated in France with the manner in which the *tirailleurs* spoke French) as follows: 'Moi, pas aller faire guerre ... ni libérer terre de France! Eux actuellement occuper terre à moi, frères devraient plutôt résister à français, ici sur terre Afrique!' (I'm neither going to war nor to liberate France! They now occupy my land, brothers must resist the French, here in the land of Africa!).[23] Finally, Muslim religious leaders persuade the soldier to enlist. If there is any criticism here regarding the role of African Muslim leaders, it is very subtle. 'Why do we have to go to war in France?' asks another African recruit and the answer is twofold: first, the French might bestow freedom on their colonies in return for African participation in war; second, the soldiers will be the first to see Paris.[24] Yet there is no mention of the fact that the French abstained from granting its African colonies freedom at the end of the war or that most *tirailleurs* never reached Paris. In fact, Charles de Gaulle 'whitened' the French army before the victorious troops entered Paris in August 1944.[25]

Like Bouchareb's film, the audience for Samb's comic books is the general French public as well as the immigrants living in France. He targets the younger audience (by way of cartoons), to expose them to forgotten chapters in French history. In a radio interview Samb explained that his aim was to revive the memory of the *tirailleurs* and expose readers to the hardships they had endured during the two world wars.[26] It seems that he had hoped African youth would feel less alienated by knowing of African participation in these sacred moments in French history and in a

---

[22] Samb, *Tirailleurs Sénégalais*, p. 37.   [23] Ibid., p. 7.   [24] Ibid., p. 5.

[25] Le Naour, *La Honte*, pp. 247–8. According to Le Naour, this process continued during the autumn and winter of 1944. The sixth regiment of the *tirailleurs sénégalais*, for example, that was originally ninety per cent black, had no black soldiers at all by October 1944.

[26] RFI, 27 March 2005.

parallel way, French youth would see immigrants as brothers in sacrifice rather than as foreigners.

As we have seen, Africans in France, whether recently arrived illegal immigrants or well-established descendants of immigrants (who hold French citizenship), foster similar kinds of silences with regards to the *tirailleurs*. While breaking the silence regarding the contribution of African colonial soldiers, they create other silences. For instance, they, too, abstain from a public discussion regarding the forced recruitment of Africans and the wars of decolonisation in which Africans participated on behalf of the French. This narrative, in fact, obscures the fact that military recruitment was simply part and parcel of the French colonial repression in Africa. Now let us turn to Senegal in particular and consider the silences embedded in the official commemoration of the *tirailleurs*.

Silences within official commemoration in Senegal

Until quite recently, Senegal did not commemorate the *tirailleurs sénégalais* at all. Following independence (in 1960), the Senegalese government did not remove colonial war memorials erected by the French in central cities, primarily Dakar and Saint Louis. However, no attention was paid to these monuments. In the 1980s, Abdou Diouf's government removed several colonial monuments from the centre of Dakar. This was done mainly in order to appease public protests against France's neo-colonial relations with Senegal. One of the monuments removed was a memorial for French and African soldiers who perished in the First World War. This memorial, popularly known as the 'Demba and Dupont Monument', depicted two soldiers – an African and a Frenchman – raising their rifles above the inscription: '*Vers la victoire*'. It was relegated to a Catholic cemetery on the city's outskirts, undoubtedly a marginal site in a predominantly Muslim country.[27] This removal reflected the marginality accorded by the Senegalese government to the commemoration of the *tirailleurs*.

---

[27] www.ldh-toulon.net/article.php3?id_article=298. On the monument and its various movements see Ruth Ginio, 'African colonial soldiers between Remembrance and Forgetting: The Case of Post-colonial Senegal', *Outre-mers: Revue d'histoire*, 94: 350–1 (2006), pp. 141–55 and Brigitte Reinwald, 'Recycling the Empire's Unknown Soldier – Contested Memories of French West African Colonial Combatants' War Experience', in Indra Sengupta (ed.), *Memory, History and Colonialism: Engaging with Pierre Nora in Colonial and Postcolonial Contexts*, Supplement of the Bulletin of the German Historical Institute, No. 1 (London, 2009), pp. 37–70. I would like to thank the author for sending me her article before its publication.

Only in 2004, following a grand French ceremony commemorating the African soldiers who liberated Provence in 1944, did the Senegalese government issue a law that established 23 August as the annual Memorial Day for the *tirailleurs* (not only the Senegalese) who perished in the two world wars. In addition, it initiated a major commemorative project whereby Place de la Gare in central Dakar (renamed Place du Tirailleur) was designated to be the memorial site for the two world wars. This project, completed in 2006, saw the return of Demba and Dupont; the forgotten monument was reinstalled in the new square.[28]

The above mentioned changes encouraged public commemoration of the soldiers of the two world wars, but at the same time enhanced certain silences. The choice of date for Memorial Day and its definition can be understood as silencing mechanisms. The commemorated soldiers are only those who perished in the two world wars while the others are ignored; 23 August is the day on which the city of Toulon in the south of France was liberated, an event in which an especially large proportion of African soldiers participated. The focus here, once more, is on the Second World War and the *tirailleurs'* heroism in France.

The Senegalese government takes care to include veterans in official ceremonies. Veterans thus contribute to the enforcement of the narrative of a past of shared glory and sacrifices, even if like all veterans, they carry personal recollections of war, which sometimes contradict this narrative. Veterans take part in this official commemoration in large part to support their demands for equal pensions.[29] Nevertheless, Reinwald observes that as veterans' frustration increases due to the delay in the payment of pensions, they might begin to challenge the official narrative of Franco-Senegalese brotherhood.[30]

How can we explain this official Senegalese line? Emphasising the soldiers' participation in the two world wars and their sacrifices for France helps the Senegalese government construct amicable relations with France; Senegal is thus not a nation of victims who deserve recompense, but rather one of equal partners, worthy of respect and gratitude. This point is evident in a documentary on the *tirailleurs* produced by the

---

[28] www.aps.sn/dossier_tirailleurs.htm.

[29] In 1950 France equated *tirailleurs*, pensions to those of French soldiers, but nine years later it decided to return to a lower pension payment, after African colonies gained their independence. Therefore, after 1 January 1961, the French state paid its pensioners in those countries at a fixed rate, which it raised irregularly. Ever since then, African veterans' organisations struggled for the equation of their pensions. On this struggle and the narrative it produced see Gregory Mann, *Native Sons: West African Veterans and France in the Twentieth Century* (Durham, NC and London: Duke University Press, 2006), pp. 183–209.

[30] Reinwald, 'Recycling the Empire's Unknown Soldier', p. 67.

Senegalese government in 2004. In the film, titled *Devoir de Mémoire* (A Duty to Remember), the incumbent President Abdoulaye Wade asserts: 'We want to show to the world that we had done our bit, that we had contributed. This can become a basis for a new kind of relations because we are being marginalised in this world. We live on the periphery of the economic evolution of the world. Perhaps this is not done consciously or deliberately, I do not think so. But it is the historical evolution in which we are on the margins and I think this is unacceptable. This is why we struggle to gain our place.'[31] No wonder much is left to oblivion when commemoration is primarily about contemporary relations between Senegal and France.

But there is one event that is not so easy to ignore in Senegal – the French violent repression of a *tirailleurs'* uprising in Camp Thiaroye, near Dakar, on 1 December 1944. The events of Thiaroye contradict the narrative of Franco-African brotherhood and of shared glory and sacrifices. The story of the commemoration of Thiaroye demonstrates the flexibility of the boundaries of silence. At the same time, it also shows that breaking the silence surrounding the events at Thiaroye can nevertheless keep on obscuring its significance.

Shifting boundaries of silence: Commemorating the uprising at Thiaroye

In November 1944, after long periods of imprisonment in German camps, 1,280 African soldiers returned to Dakar and were placed in a camp outside the city. The poor conditions in the camp combined with the refusal of the French commanders to pay the soldiers' wages for their period of captivity or to give them a demobilisation premium precipitated a revolt. The men refused to be transported back to their respective colonies, knowing that if they returned home, their chances of receiving their due payment were zero. The soldiers prevented General Dagen, commander-in-chief of the forces in the Dakar area, from leaving the camp. The French declared these actions constituted a mutiny. A special commando of *tirailleurs sénégalais* from Saint Louis and the Dakar Gendarmerie took over the camp and on the morning of 1 December

---

[31] *Devoir de Mémoire*, documentary film produced by the Republic of Senegal in collaboration with Cheick Tidiane Ndiaye (2004, 23 mins.). I would like to thank Professor Ibrahima Thioub from Cheick Anta Diop University in Dakar for giving me a copy of the film. The documentary discusses the injustices suffered by the *tirailleurs* and does not ignore Thiaroye, but the main grievance is related to the lack of recognition of the soldiers' contribution to France.

opened fire on the soldiers, killing thirty-five and wounding many more.[32]

Tirailleurs who took part in the repression later claimed that the French led them to believe that they were sent to confront German internees refusing to hand over their arms.[33] In any case, the fact that the actual killing of the protesting soldiers was performed by other *tirailleurs* was hardly ever mentioned in later years.

Following the repression of the revolt, the French military authorities censored letters and news reports about the events of Thiaroye. Until quite recently, the French ignored Thiaroye and attempted to erase its memory. Only in December 2004, on Thiaroye's sixtieth anniversary, did the French Minister of Cooperation and Francophony, Pierre-André Wiltzer, refer publicly to the event. Speaking on behalf of President Chirac, he noted that Thiaroye was a tragic and shocking event, which stained France's image.[34] This was the first time ever that the French government acknowledged its responsibility. But this French silence regarding Thiaroye is not a surprising one. What concerns us here is not the silence of the colonisers but rather the less obvious one of the colonised.

Initially, there was much talk of these violent events. In spite of the French army's efforts, news about Thiaroye spread like wildfire among the Africans serving in the Allied units. After 1947, censorship was lifted from the debate over the amnesty for soldiers who were arrested for their part in the mutiny. African veterans and civilians were well aware of the event, which came to be known as 'the massacre of Thiaroye'. Reinwald, who collected oral histories among veterans, states that 'Thiaroye leaves no African veteran – whether contemporary or younger – untouched.'[35]

On the official level, however, the reaction to Thiaroye was more complex. Immediately after the events, in 1944, Léopold Sédar Senghor, poet and politician (who would later become Senegal's first president in 1960), published a poem opening with the following line: 'Prisonniers noirs, je dis bien prisonniers français, est-ce donc vrai que la France n'est plus la France?' ('Black prisoners, and I insist French prisoners, is it true that France is no longer France?').[36] Senghor was shocked by France's ingratitude towards its African soldiers. Nevertheless, as a politician, he erased Thiaroye from the Senegalese national narrative, placing his country's

---

[32] On Thiaroye, see Myron Echenberg, 'Tragedy at Thiaroye: The Senegalese Soldiers' Uprising of 1944', in Peter Gutkind, Robin Cohen and Jean Copans (eds.), *African Labor History* (Beverly Hills and London: Sage Publications, 1978), pp. 109–27.

[33] Reinwald, 'Recycling the Empire's Unknown Soldier', p. 57 note 51.

[34] *Libération*, 1 December 2004.

[35] Reinwald, 'Recycling the Empire's Unknown Soldier', p. 58.

[36] Léopold Sédar Senghor, 'Tyaroye' (from *Hosties noires*), in *Œuvre poétique* (Paris: Points, 1990), pp. 90–1.

relations with France in the forefront. Successive Senegalese governments continued to neglect Thiaroye and its site, leaving the place unmarked. And yet this erasure was not wholly successful. For many Africans, Thiaroye became a symbol of colonial repression. Before independence in 1960, various anti-colonial movements and associations, such as the West African movement *Rassemblement Démocratique Africain*, strove to turn Thiaroye's military cemetery (where the victims of the massacre were buried) into a memorial site. In the years that followed independence, opposition groups held clandestine ceremonies there. The commemoration of Thiaroye became a way to challenge the ruling party at a time when opposition parties were incorporated or banned and the regime in Senegal became a one-party system.[37]

The move to a democratised multi-party political system in the mid 1970s led to further attempts at breaking the official silence regarding Thiaroye. In 1981, the Senegalese author and playwright Boubacar Boris Diop published *Thiaroye, Terre Rouge* (Thiaroye, Red Soil). This play focused on the discrimination against African soldiers and depicted their killing as a carefully pre-planned act. In the last scene, the slain soldiers are resurrected and one points at the audience saying: 'Look at them; they came to see a play and they say to themselves: "It is beautiful like poetry, the death of the innocent!" I tell you: You have no right to feel warm and peaceful while we are rotting under the ground!'[38] Diop points this finger of accusation at those in Senegal who participated in the silence over Thiaroye.

More influential than Diop's play was Ousmane Sembene's 1987 film *Camp Thiaroye*. Despite many historical inaccuracies, it further lifted the veil of silence about this subject.[39] Popular Senegalese music since the 1990s also makes reference to French discrimination and to Thiaroye, arguing that French exploitation of Africans did not end with independence.[40]

The events at Thiaroye have now been commemorated. Since 2004, this story entered official commemoration, and the government finally refurbished the cemetery and constructed a monument at its centre.[41] On

---

[37] Reinwald, 'Recycling the Empire's Unknown Soldier', p. 59.

[38] Boubacar Boris Diop, *Le Temps de Tamango* (Paris: L'Harmattan, 1981), p. 203. This theme of the 'return of the dead' was originally brought to the fore by Abel Gance's film *J'accuse* in 1918. See Jay Winter, *Sites of Memory, Sites of Mourning: The Great War in European Cultural History* (Cambridge University Press, 1995), pp. 18–22.

[39] Ousmane Sembene (dir.), *Camp de Thiaroye* (Algeria, Tunisia, Senegal, 1988, 153 mins.).

[40] For example, Ismaël Lo, 'Nassarane', *Iso* (Paris, 1994). Attempts to break the silence around Thiaroye took place in France as well by French and African artists, journalists and historians. See for example Bouchareb's short film *L'Ami, Y'a Bon* (2004, 9 mins.) and Armelle Mabon's documentary film *Oubliés et Trahis* (2003, 53 mins.).

[41] Colonel Mamadou Lamdou Touré, *Les Tirailleurs Sénégalais: Leurs Combats, leurs Gloires, leur Heritages* (Dakar: Les 3 Orangers, 2005), p. 49.

the Memorial Day for the *tirailleurs*, the president lays a wreath in memory of the *tirailleurs* who were killed in Thiaroye. But in fact, a closer look reveals that in spite of these commemorative gestures, much remains obscured. First, the president does not lay the wreath on the day of the massacre – 1 December; rather on the official memorial date, 23 August, marking the liberation of Toulon in the south of France in 1944. Secondly, nowhere in the cemetery can one find a description of the historical events that led to the death of the soldiers. The only words inscribed on the newly built monument are: '*À nos morts*' (To our dead). The layman strolling into the cemetery will neither know how these men died nor why. Speech, we see, can sometimes lead to forgetting as well.

Conclusions

Unlike the silences embedded in the French story of the *tirailleurs sénégalais* and that of colonialism in general, African silences seem surprising at first glance. It is clear why the French government was hesitant in acknowledging the brutal repression at Thiaroye. Less obvious are the sources of African silences. Those produced by Africans living in France, be they French citizens or illegal immigrants, are the outcome of attempts to become an integral part of French society. Africans in France tend to highlight a shared past of sacrifice. Illegal immigrants use this historical argument mainly as a political tool to demand the regularisation of their status. African Frenchmen and women highlight it in order to enhance a sense of belonging, especially relevant to alienated African youth living on the margins of society. They target the French public in an attempt to make it more receptive to the assimilation of immigrants.

African silences in Senegal are encouraged primarily by the official line, emphasising a long-lasting friendship between the two states. Some African leaders prefer the image of their people as supporters of the ex-colonial power rather than as victims of colonialism. This past brotherhood-in-arms justifies present demands for economic aid and close diplomatic relations.

Hence, as we see, both colonised and coloniser have their reasons to maintain silences. Yet we also discover that the boundaries of these strategic silences are seldom static. Changing political circumstances, cultural responses and academic research based on oral interviews, can at any given point change the boundaries of silence or even totally break it; if silence is socially constructed, it can also be socially reshaped and deconstructed.

8   Now that all is said and done: Reflections on
the Truth and Reconciliation Commission in
South Africa*

Louise Bethlehem

The witness: speaking out

In 1998, four years after the transition to democracy in South Africa, a
five-volume Report answerable to the formal mandate of South Africa's
Truth and Reconciliation Commission (TRC) was tabled on the public
agenda there. The Commission, a crucial dimension of South Africa's
negotiated settlement, was empowered to grant amnesty to politically
motivated perpetrators of all affiliations in return for the full disclosure
of their offences. But the Commission's power to confer amnesty did not
exhaust its role. No less significantly, the Truth and Reconciliation
Commission was instituted in order to "[afford] victims an opportunity
to relate the violations they suffered" and was required to "[report] to the
Nation about such violations and victims."[1]

Through the workings of its various committees, the TRC called forth
individual and collective acts of testimony on an unprecedented scale.
The narratives of approximately 22,000 victims were elicited and processed.[2] Roughly ten percent of these were heard in the public hearings
across South Africa which became the hallmark of the TRC. Such acts of
breaking silence were integral to the "restorative justice" that the
Commission sought to implement. In the words of its Report, "People
came to the Commission to tell their stories in an attempt to facilitate not
only their individual healing process, but also a healing process for the
entire nation."[3] Testimony was seen as fundamental to the catharsis
deemed necessary for the therapeutic reconstitution of the post-apartheid

---

* In memory of Tania Forte whose anthropology remains, in her absence, a summons to
  witness.
[1] "Promotion of National Unity and Reconciliation Act," No. 34 of 1995, www.doj.gov.za/
  trc/legal/act9534.htm, accessed 15 July 2007.
[2] Don Foster, Paul Haupt and Marésa de Beer, *The Theatre of Violence: Narratives of
  Protagonists in the South African Conflict* (Pretoria: Institute for Justice and
  Reconciliation, HSRC Press, James Currey, 2005), p. 22.
[3] Truth and Reconciliation Commission, South Africa, *Report*, 5 vols. (Cape Town: Juta and
  Co., 1998), vol. 5, p. 69.

nation, an understanding incipient in Archbishop Desmond Tutu's remarks in his opening address to the Commission as its Chair. "We are a wounded people" he stated. "[...] We all stand in need of healing."[4]

One year after the initial TRC report, another document would emerge into the public domain as South Africans continued their reckoning with the apartheid past: J. M. Coetzee's 1999 novel, *Disgrace*.[5] The novel was the immediate focus of international acclaim, earning its author the Booker Prize for an unprecedented second time. But within South Africa, *Disgrace* was the subject of some notoriety – controversial precisely to the extent that it resonated with the unresolved tensions of the post-apartheid moment. The novel seemed to tap a malaise that still resided in the nation as a bitter residue of the apartheid past. Its pessimism was irreconcilable with the reconciliatory passing of judgment on that very past which the Truth and Reconciliation Commission apparently offered.

In the analysis that follows, I will chart the manner in which *Disgrace* interrupts the Truth and Reconciliation Commission's elaborate, even extravagant, staging of speech for the newly democratic South Africa. I offer the novel as one point of entry into the shared concerns of this volume: memory and the social construction of silence. But in doing so, I am not making a claim for the evidentiary status of *Disgrace*. The novel pointedly does not record the working of the Truth and Reconciliation Commission in the manner of Antjie Krog's remarkable *Country of My Skull*, a documentary text heightened by extraordinary moments of fic-tionalization.[6] It does not entertain the elegiac quality of Ingrid de Kok's poetry, elicited in response to the testimony of victims who appeared before the Human Rights' Violations Committee.[7] Nor does it contain uncompromising criticism of the Truth and Reconciliation Commission along the lines of Njabulo Ndebele's scathing work of metafiction, *The Cry of Winnie Mandela*.[8] Crucially for our purposes, however, *Disgrace* inter-rogates the conditions of possibility of testimony at a time when few South Africans questioned the axiom that the Commission's very capacity to give voice to the stories formerly silenced by the apartheid regime itself served as a sufficient measure of political transition.

Whereas access to speech is posited as properly, or better still, justly restorative within the discursive regime of the Truth and Reconciliation

---

[4] Desmond Tutu, *No Future without Forgiveness* (London: Rider Books, 1999), p. 87.
[5] A sixth volume of the TRC Report reviewing the findings of the Amnesty Committee, together with a seventh volume listing all victims was presented to President Thabo Mbeki in March 2003.
[6] Antjie Krog, *Country of My Skull* (Johannesburg: Random House, 1998).
[7] Ingrid de Kok, *Seasonal Fires: Selected and New Poems* (New York: Seven Stories Press, 2006).
[8] Njabulo S. Ndebele, *The Cry of Winnie Mandela* (Cape Town: David Philip, 2003).

Commission, it is more skeptically weighted in *Disgrace*. In line with Coetzee's longstanding mistrust of a mimetic poetics,[9] the TRC is literally absent from his text. The novel unsettles the claims of the Commission, while clearly remaining irreducible to the latter's institutional mechanisms, or discursive repertoires. Through positing the novel as an oblique response, nevertheless, to the testimonial practices associated with the Commission, I seek to revisit the latter. What silences might still inhere in the South African social fabric, I will ask, despite the public culture of confession, which the Commission instituted there?

This attempt to listen differently to the Truth and Reconciliation Commission is strung out between affirmation of the Commission and a certain unwillingness to allow this very affirmation to become prematurely triumphant. Yet this note of anticipatory caution must itself attend on a frank enumeration of the Commission's achievements. They are not inconsiderable. Let it not be forgotten that apartheid generated its own forms of silence, its own patterns of denialism and official mechanisms of deniability. So much so, that the Afrikaans novelist André Brink once stated that the writer's function under apartheid was to ensure that "the terrible excuse of Nuremberg is not heard again."[10] Brink holds the distinction of being the first white Afrikaans novelist to have had his fiction banned by the State. The apartheid regime was notorious, among other things, for the incommunicado detention and solitary confinement of activists; for banning orders restricting dissidents' freedom of speech, movement, and association; as well as for a punitive apparatus of censorship which strenuously limited the circulation of information in the written and electronic media. Apartheid South Africa shared the features of many other zones of political emergency where, as Allen Feldman reminds us, "the normalization and routinization of violence was accompanied by structures of deniability built into the very strategy of violent enactment. In other words, political terror not only attacks the witness but also the cultural capacity and resources needed to bear witness, particularly if we consider cultural memory as a performative medium requiring agents, spaces, and reserved temporalities for anamnesis."[11] The Truth and Reconciliation Commission, viewed as a performative medium in Feldman's sense, provided institutionalized redress for the occlusion of witness in apartheid South Africa.

---

[9] David Attwell, *J. M. Coetzee: South Africa and the Politics of Writing* (Berkeley, Los Angeles, Oxford: University of California Press; Cape Town, Johannesburg: David Philip, 1993), pp. 10–17.

[10] André Brink, *Mapmakers: Writing in a State of Siege* (London and Boston: Faber and Faber, 1983), p. 152.

[11] Allen Feldman, "Memory Theaters, Virtual Witnessing, and the Trauma-Aesthetic," *Biography* XXVII, 1 (2004), p. 172.

Through the mechanism of the Truth and Reconciliation Commission, the South African body politic was able to move from quiescence to revelation in tandem with the witness who moved from the quietude that necessarily precedes address as is its physical precondition to speech.[12] Witness in the present, witness before the Truth and Reconciliation Commission, allowed the victim to renegotiate the absence of past witness and thus to create the retrospective condition of its possibility so that the therapeutic reintegration of the self might be facilitated.[13] But the implications of testimony exceeded the circumference of the individual witness, not only because testimony elucidated the contours of a collective past, but also because the performance of testimony inscribed a "discontinuous historicity" in the public sphere, as Richard Wilson has argued. The Commission can be said to have enacted a temporal rite of separation wherein the new nation separated itself from its past in a foundational act of self-division.[14] Thus, the act of breaking silence under the mantle of the Commission can also be said to contain a certain excess which is irreducible to the referential content of the narratives it staged. The excess which emerges from testimony is, at a certain level of abstraction, nothing less than the disjunctive sovereignty of the new South Africa under non-racial constitutional nationalism[15] – even if this discontinuity is one aspect of the Commission's rationale that *Disgrace* will serve to cast into question. But if the TRC implicitly speaks in excess of the speech it facilitates, it also inscribes certain forms of lack. This is neither a matter of cynicism, nor of selective memory in its agential aspects, that is to say, as related to the vagaries of individual testimony. Rather it proceeds from certain constraints that are as much structural as ideological.

The witness: spoken to

The witness speaks; certain consequences attend. But in a sense, the victim does not speak until spoken to, until interpellated under the summons of the Truth Commission. That this summons is necessarily selective has long been noted. That it allows for the articulation of certain social

[12] Amit Pinchevski, "Freedom from Speech (Or the Silent Demand)," *diacritics* XXXI, 2 (2001), p. 74.
[13] See Dori Laub for this argument with respect to Holocaust testimony: "Truth and Testimony: The Process and the Struggle," in Cathy Caruth (ed.), *Trauma: Explorations in Memory* (Baltimore and London: Johns Hopkins University Press, 1995), pp. 69–70.
[14] Richard A. Wilson, *The Politics of Truth and Reconciliation in South Africa: Legitimising the Post-Apartheid State* (Cambridge University Press, 2001), pp. 16–17.
[15] Ibid., pp. 1–18.

truths and silences others has, and must, also be stated. Existing critiques of the TRC have focused on its procedural, gendered, and performative dimensions. In the first instance, it has been observed that the Commission avoids "race" and "racism" as analytical and political categories, leading to an emaciated understanding of social causation.[16] Moreover, critics have argued that the TRC's focus on gross violations of human rights obscures the ability to see apartheid in appropriately structural and systemic terms.[17] If issues such as the dispossession of black South Africans and their forced removals from their land are not addressed, argued Mahmood Mamdani, then the injustice accessed by the TRC is no longer that of apartheid in its specific social manifestations: forced removals, pass laws, broken families. Mamdani cautions against a definition of justice limited to human rights abuses – detention, torture, or murder – committed within the legal framework of apartheid. "The Commission's analysis," he argues, "reduced apartheid from a relationship between the state and entire communities to one between the state and individuals," thus obliterating what he holds to be a "central characteristic of apartheid."[18]

The structural omissions of the TRC were compounded by its mandate. The Commission was empowered to adjudicate only politically motivated acts of human rights violation, leaving it ill-equipped to process and record the fractal causalities of the internecine conflicts which occurred at the time of the negotiated transition (1990–4) between the African National Congress and the Inkatha Freedom Party. An estimated 14,000 South Africans died in these conflicts, more fatalities than were incurred during the mass insurrection and state repression of the entire decade of the eighties.[19] Perpetrators of

---

[16] Deborah Posel, "The TRC Report: What Kind of History? What Kind of Truth?," in Deborah Posel and Graeme Simpson (eds.), *Commissioning the Past: Understanding South Africa's Truth and Reconciliation Commission* (Johannesburg: Witwatersrand University Press, 2002), p. 165; Madeleine Fullard, *Dis-placing Race: The South African Truth and Reconciliation Commission (TRC) and Interpretations of Violence* (Braamfontein: Centre for the Study of Violence and Reconciliation, 2004).

[17] See inter alia Mahmood Mamdani, "Reconciliation without Justice," South *African Review of Books* XLVI (1996), pp. 3–5; Mahmood Mamdani, "A Diminished Truth," in W. James and L. de Vijver (eds.), *After the TRC: Reflections on Truth and Reconciliation in South Africa* (Athens, OH: Ohio University Press; Cape Town: David Philip, 2000), pp. 58–61; and Mahmood Mamdani, "Amnesty or Impunity: A Preliminary Critique of the Report of the Truth and Reconciliation Commission of South Africa (TRC)," *diacritics* XXXII, 3–4 (2002), pp. 33–4. See also Jeremy Cronin, "A luta dis-continua? The TRC Final Report and the Nation Building Project," paper presented at "The TRC: Commissioning the Past" Conference, University of the Witwatersrand, June 11–14, 1999; and Posel, "The TRC Report."

[18] Mamdani, "Amnesty or Impunity," pp. 33–4.   [19] Wilson, *The Politics of Truth*, p. 63.

violation could not easily be differentiated from victims in such contexts, as the epistemology of the Commission required. Nor could the economic causalities of specifically situated nodes of violence, such as occurred in the blood-soaked Kathorus township, be rendered legible.[20] The intricately blurred relationship between criminal and political activities during the final phases of apartheid proved similarly resistant to the Commission's grasp.[21]

Admittedly, the Commission's selection of "window cases" for public hearings did allow for some flexibility in elucidating the interpretive grids and phenomenologies of victims. Some caution is appropriate here, however. The pragmatic aspirations of witnesses did not always coincide seamlessly with the Commission's priorities.[22] Nor were their performances undifferentiated. Whereas the Commission's statement forms or "protocols" were premised on the forms of rationality associated with a literate bureaucracy and privileged statistical analysis and data-processing,[23] many witnesses favored the performance repertoires of oral culture.

This point deserves emphasis, particularly with respect to women's testimony. Consider that women were often cast as "secondary witnesses" before the Human Rights' Violation Committee where they testified regarding the violation of a kinsman – husband, brother, or son. Their own experiences, as critics have pointed out, were subordinated to this orientation-towards-the-other. Such testimony does not, at first sight, appear to address the harm suffered by these women in their own right. Yet evidence of injury to the self can be made to emerge from women's oral testimony, Fiona Ross has argued, despite the fact that the Commission does not typically elicit certain repertoires of response to apartheid – particularly that of the female political activist.[24] The

---

[20] Phillip Bonner and Noor Nieftagodien, "The Truth and Reconciliation Commission and the Pursuit of "social truth": The Case of Kathorus," in Posel and Simpson (eds.), *Commissioning the Past*, pp. 173–203; Ivor Chipkin, "Nationalism as Such: Violence during South Africa's Political Transition," *Public Culture* XVI, 2 (2004), pp. 315–35.

[21] Piers Pigou, "False Promises and Wasted Opportunities? Inside South Africa's Truth and Reconciliation Commission," in Posel and Simpson (eds.), *Commissioning the Past*, p. 43; Wilson, *The Politics of Truth*, pp. 81–94.

[22] Wilson, *The Politics of Truth*, p. 129; Heidi Grunebaum-Ralph, "Re-Placing Pasts, Forgetting Presents: Narrative, Place and Memory in the Time of the Truth and Reconciliation Commission," *Research in African Literatures* XXXII, 3 (2001), pp. 198– 212.

[23] Wilson, *The Politics of Truth*, pp. 33–61; Lars Buur, "Monumental History: Managing Truth in the Everyday Work of the South African Truth and Reconciliation Commission," in Posel and Simpson (eds.), *Commissioning the Past*, pp. 77–80.

[24] Fiona C. Ross, *Bearing Witness: Women and the Truth and Reconciliation Commission in South Africa* (London, Sterling, Virginia: Pluto Press, 2003), pp. 51–9.

absence of certain kinds of referential content in women's testimony, arising from the Commission's inattentiveness to the patterning of agency that devolves from women's constructs of domesticity and temporality,[25] might well signal the lacuna we are calling "silence" but this silence is neither empty nor meaningless. "Power traverses the unsaid" claims Ross. "It alerts us to the need for care: diverse ways of telling have different qualities, and silences are not neutral or homogenous or uniform in their effects."[26]

Not by way of illustration

The notion of illustration provides a means of condensing many of my concerns with the Commission's production of what can loosely be termed "secondary" silences. "To illustrate," writes Adam Sitze, 'is not merely "to illuminate" or "to clarify." It is also "to demonstrate or prove by way of example or instance."[27] To some extent, the singularity of individual testimony before the Truth Commission is necessarily undermined by the synecdochal or part-whole relations obtaining between the witness and the "apartheid past." This is not to suggest that testimony is cynically instrumentalized. Rather, Sitze claims, we would do well to consider these constraints to derive from the Commission's purchase over sovereignty: "*No public testimony that does not already represent the new nation* was the silent injunction of the normative power that, prior to any single public testimony, established the possibility of reading any singly public testimony as an illustration of apartheid as a whole."[28] Singular testimony, reiterates Sitze, "cannot be separated from the techniques of filtration, selection, and exclusion that preceded and produced the specifically illustrative power of testimony given before the Commission."[29] Put differently, the construction of the victim as universal subject or as template for the citizen of the newly sovereign state translates, through traducing, the singularity of the victim who testifies in her own name. This is the most general condition of testimony under the sovereign contract of the Commission. It constrains, but does not wholly preclude, the emergence of something else: an ambiguous

[25] Ibid., pp. 42–5.   [26] Ibid., p. 50.
[27] Adam Sitze, "Articulating Truth and Reconciliation in South Africa: Sovereignty, Testimony, Protest Writing" (unpublished Ph.D. dissertation, University of Minnesota, May 2003).
[28] Ibid., p. 30, emphasis in original.   [29] Ibid.

residue, a residual ambiguity that cannot wholly be recuperated under the sign of the reconstituted post-apartheid State.[30]

Staging such a disruption courts the risk of falling back upon mere exemplarity. I will nevertheless evoke its possibility in deference to the speech of a black South African woman whose elliptical address helps circumvent "illustration".[31] Eunice Nombulelo Ngubo enacts the hiatus as we have anticipated when she stakes a claim to social reparation that has distinctly unsettling reverberations. "The reason why I came before the Commission is because we do not have a home. We stay in shacks. If the Commission could build us a house please."[32] Ngubo, who twice lost her home in the Cradock township when it was burnt down after her brother was accused of being a police informer, reminds us that not "all is quiet" for the deponent before she speaks.[33] Despite her liberation into speech, which is precisely one mark of the citizen's freedom in post-apartheid South Africa, Ngubo does not testify in advance of the range of possibilities that the Commission establishes. The deviant syntax of her singular appeal may be set against the "silent injunction"[34]

---

[30] For a similar claim, see Mark Sanders: "[Witnesses] were, in practice, sometimes able to state demands in terms other than those anticipated in the vocabulary of universal human rights," in *Ambiguities of Witnessing: Law and Literature in the Time of a Truth Commission* (Stanford University Press, 2007), p. 4. I have mobilized the term "ambiguity" here in order to signal the broader contours of Mark Sanders' finely nuanced and theoretically innovative treatment of the Commission. Sanders extends the insight I have quoted in order to elucidate a "systematic ambiguity" which the TRC hearings set to work, relating this to a propensity "in the law itself that comes into play when it solicits and elicits testimony" (ibid., pp. 4, 5). This potentially transformative capacity, or strictly speaking "agency" (given that Sanders exploits the etymology of ambiguity to signal "an acting on both sides," ibid., p. 5), arises at the interface between the law and the literary: "Although, from the point of view of law, testimony is to be verified, it is, strictly speaking, unverifiable at the moment that it is elicited. This moment of unverifiability establishes the dependence of law on literature. [...] In fact, I would argue that what we call the literary actually depends on the law suspending its procedures of verification in order to hear the narration of the witness" (ibid., p. 6). This analysis deserves much fuller consideration than I am able to give it here.

[31] For a different consideration of the problem of reducing women, or "the woman," to a merely exemplary status, see Sanders' chapter, "Hearing Women," in *Ambiguities of Witnessing*, pp. 59–86.

[32] Eunice Nombulelo Ngubo, cited in Jillian Edelstein, *Truth & Lies: Stories from the Truth and Reconciliation Commission in South Africa*, with an introduction by Michael Ignatieff and an essay by Pumla Gobodo-Madikizela (New York: The New Press, 2002 [2001]), p. 88.

[33] I am drawing here on the work of Amit Pinchevski who mobilizes Martin Buber, *Between Man and Man*, trans. Roger G. Smith (Boston: Beacon, 1965), p. 10, to stress that neither speaker nor addressee subsist outside of an essentially reciprocal relation. Address does not proceed from a vacuum, all is not quiet. "It is my contention," writes Pinchevski, "that free speech is never carried out in an "Otherless" sphere, that is, untainted by the Other's demand to be responded to" (Amit Pinchevski, "Freedom from Speech (Or the Silent Demand)," *diacritics* XXXI, 2, p. 72).

[34] Sitze, "Articulating Truth and Reconciliation," p. 30.

that institutes the Commission's sovereign power. This is a source of prescription: literally, a writing-in-advance of Ngubo's subjectivity in terms of the Commission's normative category of victim. But she simultaneously eludes prescription through a polite insistence on forms of social redress or reparation that the Commission will not provide.[35]

Ngubo does not, however, elude the harm – homelessness – that persists beyond the Commission's mandate to adjudicate harm; that persists, furthermore, as a direct consequence of apartheid's violently unequal allocations of land, capital and social capital. It is this latter determinant that I seek to stress. What is at stake is less the incapacity of the Commission to go beyond its formal mandate, than the continuing inscription of racialized forms of structural inequality whose historical formation the terms of this mandate failed to stage in full. The absence of redress for Ngubo and others, arguably a consequence of the systemic forgetfulness the Commission institutes with respect to the deep structures of social and economic organization under apartheid, evokes the inadmissible persistence of apartheid governmentality, even now that all is said and done. This is precisely the unspeakable substrate of Ngubo's appeal: nothing less than the survival/*survie* of apartheid, with respect to the homelessness of black African witnesses.[36] Ngubo's singular claim reveals the inadequacy of a logic of redress which takes the individual victim as its primary unit of analysis. Something else is instantiated, the illustration fails, or rather, it does not reach the injury apartheid inflicted on the witness and on countless others.

Or it fails in a certain sense. For illustration is etymologically, as Adam Sitze reminds us, a ceremonial or ritual purification ("lustrace"). Given this, "full" sense of the word, Sitze is able to argue that "The Truth Commission clarified the truth of apartheid by way of instantiation, but it also ritually purified the new South Africa of apartheid – and, perhaps inevitably, produced a purified concept of apartheid itself."[37] It is precisely the illusion of the purge (a fully reconstituted South Africa; an apartheid written in the

---

[35] The reparations program of the TRC was unevenly realized. For a definitive treatment, see Sanders, *Ambiguities of Witnessing*, pp. 114–46. See also Brandon Hamber and Richard Wilson, "Symbolic Closure through Memory, Reparation and Revenge in Post-Conflict Societies," paper presented at the Traumatic Stress in South Africa conference hosted by the Centre for the Study of Violence and Reconciliation in association with the African Society for Traumatic Stress Studies, Johannesburg, South Africa, 27–29 January 1999.

[36] I owe the equation of persistence and *survie* to Adam Sitze ("Articulating Truth and Reconciliation", pp. 66–77), following Louis Althusser, *For Marx*, trans. Ben Brewster (New York: Verso, 1997 [1969]). For Althusser, as Sitze reminds us, the paradigmatic instance of *survie* relates to the residual persistence of Tsarism in post-revolutionary Russia.

[37] Sitze, "Articulating Truth and Reconciliation," p. 28.

lower case) that Eunice Nombulelo Ngubo dispels. It is, moreover, the consolation of the purge that comes most forcefully under criticism in J. M. Coetzee's portrayal of the post-apartheid South African farm as – literally – purgatory, a site where the detritus of the "purge" lives on.[38]

Over the body of the woman

Coetzee's novel recounts the "disgrace" of academic David Lurie, judged to have sexually harassed one of his students. Lurie admits his guilt before the "secular tribunal" of a committee of inquiry but refuses its demand for repentance:[39] "They wanted a spectacle: breast-beating, remorse, tears if possible. A TV show, in fact. I wouldn't oblige."[40] He subsequently seeks "refuge" on his daughter's farm in the Eastern Cape.[41] Lurie's refusal to perform the public remorse required of him might be adduced as oblique criticism of the apparatus of confession in post-apartheid South Africa in its most spectacular instantiation – the mediation and mediatization of perpetrators' guilt by means of the Truth and Reconciliation Commission. Coetzee has, in fact, long been concerned with the movement from confession to an achieved absolution, perfected in its religious and linguistic dimensions as *"the end of the chapter"* whose attainment is the goal of confession.[42] Mark Sanders raises this concern to particular prominence with respect to the syntax of the narrative in Coetzee's text. David Lurie tarries in disgrace, Sanders argues, and teaches us an object lesson concerning the illusion of tense – the "perfective" – whose function is precisely to convey the completion of an action.[43] The full transformation of apartheid, Coetzee suggests, is unachieved – a recognition enfolded in the interplay between the formal dimensions of the literary text and its representational content.

As for this content, *Disgrace* is resistant to unequivocal restatement precisely to the extent that a thematization of silence lies at its core. The text has, as one of its climactic moments, a scene in which Lurie is set alight by three black assailants. Imbedded in the record of violence focalized through Lurie lies yet another tale – that of his daughter, Lucy, raped by the very same men. Lucy refuses to speak publicly of the rape, jealously guarding her right to silence: "You want to know why I have not

---

[38] J. M. Coetzee, *Disgrace* (London: Secker and Warburg, 1999), p. 91.   [39] Ibid., p. 58.
[40] Ibid., p. 66.   [41] Ibid., p. 65.
[42] J. M. Coetzee, "Confession and Double Thoughts: Tolstoy, Rousseau, Dostoevsky," in David Attwell (ed.), *Doubling the Point: Essays and Interviews* (Cambridge, Mass.: Harvard University Press, 1992 [1985]), p. 253, emphasis in original.
[43] Mark Sanders, "Disgrace," *Interventions* IV, 3 (2002), p. 371.

laid a particular charge with the police. [...] The reason is that, as far as I am concerned, what happened to me is a purely private matter. In another time, in another place it might be held to be a public matter. But in this place, at this time, it is not. It is my business, mine alone."[44] Lucy's response deliberately bypasses what she terms the abstractions of "[g]uilt and salvation"[45] in favor of a more pragmatic determination to see the black rapists as "debt collectors, tax collectors"[46], given the legacy of apartheid. Rather than lay charges of rape, the silent Lucy offers her lesbian body, pregnant with a child she refuses to abort, in concubinage to her black neighbor Petrus as her bid for inclusion in the old-new patriarchy of post-apartheid South Africa.[47]

Disgrace is quite deliberate in casting rape as an open, albeit unspeakable, secret. The novel deliberately interrogates questions that might initially appear to be self-evident: Who may testify to rape? When and how can rape, as signifier, be articulated in language? We grope together with David Lurie towards certain tenuous understandings:

Words are beginning to take shape that have been hovering since last night at the edges of [Lurie's] memory. Two old ladies locked in the lavatory / They were there from Monday to Saturday / Nobody knew they were there. Locked in the lavatory while his daughter was used. A chant from his childhood come back to point a jeering finger. Oh dear, what can the matter be? Lucy's secret; his disgrace.[48]

Lucy's "secret" hovers on the boundaries between private and public knowledge. In contrast to the visible evidence of male bodily suffering in *Disgrace* – particularly Lurie's own – the text does not disclose immediate evidence of female violation, suspending the signs of rape as the gestation of a hybrid child. "[O]ver the body of the woman," states the text, "silence is being drawn like a blanket."[49]

---

[44] Coetzee, *Disgrace*, p. 112.   [45] Ibid.   [46] Ibid., p. 158.
[47] Lucy stands at the core of the controversy the novel has aroused. For some white readers, she conveys pessimism regarding the viability of whiteness in post-apartheid South Africa. The "Lucy syndrome" (Dan Roodt in Roodt "Brief aan Beeld oor Carel Niehaus se anachronistiese tirade," *Praag*, 2000. Online: www.praag.org/briewe-argiefl.htm) seems to advocate white self-abnegation as atonement for apartheid (see Mike Marais, "Very Morbid Phenomena: "Liberal Funk," the "Lucy-syndrome," and J.M. Coetzee's *Disgrace*," *Scrutiny2: Issues in English Studies in Southern Africa* IV, 1 (2001), pp. 32–8). Some black South Africans, on the other hand, have read Coetzee's text as deeply racist. The African National Congress notoriously submitted the novel to the South African Human Rights Commission's inquiry into racism in the media in April 2000 on the grounds of its stereotyping of blacks. For fuller discussion of the ANC submission and the issues it raises, see David Attwell, "Race in Disgrace," *Interventions* IV, 3 (2002), pp. 331–41 and Peter McDonald, "Disgrace Effects," *Interventions* IV, 3 (2002), pp. 421–30.
[48] Coetzee, *Disgrace*, p. 109.   [49] Ibid., p. 110.

The simile is telling, not least for its implicit coupling of speech with revelation and silence with screening, or a putting out of view. These oppositions are by no means accidental. Elsewhere I have argued that the particular narrative economy of the novel places gendered constraints on the transmission of the forms of knowledge which accumulate around its various bodies such that it is male suffering, male sexual pleasure which speaks its own name, and which moreover can be seen to be spoken.[50] Although Lucy's homosexual desire is never openly staged in the novel, her lesbianism disrupts the codes of "compulsory heterosexuality"[51] in which the novel subsists. More significantly, for our purposes, her female body subverts the forms of literal referentiality that govern the visual representation of the abject male body in *Disgrace* wherever the male focalizer is permitted to figure his wounded body as the amanuensis of violence. Lucy's silence in this reading allows her to deflect the signifier "rape" and so to prevent its legibility as a derivative linguistic scar. Lucy remains outside the codes of signification that make of the wound or scar a sign. But it is not only David Lurie who reads his scarred body as faithful mimetic inscription, the material signifier of the signified "victim." The legibility of the wounded body in the novel, I am arguing, subsists within the larger cultural visibility of the "scar-as-sign"[52] at a time when the victim's embodied performance before the TRC raised the body to particular salience for the post-apartheid imaginary.

Traffic in bodies

In a prescient analysis of the Truth and Reconciliation Commission as early as 1996, Gary Minkley, Ciraj Rassool, and Leslie Witz suggested that it served as a "threshold for the remembrance of apartheid ... in the expanded sense of the gaze."[53] At the visual core of the TRC hearings, the authors claim, were "descriptions, representations and conflicts around bodies in various states of mutilation, dismemberment, and internment within the terror of the past. Again and again, witnesses

---

[50] Louise Bethlehem, "Aneconomy in an Economy of Melancholy: Embodiment and Gendered Identity in J. M. Coetzee's *Disgrace*," *African Identities* I, 2 (2003), pp. 167–85.
[51] Adrienne Rich, "Compulsory Heterosexuality and Lesbian Existence," in C. R. Stimpson and E. S. Person (eds.), *Women: Sex and Sexuality* (University of Chicago Press, 1980), pp. 62–91.
[52] Bethlehem, "Aneconomy in an Economy," p. 172.
[53] Gary Minkley, Ciraj Rassool, and Leslie Witz, "Thresholds, Gateways and Spectacles: Journeying through South African Hidden Pasts and Histories in the Last Decade of the Twentieth Century," paper presented at the conference "The Future of the Past: The Production of History in a Changing South Africa," University of the Western Cape, July 10–12, 1996, p. 8.

made claims in respect of body parts and human remains, making their visibility, recovery and repossession a metaphor for the settlement of the pasts of apartheid."[54] Following Minkley, Rassool, and Witz, I have elsewhere traced the epistemological, semiotic, and social dimensions of the Commission's resolutely "corporeal dominant," that is to say, its mediation of trauma rooted in individual bodies whose visible scarring and abjection, on display before the Truth Commission, serves to guarantee the veracity of the history the Commission inscribes.[55] The Truth Commission's turn to the body seems to promise immediacy of reference, and the facticity of a resolutely material (because corporeal) historical narrative. But the body cannot be judged to constitute a literal sign that is simultaneously external to the linguistic system it appears to ground without a serious misrepresentation of the complex relations that make the one co-implicit in the production of the other, as Judith Butler has claimed.[56] It is crucial, I am arguing in the wake of Butler, to retain awareness of the indissoluble trace of signification that adheres to the body even though the body seems to efface discourse in favor of sheer materiality. The body of the victim does not silently speak a supplementary truth – one anterior to the very words that the deponent articulates – as in the account of certain realist epistemologies. It is, instead, a particular "scopic regime" in Allen Feldman's sense – an ensemble of visual practices that produces a socially sanctioned form of facticity[57] – which allows the sight of the violated body to be stabilized as the site of memory.

The forensic privileging of the body that derives from the Commission's particular approach to truth is acutely pertinent when the status of women's testimony is considered. Following representations concerning the Commission's disregard for the specifically gendered nature of violence in apartheid South Africa,[58] the Commission instituted a series of corrective

---

[54] Ibid., p. 9.

[55] Louise Bethlehem, *Skin Tight: Apartheid Literary Culture and its Aftermath* (Pretoria, Leiden: Unisa Press, Brill, 2006), pp. 77–91.

[56] Judith Butler, *Bodies that Matter: On the Discursive Limits of "Sex"* (New York and London: Routledge, 1993), p. 30; Judith Butler, "How Can I Deny that these Hands and this Body are mine," in T. Cohen, B. Cohen, J. H. Miller, and A. Warminski (eds.), *Material Events: Paul de Man and the Afterlife of Theory* (Minneapolis and London: University of Minnesota Press, 2001), pp. 256, 257.

[57] Allen Feldman, "Violence and Vision: The Prosthetics and Aesthetics of Terror," *Public Culture* X, 1 (1997), p. 30.

[58] Notably, by Beth Goldblatt and Sheila Meintjies, see "Gender and the Truth and Reconciliation Commission: A submission to the Truth and Reconciliation Commission," 1996 www.doj.gov.za/trc/submit/gender.htm (accessed 4 September 2007).

measures, including Special Women's Hearings.[59] But the Commission's very instantiation of the category of "women" in response to considerations of gender, Fiona Ross has argued, is disturbing. In her view, the production of "woman" as a distinct locus of harm cannot be separated from the Commission's understanding of injury, restricted to violations of the right to bodily integrity.[60] "The emphasis on that which is visibly embodied," Ross writes, "denies the forms and consequences of a political agency configured in relation to state power and cruelty's effects. The Commission's findings on women, clustered as they are around an idea of bodily violation and couched in the passive tense, do not give due weight to the challenges faced by those constituted as agents in opposition to the state, particularly in the face of cruelty."[61] This predisposition translates into the Commission's foregrounding of rape as exemplary of the gendered violence directed against South African women.[62] This is not to deny that a critical interrogation of sexual violence, particularly sexual violence against women, is indeed of pressing concern for South Africa, which is widely considered to have the highest incidence of rape in the world. But the fictional precedent of Lucy Lurie cautions us regarding the words that take shape around the violated female body. A black South African political activist, Yvonne Khutwane, has, implicitly, already said as much.

In a nuanced engagement with Khutwane, anthropologist Fiona Ross traces "the distillation of testimony" through its representation, by Khutwane, before the Commission in written and oral form, in the media, and subsequently by Khutwane upon later reflection.[63] The analysis pivots on the fact that Khutwane's deposition regarding, among other things, the torture and abuse of political prisoners, did not initially include an account of the sexual violation she later recounted in a public hearing in Worcester in the Western Cape in June 1996. But the specifically sexual dimension of Khutwane's violation was heightened, Ross argues, to the detriment of other aspects of her oral testimony through the interventions of one of the Commissioners.[64] Rape emerged into prominence despite Khutwane's sustained unwillingness to talk about this particular facet of

---

[59] Four special hearings on youth and children were also conducted. Their findings are contained in the *Report*, vol. 4, chs. 9 and 10. See Karin Chubb and Lutz Van Dijk, *Between Anger and Hope: South Africa's Youth and the Truth and Reconciliation Commission* (Johannesburg: Witwatersrand University Press, 2001), for a book-length analysis of the Youth Hearings. Ross deals with the under-representation of the testimony of young women, in particular, in the Commission's proceedings. Her chapter "Considerations of Harm" (*Bearing Witness*, pp. 103–32) offers a partial corrective.
[60] Ross, *Bearing Witness*, pp. 11, 19.   [61] Ibid., p. 76.
[62] Ibid., pp. 24–5.   [63] Ibid., pp. 77–102.   [64] Ibid., p. 88.

her experience as a political detainee. In the scripting of the public hearing, as well as in concurrent newspaper representations and in the unusual weight given to Khutwane's testimony in the Commission's Report,[65] sexual violation becomes "the traumatic event and the primary violation."[66] This outcome, writes Ross, "appears to be predicated on an assumption that that which happens to or is inflicted on the body endures as pain remembered in a different and more profound fashion than the pain of, for example, a loss of community trust and engagement". The prioritization of the body as the locus of pain contrasts sharply with the subjective priorities of Khutwane herself who implicates gossip, scandal, and rumour to account for her ongoing victimization by her community subsequent to her detention.[67] Khutwane's reticence to recapitulate sexual violation moves us beyond what Wendy Woodward, Patricia Hayes, and Gary Minkley term "undifferentiating" or binary constructions of voice versus silence,[68] foregrounding our need to become cognizant of "a spiralling continuum, a genealogy of voices and voicing."[69] Khutwane stages a shifting encounter between speech and silence, Ross argues, such that "spoken words and silences sculpt one another and may take on a kind of tangibility, a traceable life of their own".[70]

This interdependence makes it possible to bring Khutwane's testimony into confluence with J. M. Coetzee's novel. In both instances, the act of listening for silences asks of us to attend to the relational dimensions of the unvoiced: its subjective weight; its communities of witness; its genealogy; its historicity; "[t]his place being South Africa."[71]

This place being South Africa

Moving the relationality of the speech act into prominence, precisely when it is speech itself that is being withheld, has allowed us to access the affective dimensions of silence as well as its tacit – or tactical – freight. Lucy Lurie speaks to the activist and detainee Yvonne Khutwane along this axis, across the ontological divide of fiction. But this is not all that can

---

[65] Truth and Reconciliation Commission, *Report*, vol. 3, p. 448; vol. 4, p. 298; vol. 5, pp. 352–3. See also Ross, *Bearing Witness*, pp. 91–2.
[66] Ross, *Bearing Witness*, p. 89.   [67] Ibid., pp. 97–8.
[68] Wendy Woodward, Patricia Hayes, and Gary Minkley, "Sounding the Spaces: Some (Re) locations of Voices and Silences in Recent Colonial and Literary Debates [work in progress]," in Relocating Literature: Africa and India Conference Proceedings, University of the Witwatersrand, 2001. Reprinted in Woodward, Hayes, and Minkley (eds.), *Deep hiStories: Gender and Colonialism in Southern Africa* (Amsterdam and New York: Rodopi, 2003).
[69] Woodward, Hayes, and Minkley, "Sounding the Spaces," p. 324.
[70] Ross, *Bearing Witness*, p. 101.   [71] Coetzee, *Disgrace*, p. 112.

be said. What I am terming the relationality of silence is no doubt a component of those intersections between the social and institutional constraints on memory, on the one hand, and the singularity of a life recalled, on the other, such that the phenomenology is never entirely divorced from the swell of ideology. Yet the type of work that I am calling upon the phrase "the relationality of silence" to perform does not simply coincide with "the social construction of silence" as shorthand for, say, forms of denialism. Rather relationality returns us to the political as constitutive of the very emergence of the latter; returns us, moreover, in the work of such critical theorists as Judith Butler, to the political as a site of vulnerability where the duty of mourning, or its possibility, is incipient. Reconciliation entails a leaving behind of a painful past and of elements of suffering in it.

In exploring the question of "What makes for a grievable life?," Butler observes that "[Each] of us is constituted politically in part by virtue of the social vulnerability of our bodies – as a site of desire and physical vulner-ability, as a site of a publicity at once assertive and exposed. Loss and vulnerability seem to follow from our being socially constituted bodies, attached to others, at risk of losing those attachments, exposed to others, at risk of violence by virtue of that exposure."[72] The trajectories of grief which Butler delineates may well, she points out, derive specifically from the heightened vulnerability of women or communities to the sundering of ties by violence.[73] When endured, grief, for Butler, sets in motion the self's dispropriation from the self.[74] "Freud reminded us that when we lose someone, we do not always know what it is in that person that has been lost. So when one loses, one is faced with something enigmatic: something is hiding in the loss, something is lost within the recesses of loss."[75] Mourning thus makes the self inscrutable. "On one level, I think I have lost 'you' only to discover that 'I' have gone missing as well. At another level, perhaps what I have lost 'in' you, that for which I have no ready vocabulary, is a relation-ality that is composed neither exclusively of myself nor you, but is to be conceived as *the tie* by which those terms are differentiated and related."[76]

It is such relationality, I contend, that the silence of "Lucy Lurie," the reticence of Yvonne Khutwane, traverses. Enigmatic in itself, their with-holding of speech calls out for interpretation. Yet for interpretation to

---

[72] Judith Butler, *Precarious Life: The Powers of Mourning and Violence* (London and New York: Verso, 2004), p. 20.

[73] Ibid.

[74] The term dispropriation does not arise in Butler's discussion here, but is central to Sanders' interventions in *Ambiguities of Witnessing*: "A term I take up from a discussion of Levinas and Derrida by Thomas Keenan, "dispropriation" refers to an entity's not being proper, or identical to itself' (p. 8). See also Thomas Keenan, *Fables of Responsibility: Aberrations and Predicaments in Ethics and Politics* (Stanford University Press, 1997).

[75] Butler, *Precarious Life*, pp. 21–2.   [76] Ibid., p. 22, emphasis in original.

ensue, silence must be positioned within a skein of social relations where its very opacity requires that we adjudicate these relations anew. An engagement with the work of mourning, I am suggesting, provides one axis of revaluation. Violence has dispropriated the self, for "Lucy Lurie" as for Yvonne Khutwane, requiring that each mourns her own fractured personhood. Yet more broadly speaking, their specifically gendered vulnerability and its insertion into the "long durée" of apartheid, call us into ethical and political account as a consequence of the relationality which attending to their silence casts into relief. Each woman invites us to anticipate a state of mourning in which we are also rendered bereft of a "ready vocabulary" for what we have lost. Lucy Lurie and Yvonne Khutwane silently ask us to intuit that this "lost object" is precisely a proper form of sociality which might allow the vulnerability of the self to be safely sustained.

Apartheid South Africa notoriously denied such sustenance to black and coloured South Africans, to its white conscripts, as well as to homosexuals of all races. But to state that apartheid governmentality was profoundly unmindful of such vulnerability is also to anticipate the question of how violation was – or more accurately, was not – commemorated. Apartheid, Mark Sanders has recently argued, was itself "a proscription on mourning, specifically of the other."[77] The claim is a powerful one. It defamiliarizes epistemic assumptions regarding the constitution of apartheid even as it reorients us to the primacy of mourning practice in the workings of the Truth and Reconciliation Commission. When the testimony of witnesses, says Sanders, "includes calls for reparation, it registers what apartheid is understood, or felt, to have taken away. When such calls involve mourning and condolence, memory inevitably shades into acts of commemoration. Addressing what [apartheid] repressed, disavowed, or foreclosed, [such calls] inevitably produce signs of what apartheid was or, more strictly speaking, will have been."[78] Sanders conceives of the Commission's hospitality towards mourners and mourning as a form of reparation that itself announces a different kind of sociality, a "joining in mourning"[79] across racial divides. "Mourning would make good for the violations of the apartheid era. As a system of social separation, apartheid would be undone through condolence."[80]

Enter, in corroboration, the figure of the "comforter" who has waited in the wings of our discussion. Early on in its proceedings, the TRC hired briefers to inform witnesses about the legal implications of their testimony, to debrief them after testimony and to provide ongoing

---

[77] Sanders, *Ambiguities of Witnessing*, p. 35.   [78] Ibid., p. 39.   [79] Ibid., p. 49.   [80] Ibid.

psychological support.[81] The colloquial designation of briefers as "comforters" or "Cry People" derives from their visible presence in public hearings where they stood beside witnesses, wiping their tears and embracing them during harrowing emotional testimony. The comforter's role, to embody the mournful affective reparation which the contract between commissioner and victim underwrites, is not a referential one. She of necessity maintains her silence with respect to the veracity of the testimony she hears. She does not speak before the Commission, attesting to nothing except the singularity of the witness whom she attends and the need for us who listen to recognize the suffering the witness underwent. The comforter's speech is, in other words, interdicted by the Commission for whom she has no evidential function. Yet the comforter's interdiction, a speech-across-witness that subsists between the lines of the official record, stages a visceral recognition of the vulnerability that simultaneously grounds and may come to undermine our sociality. The comforter silently returns theory to the grounds of its etymology and to the ethical foundation of its practice – as witness.[82] Her precedent is crucial to our concerns, precisely because it renders concrete the ethical turn to the other which the silence of denialism corrodes. To the extent that such reparation animates our shared intellectual pursuit in this volume, the parameters of her remit tacitly implicate us all. In many different contexts the notion that telling the story liberates those who have suffered from violence must be contested. Silence itself can be powerfully resonant, especially when it concerns the frail and vulnerable human body. The comforter's wordless comfort is an act of recognition which we as scholars must honor not only in the texts we study but in the position we take in speaking about them. None of us can provide Ngubo with a home, but we can feel the need to go beyond commissions of reconciliation which fail to do so.

---

[81] Brandon Hamber, "The Burdens of Truth: An Evaluation of the Psychological Support Services and Initiatives Undertaken by the South African Truth and Reconciliation Commission," *American Imago* LV, 1 (1998), p. 20.

[82] It is well known that the etymology of theory couples it with witness. "Etymologically," Wlad Godzich reminds us, "the term comes from the Greek verb *theorein*, to look at, to contemplate, to survey ... The Greeks designated certain individuals, chosen on the basis of their probity and their general standing in the polity, to act as legates on certain formal occasions" (Wlad Godzich, "Foreword: The Tiger on the Paper Mat," in Paul de Man, *The Resistance to Theory*, foreword by W. Godzich (Minneapolis: University of Minnesota Press, 1986), pp. ix–xviii, p. xiv). The report of the *theoros* allowed that which was seen to become the sanctioned object of public discourse, such that "Only the theoretically attested event could be treated as a fact" (ibid.).

Part IV

The Middle East

9   Facing history: Denial and the Turkish national security concept

Taner Akçam

In September 2005, Turkish intellectuals who questioned the Turkish state's denial policy on the deportation and killings of Armenians during the First World War gathered for a conference in Istanbul. Outside, in the streets, demonstrators also gathered in protest against the conference. One of the placards read: "Not Genocide, but Defense of the Fatherland."[1] Two parallel points of view are at work here, one referring to the past, the other to the present. Both the events of 1915 and the denial policy nine decades later are framed in terms of Turkish self-defense.

One may well ask why demands from inside and outside the country, that Turkey come to terms with its past, are so vehemently rejected. In Turkey today, any attempt to open a discussion of historic wrongs is denounced as a covert move in a master plan to partition the country. Why is facing history seen as a threat to national security?

Before answering this question, I have to add that this is not just the view of the political elite, but also underpins legal decisions. In a recent judgment against journalists Arat Dink and Sarkis Seropyan, who received a suspended sentence of a year in prison, for using the term "genocide," the Turkish court stated that: "Talk about genocide, both in Turkey and in other countries, unfavourably affects national security and the national interest. The claim of genocide ... has become part of and the means of special plans aiming to change the geographic political boundaries of Turkey... and a campaign to demolish its physical and legal structure." The ruling stated further that the Republic of Turkey is under "a hostile diplomatic siege consisting of genocide resolutions... The acceptance of this claim may lead during future centuries to a questioning of the sovereign rights of the Republic of Turkey over the lands on which it is claimed these events occurred." Due to these national security concerns, the court declared that the claim of genocide in 1915 is not protected speech. To quote, "the use of these freedoms can be limited in

---

[1] See the Turkish daily newspapers for the time period between September 22 and 29 2005; here is only one example: http://webarsiv.hurriyet.com.tr/2005/09/22/hurriyetim.asp.

accordance with aims such as the protection of national security, of public order, of public security."[2]

When one discusses Turkish history from a human rights perspective, most people in Turkey become very sensitive. This extraordinary self-defensiveness originates from the breakup of the Ottoman Empire into nation-states, a process that gave rise to divergent and mutually exclusive historical accounts. From late Ottoman times to the present, there has been a continuous tension between the state's concern for secure borders and society's need to come to terms with abuses of human rights. To understand and resolve this contradiction, we need to examine the rise of two opposing historical narratives.

Until recently, the dominant narrative has been the story of the partition of the Empire among the Great Powers, which ended with the Empire's total collapse and disintegration. The foundational works by Ottomanists and Turkish historians scarcely mention the Christian peoples of the Empire. Scant reference is made to Greeks, Armenians, Bulgarians etc., as contributors to Ottoman social and political life, let alone as the victims of massacres and other gross violations of human rights. Instead, especially in Turkish historiography, Christian communities are painted as the seditious agents of the imperialist Great Powers, continually intriguing against the state.[3]

The ethnic and religious minorities, for their part, center themselves within a narrative of persecutions, massacres, and, especially in the case of the Armenians, wholesale annihilation by their Ottoman rulers. The overall theme of this history is the community's maturation and national emergence, thanks in part to the intervention of the Great Powers.[4]

In this light, Turkish controversies about facing national history, in particular the Armenian Genocide, can be understood, in part, as the deployment of two, apparently contradictory, historical narratives against one another. Whenever the proponents of acknowledgment bring up a

---

[2] Court Decree, 2nd Penal Court of First Instance for The District Of Şişli, File Number: 2006/1208, Decree Number: 2007/1106, Prosecution Number: 2006/8617.

[3] Some examples of the collections published by the Prime Minister's State Archives would be enough: *Osmanlı Belgelerinde Ermeniler (1915–1920)*, (Ankara: Başbakanlık Basımevi, 1995); *Arşiv Belgelerine Göre Kafkaslar'da ve Anadolu'da Ermeni Mezâlimi*, 'Armenian violence and massacre in the Caucasus and Anatolia based on archives,' 4 vols. (I: 1906–18, II: 1919, III: 1919–20, IV: 1920–22), (Ankara: Başbakanlık Basımevi, 1995–98); *Ermeniler Tarafından Yapılan Katliam Belgeleri, Documents on Massacre Perpetrated by Armenians*, 2 vols. (I: 1914–19; II: 1919–21) (Ankara: Başbakanlık Basımevi, 2001).

[4] It is sufficient to take a look at the books written on Armenian History, for one example: George Bournoutian, *A Concise History of the Armenian People* (Costa Mesa: Mazda, 2006).

history of human rights abuses, they are confronted with an opposing narrative, that of the decline and breakup of the Ottoman Empire.

Nevertheless, the evidence shows that these two narratives are not contradictory at all. They are two sides of the same coin; complementary perspectives on a single course of human events. Both must be sufficiently understood and appreciated in order to grasp the ambiguities and contradictions of Ottoman and Turkish history and their ramifications today. The uncertainty over the boundaries of the present-day Turkish state is a crucial element in the political conflict over how to configure a past which includes a set of events at the heart of the historical consciousness of a population which was once a minority in that state and now has its own national existence.

There have been certain moments in that history where national security and human rights became inseparably intertwined. One such moment came immediately after the First World War, between 1918 and 1923. While working out the terms of a peace settlement, the political decisionmakers were grappling with two distinct yet related issues, the answers to which determined their various relationships and alliances. The first was the territorial integrity of the Ottoman state. The second was the wartime atrocities committed by the ruling Union and Progress party against Ottoman Armenian citizens.[5]

The questions about the first issue were: Should the Ottoman state retain its independence? Should new states be permitted to arise on the territory of the Ottoman state? If so, how should the borders of these new states be defined? These questions led to the formation of two different viewpoints. The Turkish nationalist movement, under the leadership of Mustafa Kemal, favored continued sovereignty within reduced borders as defined by the 1918 Moudros Ceasefire Treaty.[6] At one and the same time, the Allied Powers and ethnic-religious groups such as Greeks, Armenians and, to a degree, the Kurds, argued for the establishment of new states on both occupied and unoccupied territory of the Ottoman Empire. The successive treaties of Sèvres and Lausanne reflected these divergent points of view.[7]

---

[5] For a detailed account of the period see Taner Akçam, *A Shameful Act: The Armenian Genocide and the Question of Turkish Responsibility* (New York: Metropolitan, 2006); especially pp. 205–349.

[6] Ibid. See also Taner Akçam, *From Empire to Republic: Turkish Nationalism and the Armenian Genocide* (London and New York: Zed Books, 2004), ch. 9: 'The Treaties of Sèvres and Lausanne: An Alternative Perspective'. An earlier version of this chapter appeared in Hans-Lukas Kieser and Dominik J. Schaller (eds.), *Der Völkermord an Den Armeniern Und Die Shoah / The Armenian Genocide and the Shoah* (Zurich: Chronos Verlag, 2002).

[7] Akçam, *From Empire to Republic*.

In history writing, the immediate post-war period is generally portrayed as one of territorial conflict among national groups. The general understanding in modern Turkey is that the Turks, who see themselves as the legitimate successors of the Ottoman Empire, defended their sole remaining territory against the Armenians, Greeks, and some of the Kurds, who were trying to carve up Anatolia into nation-states, with the help of the British, French, and Italians. The 1920 Treaty of Sèvres resolved the question of territory in favor of the non-Turkish nationalities. For the Turks, therefore, Sèvres remains a black mark.[8] For the other ethnic-religious groups, however, the significance of Sèvres is quite different. Although it did not fully reflect their demands for territory, the treaty represented an unprecedented historical opportunity to resolve the territorial issue in their favor. Conversely, the 1923 Treaty of Lausanne, which guaranteed Turkish dominance in Anatolia for the Turks, stands as a milestone and validation of their continued national existence, while the other nationalities see it as a great historical injustice, reflecting the outcome of fighting between 1920 and 1923 when the Turks won the upper hand.

To portray the period between 1918 and 1923 solely in terms of territorial conflict does not, however, fully reflect the other major concern of the day: that is, wartime atrocities committed against Ottoman Christians, and especially Armenian citizens and the punishment of the perpetrators. Although everyone agreed that punishment was necessary, there was disagreement about its severity and scope.

The victorious Entente powers took the position that "the Turks,"[9] so to speak, organized the massacres of other peoples, above all the Armenians, during the First World War. It was therefore necessary to punish "the Turks" collectively in order to rescue the subject peoples (Arabs, Greeks, Armenians, etc.) from Turkish domination. Punishing "the Turks" was to be accomplished in two phases. First, the members of the Ottoman government and other officials were to be tried for these crimes against other religious and ethnic communities. Secondly, "the Turks" were henceforth to inhabit a state that would be rendered as small and as weak as possible. A telegram sent to the Paris Peace Conference on April 3, 1919 by the Assistant High Commissioner of Istanbul, Webb, clearly illustrates this policy:

---

[8] Ibid.

[9] I place the term "Turks" within quotation marks. Although the term was used in the discussions of the time, it is clear that in explaining historical events general terms such as this are not only wrong to use, but also incorrect from the standpoint of attempting to write a history.

In order to punish all of those persons who are guilty of the Armenian horrors, it is necessary to punish the Turks as a group. Therefore, I propose that the punishment be given on a national level through the partitioning up of the last Turkish Empire, and on a personal level by trying those high officials who are on the list in my possession, and in a manner that would serve as an example for their successors.[10]

In short, casting the net as widely as possible, the Allied powers were minded to try individual suspects, and to engage in collective punishment through the dismemberment of the Ottoman state and the creation of new states on its territory. Here it is important to note that a major reason given for partition of Turkey among various national groups was the desire to punish "the Turks" for the barbarities they had committed during the war. Here is the source of the fact that today (2008) in Turkey every reference to human rights abuses in the past is perceived as a problem central to the national interest in general and to the security of the state in particular.

Recall that post-war Turkey had two political centers: Istanbul, the seat of the Ottoman Government and Ankara, the headquarters of the Turkish Nationalist movement led by Mustafa Kemal. Both the Istanbul and Ankara governments acknowledged the wartime massacres of Armenians. They agreed with the Allies that the perpetrators should be tried, and that such trials were "just and necessary."[11] However, Ankara and Istanbul vehemently opposed the punitive partition of Anatolia.

The Ankara and Istanbul governments signed a protocol in October 1919 calling for the election of an Ottoman Parliament according to the constitution. Five protocols were signed. The first protocol stated that: "1. Ittihadism – (Party of Union and Progress) or any hint of its reawakening is politically very damaging." Furthermore, "It is judicially and politically necessary to punish those who committed crimes in connection with the deportation." In the third protocol both parties agreed that the fugitive members of "Ittihat," who were wanted in connection with atrocities, were not to participate in the elections, because, as they put it: "it would be improper for individuals who are connected to the evil deeds of the Unionists, or persons who have been sullied by the nefarious acts of the deportation and massacre or other wicked actions that are contrary to the true interests of the nation" to participate in the national elections.[12]

The founder of Turkey, Mustafa Kemal, addressing the Turkish Parliament on April 24, 1920, called the atrocities a "shameful act."[13]

---

[10] National Archives, London, Foreign Office Papers, FO 371/4173/53351, folios 192–3.
[11] Mustafa Kemal, *Nutuk*, vol. III (Istanbul, 1934), pp. 193–4 (Document No.: 159).
[12] Ibid.
[13] *Atatürk'ün TBMM Açık ve Gizli Oturumlarındaki Konuşmaları*, vol. I (Ankara: Kültür Bakanlığı, 1992), p. 59.

Mustafa Kemal was not a human rights activist or an altruist, but a politician. What he believed was that the war crime trials were the price Turkey had to pay to protect its national sovereignty. The punishment of perpetrators, he wrote, "should not stay only on paper ... but should be carried out, since this would successfully impress the foreign elements." In exchange for this concession, the Turkish leadership expected a more favorable peace settlement without loss of territory.[14]

The failure of this strategy was made clear by two events in April 1920. First were the provisions of the Treaty of Sèvres proposed to punish "the Turks" by partitioning Ottoman territory. Second were the Istanbul Courts Martial, which opened in November 1918. Their aim was to judge those responsible for atrocities committed against Armenians.[15] Now under Allied pressure, the courts martial indicted virtually the entire national leadership of Turkey, Mustafa Kemal foremost among them, and sentenced them to death in absentia. When Turkish nationalists realized that their support for the punishment of war criminals would not prevent the partition of Anatolia, their attitude changed.

As Mustafa Kemal wrote on August 20, 1920, "[t]he Ottoman Government ... continues to hang the children of the homeland on accusations of [having perpetrated] deportations and massacres, which now became totally senseless."[16] Kemal meant that the policy whereby the Ottoman government punished Turks for what they had done to the Christian minorities would make sense only if Turkey got some positive result, in terms of a better treaty to secure sovereignty over Ottoman territories. However, the Treaty of Sèvres had been signed, Ottoman sovereignty was not acknowledged, and Ottoman territories were in danger of being distributed among different nations. Therefore, Kemal reasoned these "senseless" death sentences should be halted.

Today, these post-First World War courts martial in Istanbul remain a symbol of these two interwoven but distinct strands of Turkish history, "territory and borders" on the one side and "human rights," and the prosecution of those guilty of war crimes, on the other. As national sovereignty concerns became paramount, "human rights" and justice for the perpetrators

---

[14] The exact wording in his letter is: it appeared "more appropriate and beneficial for these punishments to be revealed to both friend and foe (*yârü ağyar*) through their actual implementation, rather than their mere publication in the press as notices, something that would give rise to a good number of heated debates." Mustafa Kemal, *Nutuk*, vol. III, pp. 166–7.

[15] For a detailed account of the Military Tribunals in Istanbul, see Akçam, *A Shameful Act*, pp. 270–302.

[16] Bilal Şimşir, *Malta Sürgünleri* (Ankara: Bilgi Yayınevi, 1985), p. 334. The letter was written to the first Grand Vizier of the Armistice period, Ahmet İzzet Paşa, with the aim of its contents being communicated to the British High Commission.

of war crimes were consigned to oblivion. This is one major reason why, in modern Turkey, the human rights aspect of history, including the Armenian genocide, has been suppressed and forgotten. For this reason also, any questioning of the "official history" sponsored by the state is perceived as a threat to national security.

The conclusion of this brief historical account of post-1918 courts martial is evident. Had the Western forces agreed to territorial integrity in exchange for trials in cases of "crimes against humanity," we might be talking about a very different history today.

If we step back from that moment, and try to take into account the consequences of those events, certain implications are clear. Reintegrating human rights issues into Turkish history reveals three important new perspectives. First, Mustafa Kemal's condemnation of the Armenian massacres is diametrically opposed to the current official Turkish policy of denial. Acknowledging Kemal's position during the difficult war years, could be a positive starting point for a resolution of the impasse between official denial and international condemnation of Turkey as responsible for a crime it refuses to admit even occurred. To become a truly democratic member within the society of nations, Turkey must confront this "dark chapter" of its history, this "shameful act," as Mustafa Kemal called the Armenian genocide.

Secondly, until now, the Turkish-Armenian problem has been perceived within the old paradigm which produced these conflicts, namely, the collapse of the Ottoman Empire and the clash of different ethnic or national groups over lands and boundaries. We have to change this understanding. What we need is a new paradigm and to rethink the Armenian-Turkish conflict. I suggest that we have to reposition the Armenian-Turkish conflict within the new paradigm of transitional justice, that is, as a part of the democratization effort within existing nation-states. The conflict should not be regarded as a territorial dispute, but rather as a human rights issue. Turkey and Armenia should deal with their pasts as a part of their respective democratization processes and try to redefine themselves and their perception of the other's identity.

This can be done only if we patiently disentangle the question of human rights from the question of territory or national security. The question of territory should be considered as resolved and should remain closed. The question of human rights remains unresolved and must be reopened.

Third, the concept of Turkish national security must be revised and changed. In the past Armenians, of whatever age or sex or political outlook were considered as security threats and during the Great War, they were targeted for massacres and deportations. For decades, any undiluted and positive approach towards facing Turkish history, any attempt to open a discussion of historic wrongs, has been treated as an attack on Turkey's national security. This is why Turkish authorities denounce intellectuals as traitors and prosecute them under the infamous Article 301 of the Turkish criminal code.[17]

Criminalizing historical inquiries for national security reasons is not only an insurmountable obstacle for the realization of democracy; but ironically enforcing this security concept of what can and cannot be said about the past could create a real security problem in itself. There is a clear parallel between Turkey's Armenian policy in the past and her Kurdish policy today. The same concept of national security underlines Turkey's denial of the 1915 genocide and Turkey's incapability to deal with the Kurdish question today. Just as the Armenians were deemed a threat in the past (and facing that history is also threatening today), any discussion of a democratic future for the Kurds today appears to be threatening as well.

As long as Turkey continues to juxtapose on the one hand morality (facing historic wrong doings) and on the other hand, national security, further problems will proliferate. These facets of the past are not two opposing poles that are mutually exclusive. As long as Turkey refuses to come to terms with its past for national security reasons – indeed, as long as Turkey's national security is defined in opposition to an honest historical reckoning, then its search for democracy and security, alongside its search for a viable partnership with Europe will evade her.

Historical injustices and their consistent denial by one or another state or ethno-religious group delay democratization and destabilize relationships in the volatile Middle East. For this reason, any security concept, any exercise in Realpolitik in and for the region that excludes morality and facing history is doomed to fail. Instead of denying the past, Turkish policy should re-integrate facing history into a policy of realizing her national interest.

In a volume of essays on the social construction of silence, a brief and incomplete survey of the Turkish case sharply illuminates the consequences of stifling debate, research, and the acknowledgment of past injustices. Adopting a human rights framework in the context of today's Europe makes sense on both ethical and geopolitical grounds. The end of silence may well be the beginning of the normalization of Turkey's role in Europe, in the Middle East, and in the world.

---

[17] For a list of the court cases against the intellectuals from this article see: http://bianet.org/bianet/kategori/bianet/71792/madde-301-ve-davalar.

10   Imposed silences and self-censorship: *Palmach* soldiers remember 1948

Efrat Ben-Ze'ev

Among the things they carried, to use Tim O'Brien's phrase,[1] was silence. The soldiers who fought in Israel's war of independence were no different from other twentieth-century soldiers like O'Brien. They were young, they were inexperienced, and they saw and did things they did not refer to in conversation, in writing, or in public ceremonies and commemorative events. The subject of this chapter is soldiers' silences, and the ways in which they are tacitly agreed and maintained over the years. I also will explore the ways in which the veil of silence some soldiers drew over their military service in the 1948 war started to fray, and then fall away as these men became old soldiers, and for a host of reasons, took another look at what they had done and what had happened to them long before.

Israeli's soldiers' tales of the 1948 war bore a particular imprint related to the fact that they were on the victorious side of their country's war of independence. The heroic baggage of elite troops, in this case, the *Palmach*, was greater still, since these young commandos embodied the tough, hard-working and unsentimental image of the new Israeli state. The bonds they formed lasted a lifetime, and so did the tales they told about their war. Suffice it to say that the sufferings of the Arab population, expelled en masse from their towns and villages in the course of the fighting in 1948, was not at the centre of their field of vision.

The state of Israel quickly mythologised the story of the war, and occluded evidence that injustice had been done to Palestinians thereafter gathered in refugee camps on the other side of the newly founded international borders of the state. This is hardly surprising, but it does raise a problem with respect to the way small groups of soldiers recreated their war at that time and thereafter. How do ordinary men and women tell what Samuel Hynes has termed 'the soldiers' tale', when it is part of the myth of creating a new nation?

---

[1] Tim O'Brien, *The Things they Carried* (New York: Houghton Mifflin, 1990).

The problem is that the soldiers' tale, as Hynes has framed it, is myth-destroying. It is direct and undecorated, drawing on personal witnessing and on human encounters.[2] It is intricately entwined with un-heroic memories of war.[3] In contrast, state narratives of wars of independence have a larger than life dimension, requiring completely simplified stories of good versus evil, right versus wrong, justice versus injustice and so on. What can be expunged from official narratives is less readily erased from the soldiers' tales.[4] They know better.

The Jewish (later Israeli) soldiers of 1948 were caught up between two conflicting types of tales. They were both exposed to and helped construct a simplified national narrative, yet they also experienced the complex, chaotic, unromantic, ugly side of war. On the one hand, they were part of the Zionist revolution, dreaming of a new world, wanting to frame the story of their lives and their war in terms of the future. They were active agents in the creation of what was described as a miracle; a victory of a Jewish army after 2,000 years of exile; and the chance to create a new and vibrant society where all Jews could come after the Holocaust. And in achieving this goal, they believed they had remained clean; they were decent people. On the other hand, they were the cutting edge of the 'miracle', fighters for the cause, and the 1948 war, like any other war, had its ugly side. As heroes and icons of the 'New Israeli fighter' and citizen, they had a role to play of which they were well aware. They were neither victims, nor perpetrators of crimes, according to the narrative of the new state. And yet were they so noble, so brave, so clean? No one chose the circumstances of this war; no one sought to help along the mass expulsion of the Arab population; no one put on a uniform so he could kill an old Arab woman who would not leave her home; no one set out to steal from abandoned Arab homes. And yet they did.

---

[2] Paul Fussell indicates this in his foundational study *The Great War and Modern Memory* (Oxford University Press, 1975). He quotes Sir Geoffrey Keynes recalling in 1968 an incident during the First World War. Keynes wrote that 'the pattern of war is shaped in the individual mind by small individual experiences, and I can see these things as clearly today [1968] as if they had just happened' (p. 31).

[3] In 'How to Tell a True War Story', Tim O'Brien comments that 'You can tell a true war story only if it embarrasses you' (p. 175). This embarrassment is imbedded in the messi-ness of war memories. O'Brien later adds, 'The old rules are no longer binding, the old truths no longer true. Right spills over into wrong. Order blends into chaos [...]' (p. 181), in Paula Geyh et al., (eds.), *Postmodern American Fiction: A Norton Anthology* (New York: W. W. Norton, 1998).

[4] Hynes chose the title 'the soldiers' tale' to indicate that if all soldiers' tales were put together, the outcome would be one coherent story. Yet in this chapter I am more cautious and prefer the plural, which places an emphasis on juxtaposing different tales of war. Samuel Hynes, *The Soldiers' Tale: Bearing Witness to Modern War* (New York: Penguin, 1997).

Trapped between two opposing ways of framing war – the glorious and the inglorious – the members of the *Palmach* (known as *Palmachniks*)[5] were in need of a solution to the problem. The solution was that they lied to themselves and to each other about much of what they had done. They were bound to a conspiracy of silence, constructed with half a mind, or semi-consciously, and they created stories with silences built into them. They told some tales only in the safe company of their comrades. They adopted terms that helped them sanitise harsh deeds. This chapter is about these cleansing silences and the mechanisms of keeping secrets. It is also about the capacity of old soldiers to think again.

In his seminal text, Hynes does not dwell on soldiers' silences. He examines two principle kinds of sources, those that fulfill the urge to report and those that fulfill the urge to remember. The former were written mainly during the war: journals, diaries, letters, and these texts carried the virtue of immediacy and directness. The latter were often written long after the war and are more reflective, selective and self-consciously constructed.[6] However, there is a third repository of soldiers' tales: the collection of things about which they do not speak or write. This third form of narration is, of course, a more elusive source of information; it can remain hidden for years, if soldiers are very determined neither to report nor to remember it.

And yet over time, some of these hidden stories come out. Years must pass, but in particular circumstances, soldiers may remember things a different way. In this context, interviews are important. Conversations can lead in directions remote from the original narrative. And when this happens in the framework of an interview, a tape recorder can be turned off, or erased; more conventional formulations can be found, or older terminology reintroduced. And yet, oral evidence can push aside the veil of silence in limited though significant ways.

Three methodological notes – the subjects, the time, the author

The subjects of this study are the veterans of one Jewish *Palmach* unit who fought in 1948. The *Palmach* was considered the best trained Jewish force, comprised of the sons and daughters of its elite. The unit consisted of men and women, and combined the mission of being fighters with farm work,

---

[5] The *Palmach*, acronym for *Plugot Makhatz*, elite combat battalions, were established in 1941 and dissolved in 1948, when the Israel Defence Force was created. At its peak the strength of the *Palmach* was about 6,000.
[6] Hynes, *The Soldiers' Tale*, p. xiv.

while the longer-term plan was to establish a *kibbutz*.[7] While the men were the fighters, the women mainly fulfilled auxiliary tasks. This unit numbered almost fifty members when it was first established in the autumn of 1947. This chapter is based on an ethnographic study of this unit which included twenty interviews with the veterans, an analysis of their written memoirs, their own video-tapes and other written sources. The interviews were carried out in the years 2002–05, when the members of this unit were in their mid-seventies.

The subjects discussed in the interviews spanned the period from the end of the war of 1948 to 2005. These veterans remembered their lives together as young soldiers. They had engaged in collective recollection together for the last sixty years, in powerfully bonded informal associations. These groups were and still are sites of storytelling in which the shared character of recollection time and again reconstituted the group whose stories take on a certain unity. Thus, their reunions were performative; these people came together and in the act of doing so, both described and created their shared past.

This was as true in the first years after the end of the 1948 war as it was fifty years later. The difference was disenchantment. This too was a group matter; slowly but surely they came to see their country as different from the one they had envisioned in 1948. This loss of illusions, this changed context, had an impact on the tales they told of *their* war, the war of independence.

Of course they had changed too. They were growing old; these old soldiers, these *Palmachniks*, were now in the dusk of their lives, and were prone to reflect on their trajectory, just as others do who did not serve in uniform. They had families; grandchildren, and others who asked questions. It was natural that their storytelling would take on a somewhat different character than it had done in the past.

A word is necessary too on who conducted the interviews. Full disclosure requires a comment on my own subject position vis-à-vis these veterans. Samuel Hynes noted at the very opening of his book that his deliberations on the nature of warfare may have begun fifty years earlier, when he was an American soldier in the Second World War. Flying into combat at Okinawa, he was astonished that war was not what he had expected. Hynes's voice is that of the participant, who attempts to make sense of his own experience as well as that of others. My own position is more removed. I am a woman, have never taken an active part in a war, am

---

[7] The unit was defined as *hakhshara* (sing.) in Hebrew, meaning a training group. Roughly half of the *Palmach* members were organised in *hakhsharot* (plural). On the *hakhsharot*, see Alon Kadish, *la-meshek ve-la-neshek: ha-akhsharot ha-meguyasot ba-palmach* (To Arms and to Farms: The Hakhsharot in the *Palmach*) (Tel Aviv: Tag Publishers, 1995).

a member of the younger generation, one of the children of the 1948 generation, who previously studied the narratives of Palestinian refugees of the 1948 war. Not surprisingly, I was suspect in the eyes of the *Palmachniks* who assumed that I would have a hard time understanding the way they saw their lives. As Jay Winter noted in the introduction, just like many other veterans, they had a somewhat proprietary view of 'their' past.[8] Here is one such comment in an interview:

I would like you to understand; it is difficult to judge from today's perspective and sense the emotions back then. How should I say this to you? There was such a yearning (*kemiha*) for a state and such devotion (*hitmasrut*) that everyone knew that he was about to die. There was such readiness (*nekhonut*) because of this endless yearning. I tried to explain this feeling to my children. 'Listen children, close your eyes and think of something you wish for very much' and when they opened their eyes I'd say: 'That is how we wished for a state.'

I had and have no difficulty in understanding such a statement. This chapter is an attempt to respect it and at the same time, precisely because I have lived a different life, to go beyond and behind it, to elicit what silences were hidden behind this yearning, this dedication to bring the new state into being.

1.   Silence and emotional restraint

The public display of emotion was not a positive value especially for men within the newborn Israeli society in 1948. Setting a value on emotional restraint was part of the project of building the new collectivity, which had little room for those who expressed personal sentiments in public. A rejection of individualism implied the curbing of one's emotions when in company.[9]

The narratives of those interviewed reflected this normative system. One veteran, Avremaleh,[10] noted in 2005 that when he watched soldiers' funerals on the television in recent years, he was mystified by the comrades who gather round the fresh grave and cry in public. Such behaviour, he

---

[8] See ch. 1, pp. 7–8.

[9] Oz Almog, *The Sabra: Creation of the New Jew* (Berkeley and London: University of California Press, 2000). For a more general discussion see Peter N. Stearns and Carol Z. Stearns, 'Emotionology: Clarifying the History of Emotions and Emotional Standards', *American Historical Review* XC, 4 (1985), pp. 813–36. Holocaust survivors in Israel were also expected to abstain from speaking about their past. In the case of the Holocaust, the imposed silence was part of the negation of the Diaspora and the passive role of the Jew. For a review of this topic see Anita Shapira, 'The Holocaust: Private Memories, Public Memory', *Jewish Social Studies* IV, 2 (1998), pp. 40–58; Tom Segev, *The Seventh Million: the Israelis and the Holocaust* (New York: Hill and Wang, 1994); Hanna Yablonka, *Survivors of The Holocaust: Israel After the War* (New York University Press, 1999).

[10] Note that all names and most place names have been changed.

commented, was unacceptable in 'his time'. Shaikeh, another member of the same unit, knew well how emotional repression worked back in 1948. He recalled this exchange which followed his having killed an Arab villager: 'I remember that the Lieutenant asked me [about the killing]: "Tell me – how did it feel?" And our Captain was there and said to him: "What are you talking about? Cut the bullshit"' (*ma ata mevalbel lo bamoah, tafsik lekashkesh lo shtuyot*). This comment was made in the context of admiration for the Captain who cut the discussion short; one should not waste words on how something felt. During the interview with Gad, he touched on the same theme. When I asked whether they would talk of personal matters, he replied:

> – Much less than we would today, for sure. I am certain. I think that had we been talking of these things today, we would surely speak of the burden that each of us carries from back then. It would surely be more personal than it could have been back then.
> – Why?
> – I don't know. This is the way we were brought up. This is how we were educated. Once more I am generalising but I think this was the gist of the period. Look, let us make a very unfair and imprecise comparison: Look at the Arabs today: All these *shahid*s [suicide bombers]. This kind of upbringing of a *shahid*, whereby a mother sends her son and after his death thanks God. Isn't this abnormal? Right? We cannot understand it. We will never be like that. We even tuck it into a corner so as not to speak about it. Human beings do not talk like that. That is the general atmosphere.
> So coming back from this imprecise comparison I say: We, too, were characterized by things that cannot be understood with today's sensitivity. We were tougher. We were stronger. And also, perhaps in parallel, we were less thoughtful. It is not as if we were made of a special substance. But this is the way we were brought up. I don't know whether what I'm saying would make sense to everyone but I am sure it makes sense to many of those who lived back then.

'Back then' was certainly not a passing moment but rather a powerful and enduring norm within a set of values that prevailed both before and long after 1948. Berl Katznelson, a Zionist leader, wrote following the eruption of the 1936 inter-communal violence in Palestine: 'This generation of Israel, for whom the world and his country have become gallows, knows not weeping, nor praying, nor pleading like its forefathers, yet is stubborn and standing firm like them.'[11] 'Back then' was also more evident within certain

---

[11] Bracha Habas (ed.), *Sefer Me'oraot Tartsav* (The 1936 Occurrences) (Tel Aviv: Davar, 1937), introduction by Berl Katznelson, p. 13. This rejection of weeping is evident even earlier, when Avshalom Feinberg (an underground leader in Palestine) wrote the following: 'Descendents of Bar-Kokhva! To take arms, to fight, to win or to die a hero's death, but not to cry...', in Nitsa Ben-Ari, *Dikuy ha-erotica: tsenzura utsenzura atsmit ba-sifrut ha-ivrit 1930–1980* (Suppression of the Erotic: Censorship and self-censorship in Hebrew literature 1930–1980) (Tel Aviv University Press, 2006), p. 366, footnote 38.

segments of the population who were highly committed to the national cause. The *Palmach* fighters were in many respects the vanguard of this stratum. In a poem on an unrequited love, published in 1955, Israeli poet Lea Goldberg commented critically on this norm of emotional restraint:

> This generation thinks crying a disgrace
> It will not cry for dying love
> On judgment day or nights of grace
> No tear shall wet its proud and stony face.[12]

Saying little, curbing emotions and being steadfast: these were the hallmarks of the *Palmach* soldiers. These habits, acquired early on in their lives, persisted for many decades after. However, when they reached their seventies, men like Gad were still struck by the restraint that characterised their early years; someone who had not been socialised into these ways of being could not fully understand these silences.

There were gendered differences in accepted standards of emotional comportment. While the ideal fighter was expected to be restrained, the women were permitted some emotional expression. This distinction was evident within the *Palmach* unit itself. The women's role was to care for the fighting men; they would accompany them when leaving for combat and receive them upon their return. In the early months of the 1948 war, delegations of women, or women accompanied by men, came to families and told them of the death of their loved ones. Women shared the preference for the laconic, but still, as women, they had more space to express their emotions than did men.

2.   *Sanitising Language*

Silences emerged from such rules of social comportment. But even when information or feelings were exchanged, the language used was always modulated to tone down its emotional content. A choice of words to describe the enemy was significant in order to diminish any identification with the human beings fighting on the other side of the line. For instance, the *yeshuv*'s (namely the pre-1948 Jewish population of Palestine) most common terms to describe the Arab fighters (both in 1936–9 and later in 1948) were gangs (*knufiyot*) and rioters (*por'im*). An Arab village before it was attacked was described as 'the nest of the murderers' (*ken Hameratzhim*). While these phrases were generally used, others were unique to the *Palmach*. As the *Palmachniks* faced 'difficult' military

---

[12] Lea Goldberg, *Barak Ba-boker: Shirim* (Merhavia: Sifriyyat hapoalim, 1955). I thank Yahav Zohar for the translation.

situations to deal with during the war, they were exceptionally creative in finding euphemisms for what had happened.[13]

In April 1948, the unit was fighting in the Jerzre'el valley and its surroundings. The nearby Arab villagers of Sabbarin and al-Kafrin were forced to hurriedly flee and left their farm animals behind. Rivkaleh, a member of the unit, spoke of the following events:

> By then, after the attack on [*kibbutz*] Mishmar Ha'emek, the whole area was freed (*shihreru et kol haezor*) and our friends [the men] reached *Ju'ara* [an army camp]. Many cows from the Arab villages were roaming the area, roaming freely (*histovevu hofshi*), and the *Palmach* gathered these cows (*HaPalmach asaf et haparot*) and brought them to the *kibbutz*.

Rivkaleh's language sanitised the operation: the area was freed rather than conquered; the cows of the Arab villages were roaming freely; we do not know why no one was there to tend them. The Arab villagers are altogether absent from the pastoral scene and their land is described as 'the area'. The farm animals are gathered, rather than taken as war plunder. Every moral conundrum was rhetorically buried in a few short sentences.

3.   *Death and denial*

Any cursory examination of war narratives will disclose how common it is for soldiers to sanitise language and use euphemisms when it comes to the dead.[14] Denial and euphemisms were evident when *Palmachniks* reflected on the possibility of their own death as well as that of comrades. This sense of immunity was described by Gideon in his narrative on the withdrawal from their first violent mission:

> We were ordered to withdraw and then discovered that there were two seriously wounded soldiers and for some reason ... I had to carry one of them with someone else. There were no stretchers. So we put his hands here [pointing to his shoulders] and someone else carried his legs, and walking in the mountains was not easy. It was awful. We did not think one can get killed of course. Despite the fact that the one I carried had a bullet in his head.

---

[13] For a popular dictionary of slang words, including many originating in the *Palmach*, see Dan Ben-Amotz and Netiva Ben-Yehuda, *Milon olami le'ivrit meduberet* (A World Dictionary of Spoken Hebrew) (Jerusalem: Levin Epstein, 1972).

[14] In 'How to Tell a True War Story', Tim O'Brien seems to say that in fact euphemism, or better said, recourse to metaphor, can be a 'true' way of telling a story. Lemon's death, after detonating a land mine, is best described, according to O'Brien, in metaphorical terms: '[...] and when his foot touched down, in that instant, he must've thought it was the sunlight that was killing him. It was not the sunlight. It was a rigged 105 round. But if I could ever get the story right, how the sun seemed to gather around him and pick him up and lift him into a tree, if I could somehow recreate the fatal whiteness of the light [...]' (p. 181).

The soldier that Gideon carried died. Perhaps he was already dead when Gideon was carrying him back to the base. Yet for Gideon, this was unthinkable. He elaborated further on this, adding his interpretation to it:

At some stage in war you build a barrier (*khayitz*) between yourself and what is happening around you because what is happening is an awful thing altogether. The fear. Everything that happens is something you did not want to happen.

Avremaleh described a very similar feeling:

From the first to the last battle, I was never indecisive. I didn't think that I was going to die. I didn't think that it was my last battle. At times I may have thought something could happen to others, but I never experienced an anxiety from death. I'm not a fearful type. At least I wasn't back then. I probably did change since, but back then I was stupid enough not to have any fear.

These veterans were well aware of their reluctance to admit the dangers of war. They had to measure up to their fellow soldiers, who were young and full of normal adolescent bravado. I asked Gad how the unit coped with the fact that three of their close comrades had been killed in two missions. He replied:

I am not sure I can answer this question because I think that all of us, if I may generalise, we were totally preoccupied by what we were doing and it was clear that it can happen and it happens. ... From every direction we would hear of Jews dying here and there. Yet as the situation progressed, we were less preoccupied in coping with this. Perhaps one represses. There is surely repression (*hadchaka*) here. I assume this was the condition because we would have noticed someone who would treat it differently.

Even decades later, when Gad was well aware of their past tendency to repress thoughts about death, the words he chose to speak of it were minimal: 'It can happen' or 'we were less preoccupied in coping with this'. This denial found its way to the slang of the period. The popular phrase which was used to refer to someone who had been killed was that he had 'gone to fetch something' (*halach lehavie*). Though popular among the *Palmachniks*, it disappeared from Hebrew speech and is unknown to the generations that followed.

Denial was also necessary when talking about the enemy. Many of the *Palmachniks* were born and raised in Palestine and had ongoing relations with the local Arabs. When war broke out, the neighbouring Arab – working in an orchard or shop alongside Jews – had to be transformed into 'the enemy'. The enemy was more often than not depersonalised rather than portrayed as evil. One way for the *Palmachniks* to bypass familiarity was to relate to the enemy as a foreigner.

One of the unit's most frequently repeated stories comes from the height of the fighting at the ill-fated battle of Kirin. During the battle, Shaikeh was sent with a message to his officer and came across an enemy soldier who jumped on him, and the two began to wrestle. Two comrades came to his assistance, and they managed to kill the enemy soldier. The dead man, the *Palmachniks* claimed, was a Yugoslav volunteer on the Arabs' side. Why they gave him this identity, they could not explain. Someone came up with the term 'Yugoslav', and they all took it for granted that this dead man was indeed Yugoslav.

On another occasion the unit was sent by night to attack a house near Shefa-'amr (Shefar'am, in Hebrew). Again the claim was made that it housed 'all kinds of ex-Nazis, Yugoslavs, Germans, who came to assist the Arabs.' From these narratives one gets the impression that few Palestine-born Arabs were in the ranks of the enemy. This perception complemented the hegemonic Zionist narrative according to which the Arab inhabitants of Palestine hardly fought but merely relied on foreign assistance and at one point chose to flee.[15] Hence, although the local Arabs were denounced for precipitating the war (following the 29 November 1947 UN resolution offering partition as a solution), they were also represented as cowardly, since they fled without putting up a fight. Different studies have shown that in some localities Palestinians did fight for their land.[16] The *Palmachniks* therefore constructed an imaginary enemy, one who was not their neighbours but rather veterans of the killing fields of the Second World War.

Fighting and killing such enemy soldiers caused no moral problems. When these *Palmach* units came across Arabs in flight, they were confused, troubled and ill at ease. In July 1948, the unit was stationed at an old Arab *khan*, on the road east taken by over 30,000 Arabs expelled from the towns of Ramle and Lydda.[17] The following is Gideon's description of what they saw:

> – A long procession was in front of us. It was their way East. And that was the most difficult site I witnessed during the war, I think, because I constantly saw the Jewish people going into exile. I saw a nation walking into exile with all the

[15] On the image of Palestine's Arabs in the eyes of its Jewish population see Yisrael Ben-Dor, *Dimuy ha-'oyev ha-aravi ba-yeshuv ha-yehudi ube-medinat yisrael ba-shanim 1947–1957* (The Image of the Arab Enemy in the Jewish Yeshuv and in the State of Israel 1947–1956), (Ph.D., University of Haifa, 2003).

[16] Nafez Nazzal, *The Palestinian Exodus from the Galilee 1948* (Beirut: Institute for Palestine Studies, 1978); Elias Shoufani, 'The Fall of a Village', *Journal of Palestine Studies* I, 4 (1972), pp. 108–21.

[17] Benny Morris, *A History of the First Arab Israeli War* (New Haven: Yale University Press, 2008), pp. 286–93.

consequences … They left with quilts and pillows in their hands and bit by bit lost them, until they were left with only their clothes on. The days were unbearably hot. They passed near us and we had water there, cisterns, and we gave the guys [*hevreh*] water.

One day, in the afternoon, just before the evening, someone passed and suddenly fell on the shoulders of one of us and said: Eli, Eli, Eli. Eli studied at Mikve Yisrael [an agricultural high school] and this Arab used to work there and had known him. Or perhaps he had known him from Ness Ziona [Eli's town of origin]. He begged us to allow him to sleep on the stairs of this building, this *khan*. We would not allow them to come near the *khan* fearing that one would take out a gun against us. We were only twenty people there. Eli said: OK, sleep here. The next morning we found him dead.
– Dead of what?
– A broken heart (*shivron lev*). We gave him tea in the evening and it seemed that everything was OK. But he never woke up. He wasn't a young man. And like him, many died on the track – children, babies. We saw mothers abandoning their babies – placing them under trees. We really tried to help them.

Gideon certainly expresses sympathy with these people, yet he also down plays the role of the *Palmach* in their predicament. Going into exile is a Jewish story too. When describing how they gave water to the refugees, he nicknames them 'guys' – *hevreh*, as if they are like him rather than people who have just been expelled by Gideon's army. They did not participate in whatever was causing the expulsion. They are watching a scene unfold, and offering simple forms of human assistance. The old man, notes Gideon, died of a broken heart and not from the long journey in the heat of July. There are resounding silences throughout this narrative, not only in terms of the language used but also in the sense of detachment from the very war producing these population movements. Someone else was responsible for the fact that in their midst a Palestinian refugee died of a broken heart.

In another description of the same event, appearing in a memoir written by one of these soldiers, the Arabs are described as stumbling over one another in their attempts to reach the well at the *khan*. One of their babies is on the verge of falling into the well when one of the Jewish soldiers saves him. Watching Palestinian refugees on the move in wartime was troubling to be sure, so troubling that most of the veterans refrained from mentioning the event altogether.

4.   *Killing*

One particular event was both hard to forget and hard to recall. It was the killing of an old woman at the village of Jublein. All inhabitants of this village in the eastern Galilee had fled by the time the unit arrived on the scene at the end of May 1948. Fierce fighting at a nearby village two weeks earlier may have led to the inhabitants' flight. However, as happened in many of the other villages, some elderly people were left behind in the deserted villages. Avremaleh spoke on three different occasions about the killing of an old Arab woman in this village, first saying:

We reached Jublein and there something happened that I will not tell you: an old Arab woman was killed there. That is, I can tell you without disclosing who did it. Someone saw the Arab woman and shot a burst at her and she ran and even picked up her shoe. It was important for her to hold the shoe. Then he shot another burst and another burst at her. And she died.

The passivity of the observers – all but the unnamed man who fires the shots – reverberates; why didn't they stop the shooting soldier after the first burst or the second one? Later in the interview, when reflecting on the moral consequences of the war, Avremaleh argued that his division kept to high moral norms, with the exception of this one incident:

We fought in the central front, in the northern front, in the southern front, and I remember no such [immoral] deeds other than the terrible case in Jublein when one of us killed an Arab woman simply for the sake of killing. That is terrible and I will never forget it. Otherwise, I cannot recall any improper behaviour by one of us or by people who were with us.

Here was the exception (of straying from moral norms) that proved the rule, one that was part of the self-image of Israeli soldiers not only in 1948 but thereafter. 'Purity of arms' mattered to them. But even as an exception, this incident is unsettling to the men interviewed, and Avremaleh, who returns to discuss the event a third time, tries to explain the fact that it has been erased from memory:

I want to tell you something. We were touring Kirin (near Jublein) not long ago [in May 2003] and I was walking near a friend of mine telling him: 'Let me remind you' [of the woman who was killed here]… And he says: 'I don't remember it happening.' A friend of mine who was near me in the battle. He says: 'I don't remember it happening.' I say to him: 'It couldn't be that you don't remember.' He says: 'I don't remember it happening.' And I see it in front of my eyes. I see her running up the hill. I see how she runs. She had a white shoe. She bent and he shot. I see it with my eyes. And he says: 'I don't remember it happening.' Believe me. If he says he doesn't remember, he doesn't remember. Namely, it has been erased. Just as I have erased many things.

When I asked him what the consequences of the incident were at the time, he noted that there were no consequences whatsoever. 'No one boycotted him [the killer],' he said, 'Only I boycotted him in my heart.' Like so many other issues, this too was silenced.

Although this event is described as an exception, there were other similar incidents. At one time the soldiers had a car accident in the heart of the Galilee, and some said that they killed an Arab passer-by, lest he report them to the nearby Arab villages. Others noted that they think this person they held, then described as a 'prisoner', had been released.

While these two events were described by several interviewees and found their way to the unit's chronicle (see below, pp. 194–5), the following story was recited by one veteran only. This may be due to the fact that the *Palmach* unit was dismembered at one point, and some of these soldiers found themselves fighting alongside 'new' soldiers. Thus the narratives diverged at times. The event in question happened during 'Operation Broom', in which the Jewish forces expelled the Bedouin population of the eastern Galilee.[18] Gideon asked me to turn off the tape and told me about a soldier under his command who was about to kill an Arab woman sitting on a stone in front of her tent. He turned to the soldier and prevented him from doing so. However, when Gideon looked away, the soldier shot the woman and killed her. To explain how unusual such a deed was, Gideon noted that this soldier 'has only recently come off the ship', namely, he was a Holocaust survivor, and he could not speak [Hebrew] and he looked as if he was a bit of a lunatic [*yarad mehapasim*, literally meaning 'he strayed from the lines']. In all these explanations, he portrayed the soldier as the complete opposite to the standard *Palmach* soldier – raised in Palestine, Hebrew speaking and adhering to a code of the purity of arms.[19] Perhaps to demonstrate the poetic justice of the story, he noted that the killer was himself killed shortly thereafter.

So far we have seen that the *Palmachniks* employed a variety of masking or silencing methods in the tales they told – sanitising language, denying the existence of certain events, describing the unacceptable as exceptions that prove the rule of morality, abstaining from recording sensitive tales. Yet there is another process of silencing that takes us in a different direction. This is the domain of communal secrets, tales which can be told within the collective, but never outside of it.

5. *Secrets*

The first armed encounter of this *Palmach* unit, in December 1947, was an assault on an Arab village, in retaliation for the killing of thirty-nine Jews in

[18] Morris, *A History*, p. 157.

[19] For a key study of the profile of the *Palmach* generation and its image, with emphasis on books of commemoration, see Emmanuel Sivan, *Dor Tashah: Mitos, Dyokan ve-zikaron (The 1948 generation: Myth, Profile and Memory)* (Tel Aviv: Ma'arachot, 1991).

a nearby town. The mission was to attack the village by night by breaking into the houses, using axes when needed. The soldiers were instructed to separate the women from the men and kill the men. One estimate has it that 60 to 100 Arab villagers were killed on the occasion.[20] This is how the unit's officer described the event fifty years later:

We received arms and a briefing and went off to take cruel revenge (*laasot shefatim*). We walked on the slopes of the Mountain [Carmel Mountain] and came down to the village in a few waves (*kama rashim*). At some stage they [the Arabs] noticed us and shot [at us]. We did not respond. We penetrated quickly into the village and began the action. It wasn't simple. It wasn't a nice kind of an action. We did what we were supposed to do and retreated. [...]. There are no nice battles but this one had something unpleasant [added to it]. The youngsters who returned glorified their deeds. Very soon it became tasteless and unpleasant. [...] Among these youth there were those to which this kind of wild behavior was alien but in the circumstances of this battle, this is what they were expected to do.[21]

Despite the understated tone, one can sense the officer's discomfort, when he summarises the event: 'They [the soldiers of the *Palmach* unit attacking] were good guys and the case at this village was the worst case we had.'[22] Both the officer and the soldiers were demoralised by this kind of retaliatory action. The day after this mass killing, as the men came back to their *kibbutz* base, they organised a get-together and curiously named it the 'Party of the First', drawing its name both from the date of the party, 1 January 1948, and from the title given to the action – the first battle (*Hakrav Harishon*). Indeed, the nightly attack was hardly a battle, but was so named retroactively, joining other instances of language laundering.

The 'Party of the First' soon became an annual event. During the war the unit tried to hold it once a month, though with limited success due to the ongoing fighting. Since the end of the war, these men and women have been meeting almost every year on 1 January, for sixty years (2008).

The character of this annual meeting was set during the first occasion it was held, and it has not changed much in later years. It included singing together (*shira betsibur*) a set list of Hebrew songs, reading poems (including a pacifist poem by Nathan Alterman entitled 'Don't you give them guns'), reading a translation of a Soviet text on the justification of going to war and a recitation of a war chronicle they themselves composed.

---

[20] Yoseph Argaman, *Khiver Haya Halaila* (Pale was the Night) (Tel Aviv: Yediot Ahronot, 2002), p. 74.
[21] The above-cited officer died before I began my research. The quote is taken from a book based on interviews with him and about him. Argaman, *Khiver Haya Halaila*, p. 74.
[22] Argaman, *Khiver Haya Halaila*, p. 77.

The war chronicle was written in the years immediately after the war and since 1952 has not changed much. The chronicle, ten typed pages, described the unit's war events. To accompany the chronicle, a map of Israel was hung on the wall, indicating the sites of each battle and incident. What comes as a surprise, at least to me, was that the chronicle is not at all sanitised. It is written in short laconic sentences, and is comprised of piercing descriptions, such as the following:

A little later [after the retaliation raid in the Arab village described above] an awful feeling overcomes us; a kind of a shock. The babies cry silenced by hand grenades; a woman ripped to pieces by a Sten gun; a helpless man hiding under a bed, killed by a burst of gunfire. Is this war? Is this heroism? Are these the enemies? Here is the sum of our first battle. And then comes the Party of the First.

It is evident that the Party of the First is a profoundly intimate, uncensored moment, a site at which the unsayable is said. Within the confines of the party, in the framework of a carefully worked out written text, in the ordained time – a liminal time set outside of 'regular time' – the haunting memories of war can be uttered and shared. Here is another example: 'Two days later comes the theft of property at the village of Shefar'am.' 'Each one of you [women] can order booty. Do you want a wrist watch? Fine. It is not difficult to carry/to swipe [*liskhov*].'[23]

In this way, the group's troubled conscience, their repressed collective memory, can be put to rest, at least for a time. Silence is lifted: we feel the shock of 'battle', see the looting of valuables, the killing of the innocent. Hidden stories come to light, but only in the confines of the party, the moment when old soldiers come together and speak together of things they do not say at any other time.

For decades, it was this hidden, semi-sacred collective text and its ritualised reading that brought everyone in the unit together. However, in 1998, to celebrate the war's fiftieth anniversary, the unit decided to breach this code of secrecy. All family members were invited. The songs, the poems and parts of the chronicle were shared with children and grandchildren, friends and other guests. The organisers were well aware of the risks of doing so, and began the evening with the following apology: 'There is a special format to this party and an external observer may not understand the things as we did [...]. We beg your forgiveness.'

Why did they keep this vow of silence before 1998 and break it thereafter? The consequences of bringing the story into the public domain, even when restricted to close family members, were simply too painful. As long as the *Palmachniks* felt that they had to behave as national heroes,

---

[23] The Hebrew term *liskhov* literally means to carry, but in slang it means to steal.

their public demeanour came first. They simply locked these stories in a safe place – one they shared only with each other. But as the *Palmachniks* grew old, as they reflected more and more on their past, and as the national tale of totally heroic state-builders lost its grip, they were prepared to bring these tales to the surface, or in the terms Jay Winter suggested in the introduction to this book (see p. 3), to reconfigure the landscape between memory and forgetting by adding previously hidden and protected silences to what could be said about the past.

Conclusion

The reasons why hidden stories emerged only at the end of the twentieth century are complex. History affects memory, over time. Israeli historians brought to light overwhelming evidence of the ways Arab villagers were forced to flee from their villages by Jewish troops. The unsayable became sayable: the creation of the state of Israel was accompanied by a monumental injustice to the Palestinian inhabitants of what became Israel. What Israeli soldiers did in 1948 appeared not only commonplace, but also – to those who lived to tell the story as well as to those now permitted to hear it – forgivable. These were young men and women; they did not choose that war or those circumstances. Some were more troubled by the killing of innocents than others. The culprits were not identified and pilloried. But at least their acts – their crimes – were admitted in public.

There is a vast literature on why soldiers take time before their stories get turned into tales, sold by the thousands to a reading public of millions. Part of the reason is that it always takes time to filter experiences, especially painful ones. But part of the explanation for a time lag is a sense of shame at what an individual did or what he allowed to be done by another soldier in his unit.

In addition to such personal considerations are collective ones. These mattered to the men and women of the *Palmach*. The creation of the new state was of supreme importance to them, and speaking of the ugly things done at that time could serve no purpose, or so they believed. Fifty years later, the state was an ongoing reality, and these people felt less obliged to bear the heavy weight of silence, along with the things they carried from their turbulent past.

11   Forgetting the Lebanon war? On silence, denial, and the selective remembrance of the "First" Lebanon war

Asher Kaufman

> Beirut is burning. Beirut is in flames.
> This is the chance to toss out all the trash.
> Throw conscience and freedom into the blaze.
> Clear the whole zone. Leave not a stone.
>
> Burn the books, paper burns well.
> Don't be soft, just feed the flames.
> Clean house for Passover: is someone shouting?
> Stuff a burning rag into mouth that gapes.
>
> Are there doubts? Burn those too! And pitch into the fire
> The cries, sighs, and groans.
> The stench of charred infant flesh
> Will cover over many odors.
>
> Beirut is burning. Beirut is in flames.
> Turn everything to ash, once and for all.
> Throw conscience and freedom into the blaze
> Lest tomorrow they blossom anew.[1]
>
> Hanoch Levin, 1982

On March 21, 2007, after months of deliberations, it became official. The 2006 summer war between Israel and Hizbullah was given the formal name "the Second Lebanon War."[2] The Israeli government succumbed to public pressure and not only grudgingly recognized these "events" as a war but also gave up its original plan to name it with a moralizing and nationalistic appellation, settling instead on the name that had already struck roots within the Israeli public. Naming the recent conflict as the Second Lebanon War has naturally invoked the "first" Lebanon war,

---

[1] Hanoch Levin, *Bo Elay Hayal Nehmad, Kol Ha-Ktavim* (Tel Aviv: Hakibbutz Hameuhad, 2000). Many thanks to Adina Hoffman and Alan Paris for translating the poem into English.
[2] *Haaretz*, March 22, 2007.

197

reflecting the fact that within the Israeli public a strong link has been made between the two. Indeed, during the thirty-four-day 2006 summer war, public discourse in Israel not only focused on analyzing the current confrontation per se, but was also imbued with references to Israeli memories of Lebanon. Thus, terms such as the "Lebanese trauma," the "Lebanese quagmire," or the "Lebanese nightmare," dominated media coverage and demonstrated the fact that Lebanon and the Israeli preoccupation with this country have been on the back burners of Israeli public consciousness and returned to the front as a result of this recent war. Media analysis of the war constantly referred to the 1982 Lebanon war and the consequent eighteen years occupation of South Lebanon until May 2000, in an attempt to draw parallels with 2006. All in all, there was general agreement in describing Lebanon as a rotten, violent, and irrational "black hole" into which Israel has been periodically and inadvertently drawn since 1982 and even before. Israel, in these descriptions, was portrayed at best as an innocent victim and at worse as guilty of association with this murky entity. Buttressed by a self-image of innocence, the overwhelming majority of the Jewish-Israeli public (followed by the media) pressed for a violent and retaliatory reaction against Hizbullah and Lebanon. The poor results of the war were perceived as another link in a chain of Lebanese traumas inflicted upon Israel.

One may have needed a second Lebanon war in order to awaken public awareness about the "first" war. Indeed, until the summer of 2006 the first Lebanon war had been a "repressed war" in Israeli public consciousness.[3] This may seem surprising given the fact that at the time the Israeli invasion of Lebanon on June 6, 1982 and the following months until roughly the end of September had been perceived as one of the most cataclysmic events ever experienced by Israeli society. Many commentators believed then that the war would leave a lasting impact on Israel for many years to come. It was assumed that this war would be remembered, commemorated, discussed, and debated, if not by official state agents, then at least by different agencies of the civil society. The war, after all, was described in ways that left very little doubt that it would leave an indelible scar on the delicate tissue of Israeli society. Some of the most important Israeli thinkers and commentators described it in unequivocal terms. For example, S. N. Eisenstadt, the renowned sociologist, wrote that the war transformed Israeli society, weakened its civility, increased its divisiveness, created a breakdown of many normative restraints in public behavior and weakened the feeling of shame which led to violence and growing

---

[3] Eyal Zisser, "The 1982 'Peace for Galilee' War: Looking Back in Anger – Between an Option of a War and a War of No Option," in Mordechai Bar-On (ed.), *Never-Ending Conflict* (Mechanicsburg, Pa., Stackpole Books, 2004): 193.

intolerance.[4] Or, in the introduction to *The Lebanon War – Between Protest and Compliance*, a critical book on the war, the editors wrote:

> [...] [T]he stormy public debate that the Lebanon war instigated – its relevance and gravity – has not and will not dissipate any time soon. Also, the ideological debate on the path Israel should take, on its political and security conception, on its behavioral norms, which match our moral approach, has not and will not terminate quickly. The public repercussions of the Kahan commission[5] [...] will add another dimension to the problems created by this war and will not allow the subject matter to be removed from our agenda for a long time.[6]

Given these comments, it may be surprising to learn that within a few years after the supposed "conclusion" of the war in 1985 various Israeli commentators frequently lamented the fact that the Lebanon war was anything but remembered in Israel. Already in 1987, the internationally acclaimed author Amos Oz condemned its disappearance from public memory.[7] Eighteen years later, and marking the fifth anniversary of the May 2000 Israeli withdrawal from South Lebanon, a leading journalist and a 1982 war veteran, remarked:

> If you ask most Israelis [...] [they would tell you that] these are the chronicles of that war: in'82 the IDF crossed the international boundary, fueled with the vision of Ariel Sharon of a new Middle East, reached Beirut and deported Yasser Arafat. In 2000, the army crossed the boundary again, this time southbound, fueled with the election promise of Ehud Barak. In between many people got killed. [...] Our collective memory is an amazing phenomenon. It has a life expectancy of a genetically challenged butterfly and an infinite ability to forget. [...] And so, Lebanon is the forgotten war.[8]

Indeed, it may seem that at least until the summer of 2006, the last war where Israel was engaged in a full-scale conflict was anything but remembered by the Israeli public.

In a country that is absorbed by its wars and their commemoration, this may at first seem surprising. After all, because of the dominance of the "conflict" in public as well as private life in Israel, recollection of wars and their acts of remembrance are paramount in Israeli society. As such, a whole "industry" of war remembrance has developed far beyond other

---

[4] S. N. Eisenstadt, *The Internal Repercussions of the Lebanon War* (Jerusalem: The Leonard Davis Institute for International Relations, August 1986).

[5] The Kahan Commission was an independent commission of enquiry that was assigned by the Israeli government to investigate the massacre at the Palestinian refugee camps at Sabra and Shatila. See more below.

[6] Yitzhak Ben Aharaon et al. (eds.), *The Lebanon War – Between Protest and Compliance* (Tel Aviv: Hakibbutz Hameuchad, 1983): 7.

[7] Amos Oz, *The Slopes of Lebanon* (New York: Vintage International, 1992): 1.

[8] Ofer Shelah, *Blazer*, June 2005: 58–9.

national events, perhaps only competing with the commemoration industry of the Holocaust. The frequency of wars and the general militarization of the Jewish-Israeli society seem to assist in the pervasiveness of these acts of remembrance – from memorial monuments to *Yizkor* (commemoration) brochures, from literature to film, and from private to national memorial events and services – they all provide a sense that the public memory of wars is indeed omnipresent in Israeli society. Moreover, if one were to take seriously the harsh critique set off by the 1982 invasion, one would think that the Israeli public would not hastily forget this war and its consequences. If so, how can one reconcile the magnitude of that war and the controversy it instigated, and the general sense that, at least until 2006, it was erased from public memory? Why is it that time and time again commentators have mentioned the fact that this war – and not other wars Israel has fought – was simply a forgotten war, or, a "war that did not exist?"[9]

A few immediate answers to these questions come to mind. Since the war became harshly contested a few weeks after its outbreak, it was convenient not to engage in its remembrance and, rather, to focus on more consensual wars. Also, the war did not really draw to a close but rather lingered on for eighteen long years until the Israeli withdrawal from South Lebanon in May 2000. During these years it was difficult to commemorate it, as it was not yet an event of the past, although in the public mind it was no longer considered to be a full-fledged war after September 1982. Thirdly, in December 1987, five and a half years after its outbreak, the first Intifada erupted and diverted public attention from Lebanon to the Palestinian Occupied Territories. And then, in 2000, with the eruption of the second Intifada, it happened again. Although the Israeli withdrawal from South Lebanon could have been used as a good moment for reflection on this war, the Palestinian uprising, a few months after the withdrawal, diverted again public attention to the Occupied Territories and left the Lebanese experience in the shadows.

This was made utterly clear when Ariel Sharon, the minister of defense in 1982, became prime minister in 2001. No serious public debate emerged that involved the question of his condemnation by the 1982–3 Kahan Commission (to be discussed below) as a man indirectly responsible for war crimes, allegedly confirming the impression that the war and its consequences had been completely erased from the collective memory of Israeli society.

---

[9] Nurith Gertz, "The War that Did Not Exist," in Nurith Gertz et al. (eds.), *Mabatim fiktiviyim: 'al kolno'a Yisraeli* (Tel Aviv: Ha-Universitah ha-Petuhah, 1998): 67–91.

These are all valid but circumstantial points. In this essay I propose to go beyond them and to argue that in fact it is not forgetfulness that has characterized Israeli attitude towards the first Lebanon war, but rather silence, denial, and selective remembrance. One way to examine what has happened to the collective memory of the war in Israel is to observe the political trajectory of Ariel Sharon, its prime architect. Sharon's political career seemed to have reached an abrupt conclusion, following the recommendations of the Kahan Commission which investigated the massacres at Sabra and Shatila, yet gradually and assiduously, Sharon regained his stature to the point that in January 2001 and again in 2003 he became prime minister in landslide victories. In fact, he came to be regarded by large sections of the Jewish-Israeli society as the ultimate leader, the grandfatherly, elderly, and benign figure, who could and would save Israel from its enemies and from itself. As I argue in this chapter, it was not oblivion that facilitated the reemergence of Sharon to the high stature of *the* national leader in Israel, but rather indifference to his responsibility for crimes directly committed by a Lebanese militia on Palestinians in the midst of a civil war.

The chapter is divided into four main sections. I begin with a brief description of the 1982 invasion of Lebanon followed by an examination of the debate about its justification and its morality. I focus on the moral dimension because it dominated public discourse in Israel during and immediately after the invasion. I then discuss briefly the recommendations of the Kahan Commission and their impact on the political career of Sharon. The following section looks succinctly at attitudes within state and civil society towards the war from 1982 to 2000, attitudes which, I argue, facilitated the political comeback of Sharon. The last section examines the political rehabilitation of Sharon and his place in the remembrance of the war within Israeli society. The essay concludes with some reflections on the currently accepted boundaries of commemoration of this war in Israel.

The outbreak of the war

Following an assassination attempt on the Israeli ambassador to Britain on June 4, 1982, Israeli warplanes attacked Palestinian positions in Lebanon. In less than twenty-four hours the Israeli-Lebanese border was in flames, for the first time since the July 1981 cease-fire agreement between the Palestinian Liberation Organization (PLO) and Israel. Although the Abu Nidal Palestinian splinter group was behind the assassination attempt and the PLO was quick to disclaim any responsibility, Israel targeted PLO positions in order to provoke the organization to respond, which in turn would provide it with a pretext to launch a military assault against the Palestinian organization in Lebanon. On the evening of June 5, the government of Israel held a special session and voted for a military operation in Lebanon with the declared aim "to place all the civilian population of the Galilee beyond the range of the terrorists' fire from Lebanon, where they, their bases and their headquarters are concentrated." In the same statement the operation was given the name "Peace for Galilee" and it was stated that the Israeli forces were not to attack the Syrian military unless it initiated an attack against the IDF. The government statement concluded with the declaration that "the state of Israel continues to aspire to sign a peace accord with independent Lebanon, while maintaining its territorial integrity."[10] Based on subsequent military and governmental communiques, it was also stated that the IDF would not occupy any Lebanese land beyond a roughly 40 km cut-off line from the international Israeli-Lebanese boundary. However, within a few days after the beginning of the invasion it became crystal clear that there were other objectives behind the decision to invade Lebanon. By June 8 the IDF was actively engaged in an offensive against Syrian forces deployed in Lebanon and by June 13 Israeli forces arrived in the outskirts of Beirut, connected with units of the Christian Phalanges and began an almost two-month siege of the Lebanese capital, Beirut. Thus, the three covert goals were exposed: wiping out the Palestinian military presence in Lebanon and destabilizing the Palestinian national movement, forcing the evacuation of Syrian forces from Lebanon, and installing a pro-Israeli government in the country.

At first it seemed that most objectives had been achieved. On August 27 Bashir Gemayel, Israel's most important ally and the linchpin for the success of the entire scheme, was elected president of Lebanon; and on September 1, following international mediation, the PLO concluded its evacuation from Beirut. Yet, on September 15, Gemayel was assassinated and a day later Christian Phalanges forces entered, with the direct approval of Ariel Sharon, the Palestinian refugee camps of Sabra and Shatila and for three consecutive days massacred hundreds of undefended Palestinian civilians.[11] From here it was only downhill for Israel in its Lebanese adventure.

The invasion of Lebanon was widely supported at first both in the Knesset and within the Jewish Israeli public. Yet, signs of discontent

---

[10] Pinhas Yorman (ed.), *Mivtza Shelom Ha-Galil* (Jerusalem: Merkaz ha-Hasbara, March 1983): 3.
[11] Numbers of casualties vary from 700 according to Israeli sources to 2,000 according to Palestinian sources. Lebanese authorities put the death toll at 1,200 fatalities.

were also quick to surface. It began with organizations of reserve soldiers who criticized the government for its decision to invade Lebanon and consequently refused to perform their military service in Lebanon; and it continued with growing numbers of individuals and political organizations who were appalled by the news coming from Lebanon. Information on the horrifying consequences (see below) of the invasion was flowing in abundance. The seven-week siege of Beirut accelerated the protest movement, which also began to infiltrate into the regular army. Criticism of Sharon himself, accusing him of deceiving the government and the entire public in his war plans began to emerge as well. And then the massacre in Sabra and Shatila occurred and forced the government to respond to the unprecedented mass protest movement which used the massacre to express its apprehension about the war in its entirety. Eventually, Prime Minister Begin succumbed to public pressure and ordered the establishment of an independent commission of inquiry to investigate the massacre.

The Commission of Inquiry into the Events at the Refugee Camps in Beirut, popularly known as the Kahan Commission after its head, Chief Justice Yitzhak Kahan, submitted its report the following February and concluded that direct responsibility for the massacre rested with the Christian Phalanges, while indirect responsibility rested with a few Israeli politicians and military officers, for being negligent in performing their duties. Ariel Sharon was found to bear personal responsibility "for having disregarded the prospect of acts of revenge and bloodshed by the Phalangists against the population of the refugee camps and for having failed to take this danger into consideration." The Commission recommended that Sharon himself resign, and if necessary, that the prime minister force his resignation. As for the prime minister, the Commission concluded that Menahem Begin was not directly involved in the affair but still held some overall responsibility. It nevertheless did not recommend his resignation. Seven months later, Begin resigned from office explaining his decision with the famous words, "I cannot take it any longer," and began nine years of thundering silence until he passed away in March 1992.

The Sabra and Shatila massacre and the consequent Kahan Commission and its recommendations added fuel to an already active and widespread protest movement. By then a host of forms of public protests had already flooded Israeli society creating the impression that the critical remembrance of this war would last. Consequently, Sharon was considered politically dead; after all how could a politician survive such harsh condemnation coming from a judicial commission and buttressed by an unprecedented public protest movement?

Morality of war/ morality in war

Criticism of the Lebanon war focused on two main issues: the decision to go to war and the conduct of the IDF during the war. In his book, *Just and Unjust Wars*, Michael Walzer wrote precisely about this distinction:

The moral reality of war is divided into two parts. War is always judged twice, first with reference to the reasons states have for fighting, secondly with reference to the means they adopt. The first kind of judgment is adjectival in character: we say that a particular war is just or unjust. The second is adverbial: we say that the war is being fought justly or unjustly.[12]

According to Walzer, while justice of war "requires us to make judgments about aggression and self-defense," justice in war focuses "on the observance or violation of the customary and positive rules of engagement." In 1982, criticism of "justice of war," or of the actual decision to go to war, dominated public discussion and focused primarily on Sharon and his deceitful presentation of the reasons to go to war. Sharon was accused not only of launching an unnecessary war of choice, but also of lying to the government and to the public about its scope and goals.

Criticism of "justice in war," or the conduct of the Israeli military during the war, dominated public protest as well, but within a year after the outbreak of the war, it slowly subsided. Passing judgment on the immoral conduct of the military and consequently on the society as a whole was far more sensitive than condemning the government or Sharon specifically.

Israel used extensive military power in Lebanon. An estimated 80,000–100,000 soldiers were directly engaged in the invasion and an all-out bombardment assault from ground, air, and sea preceded the advance of IDF soldiers.[13] This style of warfare was part of an overt tactic aimed at minimizing Israeli casualties even at the expense of massive Lebanese and Palestinian civilian casualties. Indeed, on the way to Beirut, the IDF either occupied or besieged major urban centers, engaging in massive shelling of Palestinian guerillas who were deployed in the midst of over-crowded civilian Palestinian and Lebanese populations. During the seven-week siege of West Beirut similar tactics were used. Large sections of the city with its 300,000 civilians were indiscriminately bombarded, and electricity, water, and food supplies were frequently cut off in order to force the PLO leadership to succumb to

---

[12] Michael Walzer, *Just and Unjust Wars*, 4th edn. (New York: Basic Books, 2006 [1977]): 21.
[13] Yair Evron, *War and Intervention in the Lebanon* (London: Taylor and Francis Books Ltd, 1987): 117.

local pressure and agree to evacuate the city. These tactics were by no means hidden. In fact, they were publicly announced by the planners of the military operation as the declared policy of the IDF.[14]

The figures of casualties and accounts from the Israeli invasion are shocking. By the end of August Lebanese police statistics showed a total of 17,825 dead and 30,203 wounded.[15] By November the police reported a total of 19,085 fatalities, 84 percent of them civilians.[16] These are mere estimates, but other international and Lebanese reports provide roughly similar casualty figures.[17] Reports of property damage also reflect the extent of destruction as a result of the Israeli assault. For example, a June 1982 UN account reported that Israeli forces had destroyed 35 percent of the houses in the Burj al-Shemali refugee camp, 50 percent in al-Buss, 70 percent in Rashidiyeh, and 100 percent in Ein al-Hilweh; also in Shatila camp, over 90 percent of the homes were destroyed or badly damaged, while all structures in Burj al-Barajneh camp were entirely destroyed. Add to these figures the estimated 800,000 civilians who were internally displaced as a result of the Israeli incursion and one gets a grim picture of the June–August 1982 invasion of Lebanon and its effect on the civilian population in the country.[18]

First-hand testimonies of Israeli soldiers, local and international journalists, international aid workers, and Lebanese themselves who bore the invasion's brunt, reflect the extent of destruction and human and material loss wrought by the invasion. For example, an Israeli officer and a famous 1948 war veteran, Dov Yermiya, wrote in his June 12 War Diary on the Israeli bombardment of the refugee camp Ein al-Hilwe in Sidon, which suffered one of the harshest assaults by the IDF:

The bombing and shelling of Ein al-Hilwe are renewed in the morning. For a number of days now, the sounds of explosions have been heard coming from one direction only. Never have I seen a war such as this. Is this a war, or a huge Israeli practice range? Supposedly, there are many terrorists who are still hiding there, and are not ready to give themselves up, despite appeals that are made to them after every cease-fire. They are warned that if they do not give themselves up, they will be killed down to the last man. Once again planes appear and drop gigantic

---

[14] See Interview of Rafael Eitan, IDF Chief of Staff, for Israel Broadcasting Authority news program in the 1997 documentary "Letters from Lebanon."

[15] *Al-Nahar*, September 2, 1982.   [16] *The Washington Post*, December 2, 1982.

[17] *Israel in Lebanon: The Report of the International Commission* (London: Ithaca Press, 1983): 18–19. See slightly smaller figures in Yezid Sayigh, *Armed Struggle and the Search for State: The Palestinian National Movement 1949–1993* (Oxford: Clarendon Press, 1997): 547.

[18] *Israel in Lebanon: The Report of the International Commission*: 49–65.

bombs on the camp. The quantity of bombs and shells that we are pouring into the camp reminds me of World War II.[19]

An American physician visiting Beirut wrote the following report in the *New York Times*:

Statistics are a game that politicians play in war. People far from the scene are having a great debate in the American press about the accuracy of death figures in Lebanon. But there is nothing subtle about the current carnage in Beirut if one can recognize blood or smell a festering wound or feel the feverish head of a dying child. There is no mystery about the scope of this tragedy if one walks the wards of the university hospital or the School of Theology [of the American University of Beirut] and sees the limbless bodies, the fractured faces, the blind, the burned. These are real people, men and women and children, hundreds of them, and no amount of sophistry can dehumanize the horrors of this war into a sterile column of figures. They were not numbers I examined but the innocent civilian debris of a war not of their making but caused by policies that have left them a stateless people. Now they have their dead and their maimed to nourish both their hatred and determination.[20]

The American ambassador to Lebanon, Robert S. Dillon, who witnessed the bombardment of West Beirut wrote the following:

Simply put, tonight's saturation shelling was as intense as anything we have seen. There was no "pinpoint accuracy" against targets in "open spaces". It was not a response to Palestinian fire. This was a blitz against West Beirut ... The magnitude of tonight's action is difficult to convey. The flare of exploding shells reflected against the cloud of smoke was an awesome sight ... a city burning.[21]

Another, and last, quotation is from one of three leading Israeli intellectuals who convened a press conference on June 22, harshly condemning the invasion:

I want to raise the question of morality and this war, the question of justice and equity. We don't yet know the extent of the losses to the civilian population in Lebanon. According to the policy of camouflage employed by the [Israeli] authorities, some claim that the number harmed was not 600,000 but merely 200,000. But for me, as one who is intent on the moral view, the number is not important. The Minister of Defense, the Prime Minister and the Chief of Staff, are those responsible, in my opinion, because they give permission to hit the civilian population. They have said that there was no choice, and they add: "we sent somebody to caution them to go out from the cities, but then we had to bomb them." But this

---

[19] Dov Yermiya, *My War Diary* (Cambridge, Mass.: South End Press, 1984): 27. The Association for Civil Rights granted Dov Yermiya, the Israeli officer mentioned above, its 1983 Human Rights Award for his activity to relieve civilian suffering in Lebanon. The army, on the other hand, released him from duty.

[20] *The New York Times*, July 24, 1982.

[21] Quoted in *Israel in Lebanon: The Report of the International Commission*: 45.

approach is immoral. The very conception of morality demands putting a limit on something that you take away from others. I am not speaking now about actual battlefields. My position is that one could forego the military aim of the conquest of Tyre, Sidon and the suburbs of Beirut, in the name of moral considerations. But we are in a jungle. Humane norms don't exist any more; morality is no more.[22]

The Israeli government rejected Lebanese and international claims as to the extent of fatalities, claiming that the casualties could not have exceeded more than a few thousand and that in any event they were mostly caused because PLO combatants used civilians as human shields.

In brief, the dilemmas of "justice in war" were as grave as "justice of war," in 1982. Information about both moral dilemmas was available to the Israeli public in major Israeli media outlets. The information was there; the question was what to do with it.

From protest to silence and denial

Within a few weeks of the invasion harsh condemnation of the war was already pervasive in the Israeli public arena. A little over a year after the invasion, mainstream Israeli journalists wrote books in Hebrew strongly criticizing the government and describing the human suffering in Lebanon caused by this "war of deception."[23] Other critical works on the war were published; some were transcripts of critical public debates, reflecting the split over the war in large sections of society;[24] others were testimonies of soldiers' war experiences.[25] Poetry soon became an important medium of protest, which was particularly noticeable given the absence of popular songs which previous wars routinely had produced. Ariel Sharon loomed high as the prime target of the protest movement, criticized primarily as the deceiving master planner and executioner of the war.

Yet, already before the supposed withdrawal from Lebanon in June 1985 (on the third anniversary of the invasion), and particularly thereafter, the Lebanon war slowly subsided into the margins of public attention. No serious protest movement developed and no major public debate evolved as Israel slowly strengthened its grip over South Lebanon.

---

[22] *Kol Ha-'Ir*, June 22, 1982.

[23] Zeev Schief and Ehud Yaari, *Milhemet Sholal* (Tel Aviv: Shoken, 1984); Shimon Shifer, *Kadur Sheleg* (Tel Aviv: Idanim, 1984).

[24] Rubik Rozenthal, *Levanon, ha-Milhamah ha-Aheret* (Tel Aviv: Sifriyat ha-po'alim, 1983); Shai Feldman and Heda Rechnitz-Kijner, *Deception, Consensus and War: Israel in Lebanon* (Tel Aviv: Jaffee Center for Strategic Studies, 1983); Menahem Dorman, *Sihot be-"Yad Tabenkin"* (Tel Aviv: Hakibbutz Hameuchad, 1983).

[25] Yesh Gevul, *Gevul ha-Tsiyut u-Zekhut ha-Seruv* (Tel Aviv: Tenuat Yesh Gevul, 1983).

This process was also directed from above as the IDF made all possible efforts to shut down Lebanon from public scrutiny.[26]

Only twelve years after the 1985 "withdrawal," the Four Mothers movement was established, launching a civil protest against the Israeli occupation of South Lebanon and awakening a public discussion about the war and its inconclusive outcome.[27] Yet, this public debate primarily focused on the futility of Israel's "presence" in the security zone and on IDF casualties – the word occupation was not used, even by the majority of the left in Israel. The moral dilemmas about Israeli misconduct in Lebanon completely disappeared from public discussion, to the point that even Israeli human rights organizations that had recorded Israeli misconduct in the Occupied Territories, did not monitor the Israeli occupation of South Lebanon.

From the very beginning of the war, public officials understood that a battle was being fought over the memory of this war in and out of Israel, and they fought back, presenting a righteous picture of the Israeli decision to go to war and of the moral conduct of IDF soldiers during the war.[28] Soon, however, the self-assurance that characterized the Israeli case was replaced by silence.

It was striking that this turn towards silence began roughly on the day Prime Minister Begin suddenly resigned his post and retired from politics. After September 15, 1983, he completely withdrew from the public eye and thereafter remained completely silent. Begin did not explain his reasons for his abrupt departure from public life. He simply and without elaboration asked for forgiveness; for what precisely? The public was left on its own to speculate.

Many people assumed that his retirement and subsequent thundering silence were related to the poor results of the war, to the death toll of Israeli soldiers, to the issue of Sharon's deception of the cabinet about what his goals were during the invasion, and to the growing rift within the Israeli society caused by the debate over the justification of the war.[29]

---

[26] See the memoirs of an Israeli senior officer, Moshe Tamir, *Milhamah le-lo Ot* (Tel Aviv: Ma'arachot, 2005): 10–11.

[27] On the Four Mothers movement see Avraham Sela, "Civil Society, the Military, and National Security: The Case of Israel's Security Zone in South Lebanon," *Israel Studies*, 12, 1 (Spring 2007): 53–78.

[28] See the different publications of the Ministry of Information and the educational kits of the Ministry of Education which were distributed in state schools, located in the library of the School of Education at the Hebrew University of Jerusalem.

[29] On Begin's retirement see Arye Naor, *Begin ba-Shilton* (Tel Aviv: Yediot Ahronot, 1993): 317–48. Naor named this chapter "The Cry of Silence."

Israeli society was unfamiliar with so much public anger following a war. Rather than becoming a tool for patriotic mobilization, as were previous wars, this war created a rift of mistrust between large sections of the society and the government. Thus, even the annual memorial events for the fallen soldiers of the war were conducted by the state with no orchestrated fanfare. They received little attention from the public as newspapers reported on them in short succinct messages on their inside pages. Politicians scarcely participated in these state-sponsored memorial ceremonies, even in "important" dates such as the twentieth anniversary of the outbreak of the war.[30]

To be sure, *Yad Labanim*, the official organization in charge of the commemoration of Israeli fallen soldiers and assistance to their bereaved families, made all possible effort to incorporate the Israeli fallen soldiers of the first Lebanon war into mainstream war commemoration. However, they faced non-cooperation from Israeli elected officials. For example, on the twenty-fourth anniversary of the outbreak of the war, on June 12, 2006, exactly one month before the eruption of the Second Lebanon War, *Yad Labanim* organized the official annual memorial service of the "Peace for Galilee War." The government's representative to the ceremony was the director of a minor state ministry and not an elected official. The chairperson of *Yad Labanim* explained: "before every ceremony we beg for a representative from the Knesset and the government. The excuses of the ministers and the Knesset members are shameful."[31] Ra'yah Harnik, one of the most prominent bereaved mothers of this war and a symbol of the anti-war protest movement, explained that every year *Yad Labanim* sends an invitation, promising that a representative of the government or the Knesset would be present at the memorial ceremony, and every year no one shows up. "I have not gone for more than ten years [because] I feel despised and humiliated,"[32] she concluded.

The Lebanon war did not disappear entirely from public awareness between 1983 and 2000. After all, Israeli soldiers were dying in Lebanon almost on a weekly basis, reminding the public, like a pesky fly, of the aftermath of the 1982 war. Nevertheless, all in all, critical discussion of the war disappeared from the public realm. As the public stopped discussing the war and as state agencies did their best to ignore it, Ariel Sharon slowly returned to the center of the Israeli political arena.

---

[30] Tom Segev, "No, It's Not Worth It," *Haaretz*, May 31, 2002.
[31] Yair Ettinger, *Haaretz*, June 12, 2006.
[32] Radio All For Peace www.allforpeace.org/viewarticle.aspx?articalid=1778&lang=3 accessed June 26, 2006.

Selective remembrance and the rehabilitation of Ariel Sharon

The political sanitization of Ariel Sharon began the moment the Kahan Commission submitted its report in February 1983 and recommended that he resign from his position as minister of defense. Sharon refused to resign voluntarily, and the prime minister only partially followed the Commission's recommendation that asked that he force Sharon's resignation. Sharon remained in the government as a minister without portfolio and soon thereafter was reinstated as a member of the important government Committee on Security and Foreign Affairs. In fact, Israeli politicians were the first to deem the recommendations of the Commission irrelevant. As early as 1984 Sharon ran for the position of chair of the Likud party (and lost by a slim margin), and after the national elections of the same year he became minister of industry in a Labor-led government. It was evident that the judicial condemnation of Sharon was insufficient within Israeli political culture to terminate his career.

Interestingly and paradoxically, Sharon thereafter actually became the focal point of Israeli memories of the Lebanon war. The massacres at Sabra and Shatila and the consequent Kahan Commission and its recommendations focused public attention on Ariel Sharon in that one context. The mandate of the Kahan Commission was limited to an inquiry as to the origins of that particular massacre; it did not include an investigation of the merits of the war in its entirety, or of any other aspects of its conduct. In other words, the Commission was not concerned with the morality of the "justice *of* war," the contested justification of the war or the question of official "deception" about war objectives. The Commission was indeed preoccupied with the morality of "justice *in* war," but only within the context of one dreadful event: the massacre at Sabra and Shatila. Thus, while the Commission did inquire about the moral conduct of IDF soldiers during the massacre, it did not engage in the more general question of IDF behavior during the entire war, from the invasion through the siege and bombardment of Beirut. Furthermore, its underlining premise was that the conduct of the IDF soldiers had to be examined separately from that of the Phalange killers who were responsible for the massacre, and that since Israel was the occupying power in Lebanon, it had to answer the charge that it failed to uphold safety and public order, especially after the expulsion of the PLO from Beirut. The massacre at Sabra and Shatila happened *after* Arafat and the PLO had left the city, the ostensible aim of the invasion.

The Commission indirectly and unintentionally exonerated the government, the IDF, and the entire state from the harsh moral questions related to the conflict before and after the massacre. By focusing on one event, horrific as it was, and by concentrating on a few senior military officers and a few politicians, most prominently on Sharon himself, the Kahan Commission helped in narrowing down the entire Lebanon imbroglio into one horrific affair. From that point on, the shadow of the war within Israeli public discourse became more and more reduced to and focused on Ariel Sharon and Sabra and Shatila.

Sharon's political rehabilitation was closely followed by the media in Israel. Every step in the ladder back to political prominence was followed by journalistic reports about his role in the war. These reports cited the recommendations of the Kahan Commission declaring him unfit to be the minister of defense, thus implying that he was unsuitable to hold any senior position in the government.[33] At the same time, each step up was met with public indifference. During the election campaign of 2001, Ehud Barak's camp used the Lebanon war, Sabra and Shatila, and the Kahan Commission in order to invoke public memory of Sharon's role in the 1982 invasion, hoping to impede his chance to win the elections.[34] As before, the public had at its disposal the relevant information about Sharon's shady conduct during the Lebanon war, but chose to ignore it. This was not a case of forgetting, but of silent exoneration.

Sharon himself kept his name in the Lebanon-related headlines through the law suits he filed against *Time* magazine and the Israeli daily newspaper *Haaretz*. *Time* was served with a suit by Sharon's lawyers following a report it published according to which Sharon allegedly had spoken with the Gemayel family after the assassination of Bashir, inciting them to avenge his death. The latter law suit focused on an article in *Haaretz* written by Uzi Benziman who stated that Begin must have known Sharon deceived him during the invasion of Lebanon. Intriguingly, Sharon was concerned to prove his innocence in both moral dimensions about justice during war. After all, the *Time* lawsuit was related to the moral issue of "justice in war," – i.e. Sharon's behavior during the war itself – whereas the lawsuit against *Haaretz* focused on the "justice of war," – the actual decision to go to war and Sharon's lies to his own prime minister and cabinet about war objectives. In both cases he was interested in facilitating his political rehabilitation by presenting his version of the invasion to the Israeli public. In this way, he himself assisted in occasionally pushing parts of the war – selective as they were – back into the public domain. Uzi Benziman wrote a memoir on this long legal battle

---

[33] See, for example, about Sharon's appointment as Minister of Finance in *Haaretz*, October 13, 1998.
[34] *Haaretz*, January 12, 2001.

(1991–2002) thus adding another platform of remembrance that focused on Sharon's role in the 1982 war. He, nevertheless, noted in a bitter tone, that the public was not really interested in this law suit, as reflected by the fact that the press provided only minor coverage of the trial.[35] The trial was terminated in November 1997 with the complete rejection of Sharon's position and the endorsement of *Haaretz* and Benziman. The judge accepted in full the claim that Sharon had deceived Prime Minister Begin, that Begin had learned about this in retrospect, and that Sharon had misled Begin and the government about his real objectives, while at the same time providing them with misleading information. Sharon did not give up and appealed to the Supreme Court. The appeal was scheduled for May 2, 2001, when he was already prime minister, and the judges' decision was heard on February 18, 2002. By then, Israel was in the midst of the second Intifada and Sharon enjoyed an unprecedentedly high rating as a popular prime minister. The Supreme Court judges rejected Sharon's appeal, based on the lack of proof of intent to defame on the part of Benziman and left it at that. A similar fate befell Sharon's other law suit.

The image of Sharon within Israeli society had undergone a radical metamorphosis. From the 1982 abyss of Sabra and Shatila to his ascendance twenty years later to the role of the "good grandfather," the man of peace, Sharon's triumph was indeed remarkable. This was in no sense a matter of forgetting, but rather of silence, selective remembrance, and denial. Sharon's political resurrection was only possible because Israelis preferred silence about the 1982 war to remembrance or forgetting. Indifference to Arab suffering, fueled by two Palestinian uprisings, one in the late 1980s and one that was sparked by Sharon himself when he went up the Temple Mount in September 2000, added to the atmosphere of silence and denial of the first Lebanon war.

Silence and indifference made Sharon's return to political life possible. That forgetting is not the key element here may be gauged by considering a 1996 documentary entitled, "How I learned to overcome my fear and love Arik Sharon." The documentary follows Sharon's campaign in support of Binyamin Netanyahu during the 1996 parliamentary elections. During this campaign, director and producer, Avi Mugrabi, a 1982 war resister who spent time in prison for his refusal to perform his military service in Lebanon, undergoes a major metamorphosis, from strongly detesting Sharon to falling completely for his warm and friendly personality. As Mugrabi is "transformed" during the documentary he paraphrases an exchange with his wife:

---

[35] Uzi Benziman, *Emet Dibarti* (Jerusalem: Keter, 2002):118.

Tammi said that she does not understand how one can make a movie about Arik Sharon. "Sabra and Shatila!" she said. "Have you forgotten Sabra and Shatila?" But I felt that some discomfort that has been burdening me for years simply vanished.

Although this documentary records an arguably cynical personal journey, symbolically it represents a transformation in attitudes not only towards Sharon, but also, by and large, towards the war. In 2001, when Sharon ran for the office of the prime minister, the Lebanon war had already been sanitized, through a process of silencing, denial, and selective remembrance, just as he had been.

Conclusions

It is not easy to attract public attention in Israel to a specific issue for an extended period of time. The pace of political events, the tension and pace of everyday life preclude it. The media follows suit; it is rare that an event will remain in the headlines for long. And yet, despite this "competition" over news space, the Lebanon war did not vanish in its entirety from media reports or from other public platforms such as fiction, films, documentaries, and academic and journalistic literature, mostly critical of the conduct of the Israeli government during the war.

Not unexpectedly, the most vigorous attempt to reinvoke the critical memory of this war and specifically its moral dilemmas has come from the Israeli left, very much a tiny minority in the country. Take for example, the 2002 book *From Beirut to Jenin*, published at the peak of the Palestinian second Intifada when Sharon was already prime minister. The authors of the book collected testimonies from soldiers who participated in the 1982 invasion, motivated by the conviction that there is a connecting immoral thread between 1982 and 2002 – and that thread is Ariel Sharon. After listening to the testimonies the authors of the book came to the following conclusion:

We listened to them, to the combatants of "Oranim plan", [the code name of the 1982 operation] and to our surprise we found out another thing: that despite the fact that everything is supposedly known, and written and remembered about the Lebanon war, that "war of deception", nevertheless, we, ourselves did not remember – and perhaps did not exactly know, or did not really want to know and remember – many things that these fourteen men told us. And most likely that we are not the only ones; that we are like the majority of the public in the country: do not know or do not remember and most certainly to not reach conclusions – otherwise how is it possible that what had happened is what is happening now, to that extent?[36]

---

[36] Irit Gal and Ilana Hamerman, *From Beirut to Jenin, the Lebanon War 1982/2002* (Tel Aviv: 'Am 'Oved, 2002): 8–9.

Through this book, the authors wanted to remind the Israeli public of the gross Israeli human rights violations in that war, and of the fact that since 1982 Sharon has carried the mark of Cain and that, consequently, he should not have been permitted to assume any senior political position. But, such calls remained isolated in the extreme margins of the Israeli political spectrum, and they stay there. This message literally fell on deaf ears, and every attempt to link 1982 with 2002 failed completely. Remembrance never turned into recognition which in turn could have been translated into political action. The power of silence was (and is) evident.

The presence of silence can be noted in another perhaps more surprising facet of Israeli public life, that of war commemoration. On the whole, Israeli wars share a certain meta-narrative of self-defense, sacrifice, brotherhood, and collectivity. Within this narrative each war has acquired specific characteristics. For example, the 1948 war was the war of independence, the moment when the nation was born. The 1967 war was the war of justified pre-emption and victory in the face of intolerable Arab provocation and threats. In this meta-narrative there is even space for the 1973 war, that conflict which marked the end of the first phase of the nation's history, its end of innocence. There was room for criticism of the military leadership of the war, though despite mistakes, the strength of the army and the nation finally prevailed. However, there is no space for the "first" Lebanon war in this narrative, for public perception about it holds that it was neither particularly heroic, nor defensive, nor foundational. To be sure, Sharon (and others) made efforts to include this war within the Israeli conventional narrative of wars by insisting that history would show that it was the most justified war Israel has ever fought.[37] But it was still a war that Israel's government chose to fight, not one forced on it by other states in the region.

With respect to commemoration, therefore, the 1982 war was problematic. The vast majority of the Israeli public as well as state agents have had no interest in evoking the moral dilemmas of this war. Moreover, fatigue and indifference have taken their toll, the result of long years of conflict that have thickened the Israeli "skin" and blurred its moral judgments. Eventually even Sharon, like the war itself, went through a process of rehabilitation. Israeli society did not "forget" the war. It simply turned it into a war whose predicament lay not in questions about morality, but at best, in questions about political errors. Thus, the Lebanon quagmire became not one that Israel concocted for itself, but a Lebanese swamp

---

[37] See particularly Sharon's speech at Tel Aviv University on August 11, 1987, cited in Nir Hefez and Gadi Bloom, *Ariel Sharon: A Life* (New York: Random House, 2006): 271–2.

into which it may very well have been a mistake to sink into in 1982. Silences of many kinds made commemoration very difficult and left the field open for the political rehabilitation of the man most closely associated with the war. The story of Ariel Sharon's political career shows clearly that silence works over the long term. Despite a wave of films, memoirs, and other recent reflections, the second war in Lebanon in 2006 did not provoke much soul-searching in the Israeli public about the first. Instead, there were kind thoughts about Ariel Sharon, suddenly struck down by a stroke, peacefully living out the last phase of his life in a coma, still beloved by most of his people.

Postscript

"Sometimes we can forget the past, but the past never forgets us," announces the preview of the acclaimed and award-winning Israeli movie *Waltz with Bashir*. Released in 2008, this animated documentary tells the personal story of the movie maker, Ari Folman, who served as a soldier in 1982 and who, more than twenty years later, embarks on a journey to retrieve his memories from the invasion of Lebanon, and particularly the massacre at Sabra and Shatila. Folman knows two things: there was a massacre and he was there, but he cannot put the rest of the pieces of the story together. To recreate this picture of the past he speaks with fellow "brothers in arms" who served with him during the war, and through these interviews slowly but surely the picture gets clearer and the horrors of the invasion and the massacre are exposed.

This visually mesmerizing anti-war movie runs through time from the present to the past and vice versa and is located, in fact, in between, in a world of nightmares and hallucinations which are further magnified by its dark animation. It concludes with real footage from the massacre, taking the viewers at once from the gripping sense of fantasy and delirium to the actual world of atrocities.

Every single one of Folman's interviewees holds within him personal memories of the war. None of them has forgotten the invasion and the massacres, even if personal recollections often contradict each other. In fact, Folman brought into the public realm memories retained by his generation which served in the invasion of Lebanon, memories which have been silenced. As I have argued, and as is clearly demonstrated in this movie, the massacre at Sabra and Shatila has become the focus of Israeli memories of the first Lebanon war. Nothing of what is shown in the movie was unknown; indeed these events were discussed numerous times before. But Folman's movie attempts to brings these events from the domain of silence to that of active remembrance.

When work on the movie began, Ariel Sharon was prime minister, enjoying unprecedented rates of popularity. Had he not entered a coma and had he been politically active when the movie came out, his popularity would not have been affected. The movie received glowing reviews in Israel and became a major commercial success, but it did not change public discussion of the 1982 invasion. In fact, it led to further self-serving statements of exoneration.

Now, in January 2009, Israel is engaged in another bloody round of its hundred-year war with the Palestinians, this time in the Gaza Strip. As one Israeli commentator wrote after *Waltz with Bashir* received the Golden Globe Award for best foreign film of 2008, "the Israeli animated and anti-war movie by Ari Folman continues to bring honor [to Israel], helping to raise the national morale of a people who need it now more than ever."[38]

Here is another, though by no means the last, twist in the evolution of the 1982 invasion of Lebanon. What began as a war of deception and evolved into a national disgrace has turned into a source of national pride.

[38] www.mouse.co.il/CM.articles_item,636,209,31854,.aspx.

Index